African Nationalism

African Nationalism offers an innovative perspective on the creation of nations and nationalism, and the role of race in nationalism overall, by bringing together a compilation of debates on African nationalism, from Pan-Africanism up to the present day.

The book examines African nationalism in comparative perspective, mainly with the UK, France, and the US: the birthplaces of modern nationalism. The author suggests that the origins of African nationalism lay outside the continent and demonstrates the similarities that abound between African nationalisms across a diverse range of countries.

This volume is important reading for students and scholars of nationalism, history, political science, and African studies.

Benyamin Neuberger was Professor Emeritus of Political Science and African Studies at The Open University of Israel. He published widely on Israeli politics, African politics, Israeli democracy, the theory of democracy, and nationalism. Previous titles include: *Rwanda 1994: Genocide in the "Land of a Thousand Hills"* (2017), *Israel's Relations with the Third World (1948–2008)* (2009), *Religion and Democracy in Israel* (1997), *National Self-Determination in Post-Colonial Africa* (1986), and *Involvement, Invasion and Withdrawal: Quadhafi's Libya and Chad 1969–1981* (1982).

Routledge Studies in Nationalism and Ethnicity
Series Editor: Timofey Agarin, Queen's University Belfast, UK

This new series draws attention to some of the most exciting issues in current world political debate: nation-building, autonomy and self-determination; ethnic identity, conflict and accommodation; pluralism, multiculturalism and the politics of language; ethnonationalism, irredentism and separatism; and immigration, naturalization and citizenship. The series will include monographs as well as edited volumes, and through the use of case studies and comparative analyses will bring together some of the best work to be found in the field.

Nations and Capital
The Missing Link in Global Expansion
Zlatko Hadžidedić

Cultural Nationhood and Political Statehood
The Birth of Self-Determination
André Liebich

Peace Settlements and Political Transformation in Divided Societies
Rethinking Northern Ireland and South Africa
Adrian Guelke

The Paradox of Planetary Human Entanglements
Challenges of Living Together
Edited by Inocent Moyo and Sabelo J. Ndlovu-Gatsheni

African Nationalism
Benyamin Neuberger
Translated by Merav Datan

For more information about this series, please visit: www.routledge.com/Routledge-Studies-in-Nationalism-and-Ethnicity/book-series/NE

African Nationalism

Benyamin Neuberger

Translated by Merav Datan

LONDON AND NEW YORK

First published in English 2023
by Routledge
4 Park Square, Milton Park, Abingdon, Oxon OX14 4RN

and by Routledge
605 Third Avenue, New York, NY 10158

Routledge is an imprint of the Taylor & Francis Group, an informa business

© 2023 Benyamin Neuberger

Translated by Merav Datan

The right of Benyamin Neuberger to be identified as author of this work has been asserted in accordance with sections 77 and 78 of the Copyright, Designs and Patents Act 1988.

All rights reserved. No part of this book may be reprinted or reproduced or utilised in any form or by any electronic, mechanical, or other means, now known or hereafter invented, including photocopying and recording, or in any information storage or retrieval system, without permission in writing from the publishers.

Every effort has been made to contact copyright-holders. Please advise the publisher of any errors or omissions, and these will be corrected in subsequent editions.

Trademark notice: Product or corporate names may be trademarks or registered trademarks, and are used only for identification and explanation without intent to infringe.

Translation copyright 2023 by Routledge.

Original Hebrew language title: *The Emergence of the New African States, Unit 4: Anti-Colonial Nationalism–The Ideological Dimension and* **chapter 10 from** *Africa in International Relations* by **Prof. Benyamin Neuberger and Dr Ella Keren** © by The Open University of Israel. All rights reserved.

Publisher's Note:
References within each chapter are as they appear in the original work.
Please note that this book contains some profanity which readers may find offensive.

British Library Cataloguing-in-Publication Data
A catalogue record for this book is available from the British Library

Library of Congress Cataloging-in-Publication Data
Names: Neuberger, Ralph Benyamin, 1943–2022, author. | Datan, Merav, translator.
Title: African nationalism / Benyamin Neuberger.; translated by Merav Datan.
Other titles: Routledge studies in nationalism and ethnicity.
Description: Abingdon, Oxon; New York, NY: Routledge, 2023. |
Series: Routledge studies in nationalism and ethnicity | "Original Hebrew language title:
The Emergence of the New African States, Unit 4: Anti-Colonial Nationalism–
The Ideological Dimension and chapter 10 from Africa in International Relations
by Prof. Benjamin Neuberger and Dr Ella Keren © by The Open University of
Israel:—Title page verso. | Includes bibliographical references and index.
Identifiers: LCCN 2022055598 (print) | LCCN 2022055599 (ebook) |
ISBN 9781032345635 (hardback) | ISBN 9781032345642 (paperback) |
ISBN 9781003322818 (ebook)
Subjects: LCSH: Nationalism—Africa. | Self-determination,
National—Africa. | Decolonization—Africa.
Classification: LCC DT31 .N43 2023 (print) | LCC DT31 (ebook) |
DDC 320.54096—dc23/eng/20221129
LC record available at https://lccn.loc.gov/2022055598
LC ebook record available at https://lccn.loc.gov/2022055599

ISBN: 978-1-032-34563-5 (hbk)
ISBN: 978-1-032-34564-2 (pbk)
ISBN: 978-1-003-32281-8 (ebk)

DOI: 10.4324/9781003322818

Typeset in Times New Roman
by Newgen Publishing UK

Contents

List of Figures	vii
List of Maps	x
List of Tables	xi
Acknowledgments	xii
Introduction	1
1 Africans, African Americans, and the Roots of Pan-African Nationalism	4
2 From Pan-Negroism to Territorial Nationalism: Nationalism without Nations	26
3 Négritude	31
4 Continental Pan-Africanism	41
5 The New Nationalism and Its Historical Heritage	52
6 The Permeation of Western Liberal Concepts	68
7 Socialist and Communist Concepts and Anticolonial African Nationalism	82
8 Radical Ideologies of National, Economic, Social, and Cultural Liberation	90
9 Opponents of National Independence	109

vi *Contents*

10 The Organization of African Unity and the
African Union   119

11 Black Zionism: The Return to Africa in Theory
and Practice   131

12 Conclusion   148

Appendix 1: Albert Memmi   150
Appendix 2: Alioune Diop   154
Appendix 3: Frantz Fanon   158
Appendix 4: Julius Nyerere   162
Index   168

Figures

1.1 A painting c.1830 by the German artist Johann Moritz Rugendas depicts a scene below deck of a slave ship headed to Brazil; Rugendas had been an eyewitness to the scene. Many enslaved Africans were transported to the Americas. The trans-Atlantic slave trade and African slavery in the Americas were major factors in the shaping of modern racism. 10

1.2 1840 depiction of field hand slaves and child, chained together while working. 11

1.3 Freetown, Sierra Leone in 1856. 14

1.4 Edward Wilmot Blyden. 15

1.5 Obafemi Awolowo. 21

1.6 Jomo Kenyatta. 22

3.1 Léopold Sedar Senghor. 32

3.2 Portrait of Aimé Césaire by Hom Nguyen for the Musée de l'Homme in 2021 for the *Portraits de France* exhibition. 33

3.3 African Fang mask used for the *ngil* ceremony, an inquisitorial search for sorcerers. Such art influenced modern European art, such as Picasso's cubism. See www.artdex.com/historical-influe nce-of-african-art-in-the-modern-art-movement/ for more information. 34

4.1 Kwame Nkrumah. Nkrumah strove to merge socialist ideals with traditional African values. To that end, he used to wear traditional, handwoven kente cloth wrappers. 42

5.1 The Great Zimbabwe is a ruined city in the southeastern hills of Zimbabwe. It was built between the eleventh and fourteenth centuries. It is recognized by UNESCO as a World Heritage Site. 54

5.2 Art from Benin: Head of a king (oba). 55

5.3 Art from Benin: One of six surviving ivory bell sculptures (egogo) used to drive away evil spirits (sixteenth century). 56

5.4 Art from Benin: Leopard's head (nineteenth century). 57

5.5 Art from Benin: Bronze head of Queen Idia (sixteenth century). 57

viii *List of Figures*

5.6 The Great Mosque of Jenné in Mali. The first Jenné mosque dates back to the thirteenth century, the current structure to the 1910s. 58

5.7 Child labor: children weaving, Cameroon, 1919. 59

5.8 Painting of the slave deck of the ship *Marie Séraphique* of Nantes (1770), representing its "cargo" (as slaves were then viewed). Enslaved Africans were transported to the Americas. The Transatlantic slave trade and African slavery in the Americas were the major factors that shaped modern racism. 59

5.9 Julius Nyerere. 62

5.10 Nelson Mandela. 63

6.1 Patrice Lumumba. 69

6.2 Kenneth Kaunda. 70

6.3 African churches: The Arch Cathedral Bethel, Lagos, Nigeria. 72

6.4 African churches: A Methodist chapel in Leliefontein, Northern Cape, South Africa. 73

6.5 Teaching staff and students at Liberia College, 1900. In earlier years, missionaries were the main agents for the introduction of written language into the school system. 74

6.6 This script was created in West Africa and was one of many scripts created throughout the nineteenth and twentieth century as an alternative to the European writing that was predominantly used. The creation of the script was part of a larger endeavor to represent African languages. The origin of the image-based logograms of the Vai script is not known. 75

6.7 Painting depicting victims of the Sharpeville massacre (which took place on 21 March 1960, Sharpeville, Transvaal province, South Africa) by Godfrey Rubens. It is currently located in the South African Consulate in London. 77

6.8 Spectator segregation (apartheid) in a sports stadium, Bloemfontein, South Africa, 1969. 79

8.1 Makonde woodcarvers at work in a FRELIMO production camp. The Makonde are famous for their ebony carvings. Other crafts, such as weaving and pottery, are also practised in the production camps. Some of the finished products are exported to Tanzania in exchange for needed domestic and military supplies. 96

8.2 FRELIMO hospital for combatants in a military camp. 96

8.3 A young student at one of the schools set up by FRELIMO. Most of the schools are outdoors. Various UN funds and programmes have been established to help meet the urgent needs of the indigenous peoples of Southern Africa in education. 97

8.4 Frantz Fanon. 101

List of Figures   ix

9.1 Photograph of Queen Elizabeth II and Commonwealth leaders, taken at the 1960 Commonwealth Conference, Windsor Castle. Front row: (left to right) E. J. Cooray (Sri Lanka), Walter Nash (New Zealand), Jawaharlal Nehru (India), Elizabeth II (UK), John Diefenbaker (Canada), Robert Menzies (Australia), Eric Louw Back (Australia). Back row (left to right): Tunku Abdul Rahman, Roy Welensky (Rhodesia and Nyasaland), Harold Macmillan (UK), Mohammed Ayub Khan (Pakistan), Kwame Nkrumah (Ghana). In Ghana there was internal conflict between people who demonstrated for immediate independence, and people who demonstrated for the gradual discontinuity of colonial rule.   114
9.2 Troops of the King's African Rifles carrying supplies while on watch for Mau Mau fighters.   115
10.1 The Institutions of the African Union at its inception.   124

Maps

1.1	Countries on the African continent.	5
1.2	Concentration of black populations following the slave trade.	6
1.3	The Caribbean Islands.	7
4.1	West Africa. In 1967, 14 West African countries established the West African Community: Benin (or Dahomey), Gambia, Ghana, Guinea, the Ivory Coast, Liberia, Mali, Mauritania, Niger, Nigeria, Senegal, Sierra Leone, Togo, and Burkina-Fasso (or Upper Volta). The member countries agreed on economic, social, technological, and cultural cooperation.	48
4.2	East Africa. The East African Community was established in 1967 with the aim of institutionalizing and tightening the economic cooperation between Kenya, Uganda, and Tanzania. Cooperation was based mainly on shared services (mail and telegraph, seaports and railways, agricultural research, statistical analysis, etc.), as well as the fields of aviation, a common higher education system, common markets, and investment regulations. The Community dissolved in 1977 due to political conflicts between the member states.	49
4.3	Colonial distribution of European languages.	50
5.1	The Maji-Maji Rebellion in German East Africa.	64
8.1	Areas in which the decolonization struggle was violent.	102

Tables

6.1 Westernized Africans and their struggle for independence   77

Acknowledgments

I am deeply grateful to Prof. Mimi Ajzenstadt, president of the Open University of Israel, which originally published the book in Hebrew, and to Routledge for their ongoing support. My deep appreciation to Dr. Ella Keren from the Department of Political Science, Sociology and Communication, for her invaluable contribution to the Hebrew version of the book. Profound thanks go to Merav Datan, who translated the book with remarkable sensitivity, creativity, and language sense. And, of course, many thanks to my wife Belina for her help, love, and patience when she copyedited the book.

Benyamin (Benni) Neuberger, March 2022

I would like to add a few words to thank the people who helped me complete Benni's project after he passed away in April 2022. I am profoundly grateful for the help, endless patience, and practical advice I received from Emily Ross and Hannah Rich at Routledge, and from Dana Knobler and Rachel Aharon-Shriki at the Open University of Israel. It is thanks to them that this book could be published posthumously.

And, finally, on a much more personal note, my deep, enduring indebtedness to Benni himself for 53 years of close partnership, love, and mutual support. When I try to think of a way to express the very essence of him as a person—as a father, as a friend, as a teacher, as a colleague, as a spouse—I cannot but recall the edict from Psalms 34:14: "Seek peace, and pursue it." (*Bakesh shalom v'rodfehu*)

בַּקֵּשׁ שָׁלוֹם וְרָדְפֵהוּ

And feel sorrow for his loss.

Belina Neuberger, September 2022

Introduction

This book addresses the conceptual-ideological dimension of African nationalism and the decolonization processes in Africa. Focusing on this dimension allows us to develop a broader view of African nationalism, and to trace the mutual influences between sociopolitical and ideological dimensions.

The ideological struggle against colonialism served as an important African arena of activity from the very outset of foreign rule, among other reasons because it began immediately after the colonial conquest and did not require the self-organization or complex mechanisms of struggle that developed later. Accordingly, a discussion of African ideologies allows us to examine, from a historical perspective, the courses of development of African worldviews over the years.

It is also important because it allows us to better understand the combined impacts of colonialism on African society from an internal perspective—as perceived and interpreted by Africans who lived and operated within the colonial experience. This issue is particularly interesting in relation to Western-educated African intellectuals who were prominent in the process of ideological "production." Their position at the intercultural junction posed dilemmas regarding their identity and required them to strike a balance and navigate a maze of sometimes vague, sometimes contradictory, morally charged perspectives and images: between "Africa" and "the West," between "tradition" and "progress," and between modern Europe, as a model to be imitated on the one hand, and colonial Europe, as an object of criticism on the other hand.

Ideology, as a systematic conceptual theory of specific social groups, has a number of goals: to shape the society's worldview, to legitimize its social order, to ensure integration among its members, and to mobilize them to action. The African ideologies to be examined here had additional functions, some of which were common to all ideologies, some of which were specific to particular ideologies, depending on the needs that emerged at various stages of the decolonization process. On the whole, it is safe to say that these ideologies helped clarify the need to change the situation in which Africans found

DOI: 10.4324/9781003322818-1

2 *Introduction*

themselves and convinced them that they were capable of doing so. Once the goals were identified, the ideologies offered action strategies to achieve them.

In the phase that involves a people's awakening, the ideological aspect provides an important key to understanding the background and reasons for the launching of a process of decolonization. During this phase, Africans and people of African descent residing outside Africa conducted a close examination of their image in the eyes of the ruling Western European culture and, in protest against this image, began seeking the roots of their cultural and historical identity, defining their relationship to colonialism and European culture, and trying to understand the meaning of colonialism for Africa. The cultural and racial ideologies that emerged at this stage only loosely corresponded with the social and political reality in Africa itself. During the 1930s and 1940s in particular, there began to emerge pragmatic and activist ideologies that still incorporated cultural concepts but the thrust of which was now directed toward Africa: they identified concrete political goals and called on the Africans themselves to mobilize in attaining them.

During the resistance phase of decolonization (primarily in the 1940s and 1950s), nationalist ideologies granted moral legitimacy to the struggle against colonialism and helped enlist support for movements aimed at abolishing it. They adopted European concepts and values, which they sought to adapt to African aims and needs. Their ideological horizon stretched only as far as liberation from colonialism as a condition for the revival of a "new Africa." It did not, however, explicitly delineate substantive issues or courses of development that would guide African states after liberation.

In those areas where the colonial powers refused to accede to the call for liberation, the crisis escalated, and the ongoing struggle generated fairly revolutionary ideologies. These ideologies justified a resort to violence, fanned the flames needed to fuel prolonged warfare, and even at the height of the struggle proposed an alternative model of independent existence, free from the exploitative nature of colonial relations. Even after the attainment of political independence, the model embodied a promise of liberation from continuing dependence on colonial powers.

All the ideological expressions centered around two common axes—anticolonialism and nationalism. The degree of overlap between them is nonetheless still a matter of debate in the scholarship on Africa. Given that all of the various ideologies expressed opposition to white rule and to the status of Africans (or those of African descent) in the sociocultural hierarchy established by Whites, there is no disputing that they are indeed anticolonial. But can they also be characterized as national ideologies?

Various studies have differentiated between the concepts of decolonization and nationalism.[1] The approach adopted here is different, mainly for two reasons. In his research on nationalism, Benedict Anderson—who holds that every human community is imagined, existing only in the consciousness of its members, and that a nation is an imagined political community—views the complex processes entailed in the conception, invention, and assimilation

Introduction 3

of collective identities as the foundations for the creation of nationalism.[2] Anderson concurs with Ernest Gellner's assertion that "nationalism is not the awakening of nations to self-consciousness: it *invents* nations where they do not exist."[3] However, unlike Gellner, who does not differentiate between invention and fabrication, Anderson views invention as creation and believes that communities or nations are distinguishable not by their "genuineness" or "falsity" but rather by "the style in which they are imagined." Ideology plays a central, if not exclusive, role in the diversity of styles in which communities imagine themselves as nations. It follows that an examination of anticolonial ideologies is important to the understanding of the development of African nationalism.

The approach that views these ideologies as national ideologies also recognizes the existence of "nationalism without nations."[4] This approach highlights one of the differences between the emergence of nationalism in Europe and its emergence in Africa: political independence in Africa preceded the creation of nations.

> The story of anti-colonial resistance is the story of the construction of a national liberation movement, more or less united, more or less representative, which seeks to incarnate the class and national struggles of the majority of the workforce. These histories cannot be appreciated or analyzed in isolation.[5]

Accordingly, this book groups the transition from colonialism to independence with the ongoing processes of the creation and formation of a shared national identity, of which ideology is an important element. Although neither the national-ideological unrest nor the processes of political and social decolonization generated a consolidated national identity at the time of independence, the construction of a nation remained a much sought-after goal for liberation movements and, in time, for African states.

Notes

1 See for example Robert M. Maxon, "Decolonization Histories," in Martin Shanguhiya and Toyin Falola (eds.), *The Palgrave Handbook of African Colonial and Postcolonial History* (New York: Palgrave Macmillan, 2018), pp. 643–657.
2 Benedict Anderson, *Imagined Communities* (New York: Verso, 1991), pp. 5–7.
3 Ernest Gellner, quoted in Anderson, p. 6.
4 Anthony Smith, *Theories of Nationalism* (New York: Harper, 1971), p. 216.
5 Aquino de Braganca and Immanuel Wallerstein (eds.), "Introduction," *The Anatomy of Colonialism*, Vol. I, in *The African Liberation Reader* (London: Zed Press, 1982), p. v.

1 Africans, African Americans, and the Roots of Pan-African Nationalism

The seeds of the nationalism that emerged in Africa during the twentieth century originally sprouted in the previous century, paradoxically outside of the African continent—among millions of forced migrants, Africans who had been brought to the American continent over the course of approximately 300 years of the trans-Atlantic slave trade, from the sixteenth to the nineteenth century. From its outset the nationalism that emerged among blacks went by different, and not always overlapping, names: "pan-Negro nationalism," "Pan-Africanism," and "black nationalism." An examination of the changing self-identification of Americans of African descent compounds the confusion. The widespread use during the nineteenth century of the racial term "negro" dissipated because of how morally charged and rife with prejudice the word had become. Instead, beginning in the latter half of the twentieth century, preference was given to a term based on color—"blacks." Later it became common practice to note the cultural-geographic origin as a fundamental element of the self-identification of blacks in America—"Afro-Americans"— and in recent years the accepted term has been "African-Americans."[1]

Pan-African nationalism has taken such varied forms at different times and places that any attempt to capture it with a single definition is doomed to fail. At times it manifested as a social movement or a political organization, at times it took the form of cultural, literary, artistic, or religious expression, and for the most part—a combination of all of the above.

Immanuel Geiss, a scholar of Pan-African nationalism, relied on three separate definitions for the concept of "Pan-Africanism":

> Intellectual and political movements among Africans and Afro-Americans who regard or have regarded Africans and people of African descent as homogeneous. This outlook leads to a feeling of racial solidarity and a new self-awareness and causes Afro-Americans to look upon Africa as their real "homeland," without necessarily thinking of a physical return to Africa.

> All ideas which have stressed or sought the cultural unity and political independence of Africa, including the desire to modernize Africa on a

DOI: 10.4324/9781003322818-2

Map 1.1 Countries on the African continent.
Source: The Open University of Israel, used with permission.

basis of equality of rights. The key concepts here have been respectively the "redemption of Africa" and "Africa for the Africans."

Ideas or political movements which have advocated, or advocate, the political unity of Africa or at least close political collaboration in one form or another.[2]

The tremendous variance among these definitions is resolvable if one views Pan-African nationalism as an *inclusive* concept that embodies diverse expressions of nationalism and applies to a community split across different political and territorial frameworks—within Africa itself or in the diaspora—and spanning different historical eras. From its inception in the nineteenth century until World War II, *racial* belonging was underscored as the basis of Pan-African identity, and therefore its definition as *Pan-Negroism* accurately

6 *The Roots of Pan-African Nationalism*

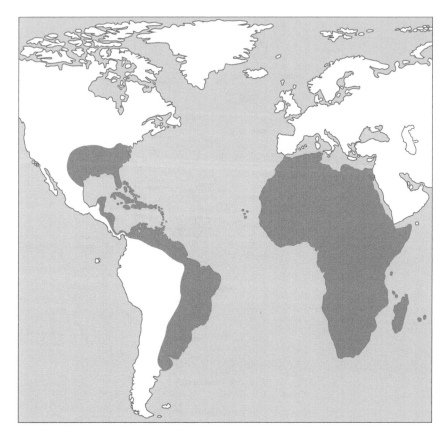

Map 1.2 Concentration of black populations following the slave trade.
Source: The Open University of Israel, used with permission.

reflects its essence and trends. After 1945 the emphasis shifted from the cultural-racial identity that characterized Pan-Negroism to the formation of an *African* identity based on more political and territorial elements. At its center was the call for national self-determination, primarily along the lines of colonial borders. The distinct racial legacy that had left its mark on Pan-Negroism remained a characteristic of the Négritude movement (see below), although its remnants are also evident in the circumscription of African political identity to sub-Saharan Africa—that is, to "black" Africa, which does not encompass North Africa. Inclusive political-continental Pan-Africanism, as the term implies, flourished only briefly, from the 1950s to the mid-1960s. Continental Pan-Africanism, on the other hand, aspired to achieve the political unification of all the states on the continent that had achieved independence or were in the process of doing so, and therefore its Pan-African framework also included the Arab states of North Africa.

The Emergence of Pan-Negroism

The national awakening of blacks in America has its origins in the shattered hopes that the US Civil War (1861–1865) would release them from slavery and enable them to integrate as citizens with equal rights in all their countries of residence across the American continent and adjacent islands, and particularly in the United States. By 1877, however, a wave of persecutions was already underway—lynchings, discriminatory legislation, and even the revocation of laws passed in the aftermath of the Civil War, which granted blacks at least formal equality. Former slaves realized that the official abolition of the slave trade, and subsequently of the institution of slavery, was not enough to emancipate them from the cruel, discriminatory, and humiliating reality into which they had been "emancipated." The distinct legacy of slavery—modern racism—left a deep impression and continued to regulate interracial power relations, even when the circumstances that originally generated it had changed.

Pan-Negro nationalism emerged in the diaspora not as a national identity within the framework of a nation-state delineated by clear territorial borders (as modern nationalism is defined), but along racial borders: people of African descent living in various countries where white culture had subordinated them and prevented them from becoming members of their national communities (nations). It is not surprising that the most prominent leaders of Pan-African nationalism were residents of the Caribbean islands (Jamaica, Barbados,

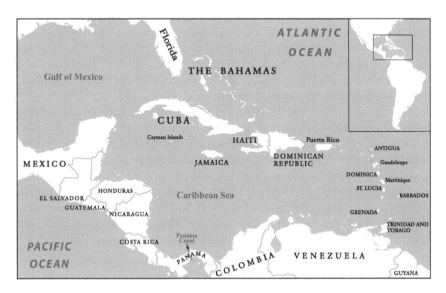

Map 1.3 The Caribbean Islands.
Source: The Open University of Israel, used with permission.

8 *The Roots of Pan-African Nationalism*

Trinidad, Guadalupe, Guyana, Haiti, and St. Thomas). These islands were destinations for trans-atlantic slave traders and also served as points for the transfer of slaves. Slavery in these areas was particularly cruel, and violent uprisings by slaves occasionally broke out in Guyana, Haiti, and Jamaica. The 1804 slave rebellion in Haiti, led by Toussaint L'Ouverture (also spelled Louverture), led to Haiti's independence from French rule. For many years Haiti served as a symbol and model for blacks, who saw it as proof of their ability to wage a war of national liberation and maintain political independence.[3] Although the gradual abolition of slavery in the Caribbean islands during the nineteenth century did not shift the balance of power between the white minority and black majority, nevertheless, alongside the ongoing oppression, higher education opportunities slowly became increasingly available to blacks, and by the mid-nineteenth century there emerged an intellectual leadership committed to struggling against racism. Among the founding fathers of black nationalism who came from the Caribbean islands were the architect of Pan-Negroism, Edward W. Blyden; leaders of black nationalism in the United States, Marcus Garvey and Burghardt Du Bois, who was born in the United States but whose father was a native of Haiti; pioneers of Pan-Africanism in the British Empire, Harold Moody,[4] Ras Makonnen,[5] and George Padmore;[6] and initiator of the first Pan-African Conference in 1900, Henry Sylvester Williams.[7] Likewise, both Aimé Césaire, a founder of the Negroism movement, which became widespread in the French colonies, and Frantz Fanon, the visionary of African radicalism, were born in the Caribbean island of Martinique.[8]

It was the ongoing slavery, degradation, racial discrimination, and oppression in America that motivated leading black intellectuals to strive for unity and solidarity among all blacks, so as to form a united front in the struggle against white rule and racism and to cultivate a sense of racial pride and dignity. In the face of White perceptions regarding their "primitive" and "uncivilized" origins, Black leaders developed an ideology of pride in their African heritage and cultivated a sense of connection and shared destiny with the homeland, Africa. The racist claim that blacks were devoid of culture and history spurred black American intellectuals to investigate their heritage, the historical and cultural roots of which are in Africa. Their studies added a dimension of historical depth to African nationalism, a dimension that is essential to any newly emerging nationalism. In the context of their struggle for complete emancipation and equal rights, black leaders and intellectuals in America underscored the racial identity of blacks—the historically, culturally, and morally unique "African personality" that need not be erased in the presence of Whites through imitation stemming from feelings of inferiority.

Nationalism as Protest against White Racism

During the trans-Atlantic slave trade, Africa became the exclusive source of human beings used for slave labor in the plantation economy that emerged on the American continent. As a result, this period saw complete congruence among the factors of racial identity, social role, and cultural value. In Western culture, accordingly, race, and skin color as its distinct marker, became a sufficient standard for determining a person's appropriate place in society and assessing an individual's character, skills, worth, standing, and level of intelligence. After centuries of slavery, the term "negro" ceased serving as a neutral, judgment-free indicator of race or color and became instead a charged term, embodying concepts such as slave, inferior, primitive, and lazy, so that naturally those to whom the term applied "deserved" the whites' discriminatory treatment. To justify the mass enslavement of Africans and the institutional discrimination against them, whites developed ideological perspectives that "proved" the superiority of the white race and inferiority of the black race. Blacks were said to be devoid of culture and history, less intelligent, controlled by their urges, and totally unproductive. Racist theories assumed that there was a hierarchy of races and that fundamental equality among human beings did not exist. The core essence of racist theory is the claim that differences between "developed" and "superior" races and nations, on the one hand, and "failed" and "inferior" ones, on the other, are attributable to biological heredity rather than social environment—namely, lifestyle, cultural values, political governance, and educational opportunities.

The black nationalism that emerged on the American continent in the nineteenth century and then reached Africa was a response to slavery, discrimination, exploitation, and degradation. It corresponded with the era of modern nationalism, which sought to emancipate oppressed people from the yoke of foreign rule and an internalized sense of cultural inferiority that had been infused into their consciousness. The struggle of blacks to achieve full civil equality in America necessitated that they confront White racism directly and strive to refute its claims and challenge its values. Indeed, Pan-African nationalism fostered the consolidation of an *independent* identity by means of the various theories it developed regarding the "negro personality" and its special contribution to humanity, as well as through the cultivation of racial pride, a focus on the richness and achievements of African culture, evidence of the history of black peoples, and of course emphasis on the basic equality among human beings, peoples, and races. Books and studies refuting racist theories appeared. Haitian anthropologist Anténor Firmin published *The Equality of the Human Races*, a response to Count Arthur de Gobineau, a theorist of modern racism, and his book *An Essay on the Inequality of the Human Races*. Firmin repudiated all the biological and hereditary explanations for the gaps between blacks and whites.

At times the opposition to racism reached the other extreme—that is, the claim that the black race is actually superior to other races. This was the position Marcus Garvey took in positing the superiority of blacks as an antithesis to white racism. A few tried to counterbalance feelings of inferiority by seeking a Black Garden of Eden in the historical past. Some Pan-Africanist thinkers argued that ancient Egyptian civilization was in fact a

Figure 1.1 A painting c.1830 by the German artist Johann Moritz Rugendas depicts a scene below deck of a slave ship headed to Brazil; Rugendas had been an eyewitness to the scene. Many enslaved Africans were transported to the Americas. The trans-Atlantic slave trade and African slavery in the Americas were major factors in the shaping of modern racism.

Source: https://en.wikipedia.org/wiki/Slave_ship#/media/File:Navio_negreiro_-_Rugendas_1830.jpg, Public Domain.

Black-African civilization, and there were those who grouped Plato, Jesus, King David, and Cleopatra with historical African heroes.[9] Efforts to highlight the achievements of African culture and its contributions to humanity as a whole continue to this day.[10]

The searing insult perpetuated by white racism was a powerful driving force behind the black national awakening in America and Africa. The "race problem," the oppression of blacks and the discrimination against them by White government and society were the fate of Africans and people of African descent alike. Their rebellion against ideologies that legitimized this situation served to unite the pioneers of black nationalism on both continents.

Pan-Negroism and Identification with the African Homeland

> Africa is our fatherland.
>
> (M. Delaney, 1861)[11]

Although a certain historical and emotional bond between the black diaspora and the African continent continued throughout the era of slavery, there were

Figure 1.2 1840 depiction of field hand slaves and child, chained together while working.
Source: https://en.wikipedia.org/wiki/African-American_history#/media/File:Illustrations_of_the_American_anti-slavery_almanac_for_1840_(cropped).tif, Public Domain.

other reasons as well for the cultivation of Africa as a homeland in the historical and cultural sense. The process of emancipation from slavery and the challenge of integrating into society required blacks to shed the racist labels that been attached to them and define their collective identity for themselves. Pioneers of black nationalism in America reacted by emphasizing the bond to Africa. They concluded that their own situation could not improve unless the status of their historical homeland was exalted. Identification with African history and cultural heritage was for them an important step in coping with arguments about their uncivilized and inferior heritage and claims that they lacked any historical or cultural identity before the arrival of whites. The transformation of Africa into a spiritual-cultural center and a truly independent political power was intended to grant blacks a proud self-identity and foster solidarity and racial empowerment. In doing so they were hoping for a breakthrough that would allow them to integrate into the national communities of whites in the various countries of America that hitherto had resisted their integration or, alternatively, to transform themselves from an oppressed community without a homeland into a nation whose unique character and roots traced back to its historical homeland, Africa.

Below are excerpts from remarks by Africans and African Americans attesting to reciprocal relations between blacks in America and in Africa.

12   *The Roots of Pan-African Nationalism*

Note the change that took place over the past century in the status of Africa and its leaders. If in the nineteenth century black nationalism in America mobilized to assist Africa, in the postcolonial era an independent Africa has been mobilizing to come to the aid of blacks in America.

American physician and journalist Martin R. Delaney, a leader of the Back-to-Africa movement, wrote in 1862:

> Our policy must be ... Africa for the African race and black men to rule them. By black men I mean, men of African descent who claim an identity with the race.[12]

Edward Blyden, a leader of the Pan-African movement and foreign minister of Liberia, wrote in 1862:

> If no Negro state of respectability be erected in Africa—no Negro government permanently established in that land—then the prejudice in question will make its obstinate stand against all the wealth, and genius and skill that may be exhibited by Negroes in North or South America. The work is to be done in Africa.[13]

In 1923, James W. Johnson wrote in the *New York Age*:

> It may be that the day is not far off when the new Negroes of Africa will be demanding that their blood brothers in the United States be treated with absolute fairness and justice.
> (James Weldon Johnson, *New York Age*, 12 May 1923)[14]

And Kwame Nkrumah, prime minister of Ghana, spoke as follows in 1958 at the First All Africa People's Conference in Accra:

> Long may the links between Africa and the peoples of African Descent continue to hold us together in fraternity. Now that we in Africa are marching towards the complete emancipation of this continent, our independent status will help in no small measure their efforts to attain full human rights and human dignity as citizens of their country.[15]

In 1897 Du Bois asserted that it was only through "Pan-Negroism" that blacks could play a part in human history, and it was in this spirit that blacks in America became attuned to developments in Africa. Reports that arrived from Africa during the nineteenth century regarding actions of colonial rulers—the mass slaughter of Africans by Belgians in the Congo, forced labor in numerous colonies, the continuing enslavement of Africans by the Arab government in Zanzibar and Pemba—sparked concern and rage and generated a sense of common destiny and connectedness between blacks in America and Africa.

The Roots of Pan-African Nationalism   13

Yet, Africa was not only a source of news about the bitter fate of blacks. On the American continent, they derived hope from accounts of the uprisings against white rule—in Sierra Leone in 1898 and in Rhodesia in 1896–1897, and especially from the story of Liberia, founded as an independent state in 1847. Only two independent African states, Liberia and Ethiopia (which managed to repel Italy's attempt at colonial occupation at the Battle of Adwa [also spelled Adowa] in 1896) served as symbols and sources of inspiration for black nationalism in America.

The deepening bond between black intellectuals and the land of their ancestors yielded many fruits: the beginnings of historical research on Africa and the emergence of philosophy and literature focused on the common fate of members of the black race. Relations between blacks across the Atlantic Ocean grew stronger thanks to gatherings in Africa and organizations and movements that emphasized the connection between the diaspora and the homeland. Particularly salient were movements that were not content with cultivating the spiritual connection to the African homeland, and instead called for a return to Africa because, in their view, this was the only means of resolving the problems facing blacks on the American continent.

"Back to Africa" and "Black Zionism"

The idea of going "back to Africa" began to take shape among black communities in the "New World" as early as the first half of the nineteenth century and manifested in practice with a small stream of "returnees." Waves of immigration to Africa intensified in times of fierce persecution, such as the racial rioting of 1829 or the passage of the Fugitive Slave Act of 1850, which required every US state to return escaped slaves to their "lawful" owners, and in the years following the Civil War and preceding World War I, when the southern US states saw many lynchings of black people. In 1847 liberated slaves from the United States founded the "free country" of independent Liberia (whose capital, Monrovia, is named after US President James Monroe). The country's leaders were immigrants from America—Americo-Liberians. As an independent African state, Liberia was a source of hope for the black nationalist movements in America and in Africa.

Liberated slaves from the United States, Canada, and Jamaica also settled in Sierra Leone, whose capital, symbolically named Freetown, became a missionary and intellectual center for all of West Africa. Most of the new settlers in Sierra Leone and Liberia were Africans rescued from slave ships that had attempted to violate the British prohibition against the slave trade but were intercepted along the shores of Africa, although as noted the settlers also included liberated slaves from the American continent who advocated an actual return to Africa. They viewed resettlement as a personal and collective solution that would put an end to oppression, persecution, slavery,

Figure 1.3 Freetown, Sierra Leone in 1856.
Source: John Leighton Wilson or an uncredited artist employed or licensed by him– From the 1856 book *Western Africa: Its History, Condition, and Prospects*, by John Leighton Wilson; https://en.wikipedia.org/wiki/Freetown#/media/File:Freetown,_Sierra_Leone_ca_1856.jpg, Public Domain.

degradation, feelings of inferiority, and loss of human dignity. They believed that this could only be achieved in the historical homeland, where blacks would not be a persecuted minority.

There were not many who viewed a return to the African homeland as a solution to the problems facing blacks in America in the nineteenth century. Most of those who advocated this idea came from the intellectual minority. Salient among them was Edward Blyden,[16] who personally put the idea into practice as he settled in Liberia and joined its leadership.

The following is an excerpt from an 1862 article by Blyden that appeared in the *Liberia Herald*:

> On our way to Washington, we stopped thirty-six hours in Philadelphia … finding that no coloured person is allowed to ride in any of the street cars, and I was shocked to see tender and delicate females of education and refinement obliged to travel on foot all the distance of that city, simply because of their dark complexion; while the rudest and most vulgar white man can avail himself of the advantages of riding.
>
> … I became indignant and sad, and felt anxious to resign my commission and return to Liberia … I felt that I would rather be a denizen of Marmora's [African chief] town, with all its attendant disadvantages,

Figure 1.4 Edward Wilmot Blyden.
Source: https://en.wikipedia.org/wiki/Edward_Wilmot_Blyden#/media/File:Edward_Wilmot_Blyden_(c._1900).jpg, Public Domain.

than be compelled, as a black man, to live in this country; that I would rather go naked and wander among the natives interior [*sic*], than occupy the position of some of the "respectable coloured people" I see here.

I thought how sad it was that so many coloured people seem disposed to cling to this land—fearing to go to Liberia, lest they die of fever. But are they *living* in this country? Their colour is the sign for every insult and contumely. Everybody and everything is preferred to them. Afraid of dying! Would it not be much better for the whole five millions of these people to leave this country, if every one dies in the process of acclimation in a land, than to remain here in servitude at the basis of society? A whole race in degradation! The idea is horrible. Is it not better to die free men than live to be slaves? Was it not under the influence of such a spirit that the first settlers of this country braved the rigours and perils of this land of savages?[17]

16   *The Roots of Pan-African Nationalism*

Being devoutly religious, blacks in America tended to invoke biblical imagery. The return to Africa thus became a modern exodus from Egypt—an exodus from slavery to freedom. From time to time there appeared a "Black Moses," who sought to bring the blacks back to the promised land—Africa. In the late nineteenth century, the return to Africa also came to be known as "Black Zionism." The choice of this term was no coincidence. Leaders of the black national revival movement drew parallels between the situation of the Jews and that of blacks in the diaspora, having no qualms about publicly declaring their identification with Zionism. Interestingly, Blyden—who, as noted, put the back-to-Africa concept into practice—had the following to say about Zionism in 1898:

> I have taken, and do take, the deepest possible interest in the current history of the Jews—especially in that marvellous movement called Zionism. The question, in some of its aspects, is similar to that which at this moment agitates thousands of the descendants of Africa in America, anxious to return to the land of their fathers ... And as the history of the African race—their enslavement, persecution, proscription, and sufferings—closely resembles that of the Jews.

> ... and it is gratifying to notice that the Zionist movement is having its effect upon the whole Jewish community ... raising them out of an indifferent materialism into spiritual contemplation, and to a more active sense of racial privileges and responsibilities.

> There is hardly a man in the civilized world—Christian, Mohammedan, or Jew—who does not recognize the claim and right of the Jew to the Holy Land; and there are very few who, if the conditions be favourable, would not be glad to see them return in a body and take their places in the land of their fathers as a great—and leading—secular power.[18]

After World War I the black community in the United States despaired of becoming an inseparable part of the White Anglo-Saxon American nation with equal rights. The politicization of blacks taking place at that time in the United States led to a revival of the back-to-Africa concept. Marcus Garvey founded a modern mass movement,[19] which aimed

> to establish a Universal Confraternity among the race; to promote the spirit of race pride and love; ... to assist the backward tribes of Africa; to assist in the development of independent Negro nations and communities; to establish a central nation for the race.[20]

Garvey's movement (the Universal Negro Improvement Association) aspired to establish a "Negro Empire" in Africa that would draw masses of blacks, from all diasporas, and endeavored to create an infrastructure for their return to Africa. Garvey founded "national" African churches, a paramilitary whose

The Roots of Pan-African Nationalism 17

purpose was to liberate Africa, and a steamship line—the Black Star—for the purpose of conveying people from the diaspora to the homeland.

During the years it was active, Garvey's movement had little impact on the conditions of blacks in America. Most of them, particularly the urban middle class, did not heed his call to return to Africa. Their main objective was to achieve equal civil rights and integrate fully into American society, notwithstanding the many hardships they faced in white society because of their race and color. They saw the cultivation of a bond with Africa as reinforcing the racist prejudice against which they were struggling and therefore as an obstacle to their struggle. The back-to-Africa idea was, in their view, inconsistent with the national loyalty to America that they sought to demonstrate to whites. The dispute between supporters and opponents of the concept was typical of debates between advocates of a distinct national identity and those who sought its abolition for the sake of assimilation into the majority society and culture.

Garvey's contribution was important in that, thanks to his scholarly and journalistic activities and organizational skills, he established the first large-scale, modern movement. Although his grand plans failed and his movement disintegrated, his contribution to the national awakening in Africa was tremendous, particularly among West African intellectuals who were strongly influenced by his personality, theory, and vision. The need for national independence, political organization, economic independence, and cultural and psychological emancipation from the yoke of whites, and the importance of an active political struggle toward these aims, found a receptive ear amidst the young and educated generation that began to emerge in British West Africa (Nigeria, the Ivory Coast, Sierra Leone, and Gambia). This generation was seeking an alternative to colonialism, and the concepts of Pan-Africanism generally and Garvey's movement specifically were sources of great influence in positioning them at the head of the anticolonial struggle that began in the 1940s. Historically, the concepts of Black Zionism and back-to-Africa, for which Garvey offered the final and most definitive articulation, had little influence on the conditions of the black masses in America but made an important contribution to the national awakening in Africa and the Africans' transition to active struggle for independence.

A national anthem expresses values, aspirations, and national character. Such was "The Universal Ethiopian Anthem" by Burrell and Ford (below), which Garvey's movement adopted as its own anthem at the Convention of the Universal Negro Improvement Association held in New York in 1920, the same gathering at which the Declaration of the Rights of the Negro Peoples of the World was drafted and adopted.

The Universal Ethiopian Anthem[21]

I
Ethiopia, thou land of our fathers,
Thou land where the gods loved to be,
As storm cloud at night suddenly gathers

18 *The Roots of Pan-African Nationalism*

Our armies come rushing to thee.
We must in the fight be victorious
When swords are thrust outward to gleam;
For us will the victory be glorious
When led by the red, black, and green.

Chorus:
Advance, advance to victory,
Let Africa be free;
Advance to meet the foe
With the might
Of the red, the black, and the green.

II
Ethiopia, the tyrant's falling,
Who smote thee upon thy knees,
And thy children are lustily calling
From over the distant seas.
Jehovah, the Great One has heard us,
Has noted our sighs and our tears,
With His spirit of Love of he has stirred us
To be One through the coming years.

Chorus: Advance, advance ...

III
Oh Jehovah, Thou God of ages
Grant unto our sons that lead
The wisdom Thou gave to Thy Sages
When Israel was sore in need.
Thy voice through the dim past has spoken,
Ethiopia shall stretch forth her hand
By thee shall all sectors be broken,
And heaven bless our dear Fatherland.

Chorus: Advance, advance ...

The Pan-African Conferences and Congresses

The first major political expression of Pan-Africanism took place in 1900, with
the convening of a global conference in London that included representatives
from Africa and all the diasporas—the United States, Canada, Britain, and
the Caribbean. The conference passed resolutions condemning racism, criti-
cizing the economic exploitation of Africa, demanding equality of rights for

blacks in the United States, and cautioning the superpowers against infringement on the territorial integrity of independent black countries—Liberia, Ethiopia, and Haiti. Pan-African congresses subsequently took place in Paris (1919), London (1921), Lisbon (1923), New York (1927), and Manchester (1945).

The following is an excerpt from resolutions of the 1919 Pan-African Congress in Paris:

> The Negroes of the world ... propose:

> That the allied and associated Powers establish a code of laws "for the international protection of the natives of Africa," similar to the proposed international code for Labor.

> That the League of Nations establish a permanent Bureau charged with the duty of "overseeing the application of these laws to the political, social, and economic welfare of the natives."

> The Negroes of the world demand that hereafter natives of Africa and the Peoples of African descent be "governed according to the following principles."

> ... The State: The natives of Africa must have the right to participate in the government as fast as their development permits in conformity with the principle that the government exists for the natives, and not the natives for the government. They shall at once be allowed to participate in local and tribal government according to ancient usage, and this participation shall gradually extend, as education and experience proceeds, to the higher offices of State, to the end that, in time, Africa be ruled by consent of the Africans.

> ... Whenever it is proven that African natives are not receiving just treatment at the hands of any State or that any State deliberately excludes its civilized citizens or subjects of Negro descent from its body politic and culture, it shall be the duty of the League of Nations to bring the matter to the attention of the civilized World.[22]

Until World War II, black Americans were the life force that drove the Pan-African movement and its congresses. Their agendas primarily reflected their interests and needs: the struggle against racism, the pursuit of equal rights for blacks everywhere, and Pan-Negro solidarity. Demands relating to the conditions of Africans under colonial rule also arose. Yet, it was only at the Manchester Congress of 1945 that leaders from Africa, including Nkrumah and Kenyatta among others, became the dominant figures in the movement, although a prominent representative role was still reserved for the founders of the movement: Du Bois, Padmore, Makonnen, and Amy Garvey, Marcus Garvey's widow.

The Impact of Pan-Negroism on Africa

The channels by which Pan-Negroism influenced the African national awakening were many. The first contacts were the work of freed slaves who came to Africa from the American continent and founded Liberia as an independent state in 1847. Likewise, thanks to "returnees" from America, Sierra Leone became a missionary and intellectual center for all of West Africa. Graduates of the first African university, Fourah Bay College,[23] established in Freetown in 1827, had a great deal of influence on the development of a new African elite. At the end of the nineteenth century, hundreds of Black intellectuals and missionaries from Sierra Leone were working in other West African British colonies (Nigeria, the Gold Coast, and Gambia). They included the first Anglican African bishop in Nigeria, Samuel Crowther; the father of Nigerian nationalism, Herbert Macaulay; and Africanus Horton from the Gold Coast, who as early as 1865 was promoting the vision of independent African nations. The national revival in West Africa as a whole was strongly influenced by the "Saro people," as descendants of formerly enslaved Sierra Leonians who migrated to Nigeria were called, and by the "Brazilians" and "Cubans"—the names given to returnees to West Africa from Latin America (mainly Cuba and Brazil).

Soldiers from Caribbean islands who were stationed in Africa as members of British military units also contributed to the spread of black nationalism. Nationalist ideas permeated the religious activities of black missionaries from America working in various parts of Africa on behalf of black national— "Ethiopian" or "Zionist"—churches.[24] These missionaries spread ideas about the black Church, black Christianity, black Jesus, black autonomy, and emancipation from the custodianship of White missionaries. The emergence of independent black churches created an infrastructure that nurtured and helped disseminate ideas of black independence and pride.

The following timeline describes the evolving relations among three figures. At the same time, it also reflects the correlation between Africa's national awakening and black nationalism in America and points to the circumstances that fostered nationalism in the Gold Coast and Nkrumah's rise to power:

> 1863 John Small of the Caribbean island of Barbados, a sergeant in a British military unit in the Caribbean, is sent to serve in the Gold Coast.
>
> 1863–1867 Small learns the language of the Fanti people and becomes acquainted with their culture.
>
> 1867–1871 Small returns to Central America—to British Honduras.
>
> 1871 Small immigrates to the United States and joins the African Methodist Episcopal Zion Church (AME Zion Church).
>
> 1896 Small is elected as AME Zion Church bishop to Africa.

1898 Small visits the Gold Coast and founds a mission of the AME Zion Church. He invites a young man, James Aggrey, to attend the AME Zion-affiliated Livingstone College in the United States.
1924 James Aggrey returns to the Gold Coast after 26 years in the United States.
1926 Kwame Nkrumah is one of Aggrey's students at Achimota College, in the Gold Coast.
1935 Inspired by Aggrey, Nkrumah travels to the United States to attend Lincoln University, a Black university.
1935–1943 While in the United States, Nkrumah specializes in Black history and is strongly influenced by the theories of Marcus Garvey.
1945 Nkrumah participates in the fifth Pan-African Congress in Manchester.
1947 Nkrumah returns to the Gold Coast and takes a leading role in the national struggle.
1957 Nkrumah becomes the first prime minister and president of Ghana (formerly the Gold Coast) when it gains independence.

Figure 1.5 Obafemi Awolowo.
Source: https://en.wikipedia.org/wiki/File:Awolowo-Obafemi.JPG, Fair Use.

Figure 1.6 Jomo Kenyatta.
Source: https://en.wikipedia.org/wiki/Jomo_Kenyatta#/media/File:Jomo_Kenyatta_1966-06-15.jpg, Public Domain.

The Pan-African movement, as noted, became an important forum for blacks from America and Africa to meet. Many African leaders received an education in the United States, where their interactions with leaders of the Black movement had a strong influence on them. Notable examples include John Chilembwe, Nkrumah, Azikiwe, and Eyo Ita,[25] who led the anticolonial struggle in their own countries after World War II, and some of whom became leaders of independent states: Nkrumah in Ghana, Kenyatta in Kenya, Banda in Malawi (Nyasaland), and Azikiwe and Obafemi Awolowo in Nigeria.

One cannot fully appreciate the national awakening in Africa, particularly in British West Africa, unless one takes into account the significant influence of the Black, Pan-Negro nationalism that emerged on the American continent. The blacks' struggle against white society and its degrading treatment of them, the consolidation of a proud, positive sense of self, their identification with the homeland and its heritage, and the cultivation of an inclusive racial sense of fraternity for the sake of achieving racial equality and, subsequently, full social equality across all diasporas, served as a model for the first generation of young, educated African leaders. The political and racial consciousness of African leaders, who ultimately took over their governments from the colonial rulers, took form and solidified thanks to their contact with leaders of black nationalism on the American continent.

Pan-Negro nationalism did not succeed in fulfilling black expectations of achieving equality and liberty in their countries of residence in the Americas. However, its contribution to the growth of political-territorial nationalism in Africa was tremendous. The failure of the movement to achieve the civil equality to which blacks had aspired and their decision to seek alternative means of struggle within American society, alongside the sobering realization that it was futile to hope that the colonial regime could be enlisted in pursuing the social, economic, and political welfare of Africans and, above all, the struggle against racism as the conceptual and moral basis of colonialism induced the young African leadership to recognize the need for anticolonial organization and action in Africa itself. Thus, the foundation was laid for the emergence of political-territorial nationalism in Africa, following which most of the African states achieved independence.

Notes

1 This multiplicity of terminology attests to the historically changing awareness surrounding collective identity, and its elucidation is necessary to ensure an understanding of the courses of development of African nationalism in all its incarnations and variety. At the same time, it can also generate much confusion, and to avoid frequent shifts in terminology we have opted for consistent use of the term "blacks."

2 Imanuel Geiss, *The Pan-African Movement* (London: Methuen, 1974), pp. 3–4.

3 In the twentieth century Haiti deteriorated into a dictatorial, exploitative regime.

4 Harold Moody (1882–1947), a native of Jamaica who studied medicine in Britain, was a moderate Pan-Africanist. He was active on behalf of Africans within European organizations and sought to promote interracial cooperation.

5 Ras Makonnen, born in 1900 in British Guyana, was a graduate of universities in the United States and Denmark. He initiated the formation of the Pan-African Federation (London, 1944) and was among the organizers of the fifth Pan-African Congress (Manchester, 1945). He worked for the government of Nkrumah after Ghana attained independence, and settled in Kenya after Nkrumah was overthrown.

6 George Padmore (1902–1959), born in Trinidad and educated in the United States, was a member of the Communist Party and a radical Pan-Africanist. Although he eventually abandoned communism, he was accused of having betrayed African nationalism. His book *Pan-Africanism or Communism* is regarded as a classic exposé on the deliberation between communism and nationalism.

7 Henry Sylvester Williams (1868–1911) was born in Trinidad and studied law in London. He was an organizer of the first Pan-African Conference (London, 1900).

8 See a detailed discussion on the role of intellectuals in African nationalism in Toyin Falola and Chukwuemeka Agbo, "Nationalism and African intellectuals," in M. S. Shanguhiya and T. Falola (eds.), *The Palgrave Handbook*, 2018, pp. 621–641.

9 Cheikh Anta Diop, *L'unité culturelle de l'Afrique noire* (Paris: Présence Africaine, 1959).

24   *The Roots of Pan-African Nationalism*

10 African-Americans continue to challenge the Eurocentric worldview with increasing determination. Recent decades have seen a flourishing body of Afrocentric scholarship centered in the United States. Its principal argument is that the Eurocentric worldview, which regards the West as the standard by which to measure other cultures, systematically continues to ignore important contributions by Africans and people of African descent to world culture and human progress. The titles of the following two publications illustrate the research approaches of the Afrocentric school of thought:

George Games, *Stolen Legacy: The Greeks Were Not the Authors of Greek Philosophy but the People of North Africa Commonly Called the Egyptians* (San Francisco: Richardson, 1976).

Martin Bernal, *Black Athena: The Afroasiatic Roots of Classical Civilization* (New Brunswick, NJ: Rutgers University Press, 1987, 1990, 2020).

The counterargument to Afrocentrism is exemplified by Mary Lefkowitz, *Not Out of Africa: How Afrocentrism Became an Excuse to Teach Myth as History* (New York: New Republic and Basic Books, 1996).

11 Geiss, p. 165.

12 Ibid.

13 Hollis R. Lynch, *Black Spokesman: Selected Published Writings of Edward Wilmot Blyden* (London: F. Cass, 1971), p. 18.

14 William John Hanna (ed.), *Independent Black Africa: The Politics of Freedom* (Chicago: Rand McNally, 1964), p. 192.

15 Vincent Bakpetu Thompson, *Africa and Unity* (London: Longman, 1969), p. 39. See also Falola and Agbo, in Shanguhia and Falola, *The Palgrave Handbook*, 2018, p. 634.

16 Edward Blyden (1832–1912), a native of the Caribbean island of St. Thomas, was among the spiritual architects of the new African nationalism. Blyden was an advocate of the Back-to-Africa movement who put the idea into practice. He emigrated to Liberia, where he served as foreign minister and was a candidate for the presidency. He wrote many articles on black history and culture, and on negro fate and pride, emphasizing the uniqueness and greatness of the "African personality." He was active in Liberia, Sierra Leone, and Nigeria in developing a modern African education that would fuse the national African heritage with the achievements of European civilization.

17 Lynch, pp. 21–22.

18 Ibid., pp. 210–211.

19 Marcus Garvey (1887–1940) was born in Jamaica, where he founded his movement in 1914. In 1916 he shifted his center of operations to New York. The Back-to-Africa movement that he headed did not believe that blacks would be able to achieve equality and social justice within White society and therefore advocated a return to the African homeland. In the early 1920s his movement numbered approximately two million supporters, most of whom were poor. Through their donations Garvey tried to establish exclusively Black-owned businesses whose profits would be used to fund the movement's activities. In 1925 he was convicted of fraud and during his two-year prison sentence the movement began to decline. Garvey, who never personally actualized the back-to-Africa concept, eventually returned to Jamaica.

20 Geiss, p. 265.

The Roots of Pan-African Nationalism   25

21 www.unia-acl.org/archive/anthem.html; https://en.wikisource.org/wiki/The_
Universal_Ethiopian_Anthem_and_How_it_Came_to_be_Written.

22 Resolutions passed at the 1919 Pan-African Congress, Paris, February 19–21,
1919, www.international.ucla.edu/asc/mgpp/sample09.

23 Fourah Bay College was established by the Church Missionary Society (CMS),
a British mission society that operated in Sierra Leone. The college was founded
after CMS despaired of recruiting sufficient numbers of European teachers and
missionaries for service in West Africa. Over the course of its 150 years the college
trained generations of educated Africans. From 1876 to 1967 the college was formally affiliated with Durham University in England, which issued the degrees
earned by graduates of the college.

24 In ancient literature Africa is often referred to as Ethiopia. As the only country
that maintained its independence during the colonial era, Ethiopia became a
modern symbol for independence during those years. Africans viewed its victory
over Italy at the Battle of Adwa as a source of pride and as proof that they are not
inferior to Whites.

25 Eyo Ita of Nigeria, who received a university education in the United States,
founded the Nigerian Youth League Movement. The thrust of his activity was
in the field of education. He advocated independent education and revival of
Nigeria's national culture. He also called for the national unification of Nigerians
despite their ethnic differences.

2 From Pan-Negroism to Territorial Nationalism

Nationalism without Nations

Studies on decolonization have identified World War II as an important turning point in the process of Africa's decolonization. The focus here is on the ideological perspectives that were associated with these sociopolitical changes. In 1945, following the conclusion of World War II, the Fifth Pan-African Congress convened in Manchester, Britain. The declarations and resolutions passed at the Congress gave clear voice to those changes, the essence of which was a transition from *Pan-Negro* nationalism to *African* nationalism.

The following are excerpts from declarations and resolutions passed at the Congress:

Resolution on West Africa:

Political

That since the advent of British, French, Belgian and other European nations in West Africa, there has been regression instead of progress as a result of systematic exploitation by these alien imperialist Powers. The claims of "partnership," "trusteeship," "guardianship," and the "mandate system," do not serve the political wishes of the people of West Africa.

That the democratic nature of the indigenous institutions of the peoples of West Africa has been crushed by obnoxious and oppressive laws and regulations, and replaced by autocratic systems of Government which are inimical to the political wishes of the peoples of West Africa.

That the introduction of pretentious constitutional reforms into the West African Territories are nothing but spurious attempts on the part of alien imperialist Powers to continue the political enslavement of the peoples.

Declaration on the Challenge to the Colonial Powers:

The delegates to the Fifth Pan-African Congress believe in peace. How could it be otherwise when for centuries the African peoples have been victims of violence and slavery. Yet if the Western world is still determined to rule mankind by force, then Africans, as a last resort, may have to

DOI: 10.4324/9781003322818-3

appeal to force in the effort to achieve Freedom ... We are determined to be free. We want education. We want the right to earn a decent living; the right to express our thoughts and emotions ... We demand for Black Africa autonomy and independence.

Declaration to the Colonial Workers, Farmers and Intellectuals:

We affirm the right of all Colonial peoples to control their own destiny. All Colonies must be free from foreign imperialist control, whether political or economic. The peoples of the Colonies must have the right to elect their own governments, without restrictions from foreign powers. We say to the peoples of the Colonies that they must fight for these ends by all the means at their disposal.

The object of imperialist powers is to exploit. By granting the right to Colonial peoples to govern themselves that object is defeated. Therefore, the struggle for political power by Colonial and subject peoples is the first step towards, and the necessary prerequisite to, complete social, economic and political emancipation.[1]

The declarations and resolutions of the Fifth Pan-African Congress undeniably reflect a genuine transformation in the nationalist Pan-African outlook. The most significant and substantive change was the shift in emphasis from a cultural-racial nationalism that aspires to recognize, unite, and represent all members of the black race across all its diasporas, to a political-territorial nationalism centered on the inhabitants of Africa itself. Various factors brought about this transition: Their disappointment with the Pan-Negro movement's ability to resolve the unique problems they faced within American societies had led American blacks to seek modes of action outside the movement and to channel their efforts toward domestic American politics. Educated young Africans whose political consciousness had taken shape within the movement then replaced the American activists in the movement's leadership, and they were not content to wage a conceptual struggle based on the ideology of colonialism—namely, racism. In 1945 it became easier than ever before to dispel the illusion that colonialism could provide effective leverage for Africa's development. Thus, the historical circumstances engendered by World War II and its aftermath greatly intensified the anticolonial struggle in Africa.

The vision of African nationalism that began to take shape in 1945 was focused not on cultural characteristics shared by all Africans, but rather on the very essence of modern nationalism—the question of political independence. If during the Pan-Negro phase the "nation" consisted of blacks from all the diasporas, then the question that emerged was: Who qualifies as the nation with the right to self-determination in the political sense? The resolutions and declarations of the Manchester Congress did not clearly delineate or define the nation in whose name the call for an independent political entity was

28 *From Pan-Negroism to Territorial Nationalism*

being issued. The definitions varied, from "the people of West Africa" or "the Colonial people" to "the peoples of the Colonies." But who exactly were these "people of West Africa"? Was this a reference to ethnic groups? Or to communities that enjoyed political independence before the colonial occupation?

The Pan-African Congress did not offer an unequivocal definition. Yet the recurring use of phrases such as "the Colonial people" and "the peoples of the Colonies" actually hint at the colonial structures themselves as a basis for demanding national self-determination despite the absence of a common sociological basis or a consolidated national identity. Indeed, the colonial state had gathered different ethnic, linguistic, and cultural communities together under one political administrative roof (the colony), and in doing so it delineated the contours of the political entity in whose name the expulsion of foreign rule was being demanded. Political independence was seen as the preliminary phase for achieving the full range of human liberties, including the right to build a nation. With the completion of this phase, African states, as demarcated by their colonial borders, would become nation-states along the lines of the national ideal prevalent in the Western world (e.g., the US, France), the cradle of modern nationalism.

Accordingly, what characterized the African nationalism that emerged after the war was its reliance on the colony as a basis for the nation that would emerge within its borders. The formation of a colonial state as a political-national framework representative of all its African inhabitants, across the entire range of their tremendous ethnic and cultural diversity,[2] is a relatively new phenomenon. Anthony Smith, a leading scholar of nationalism, described the nationalism that emerged in response to colonial rule as "nationalism without nations." The future mission of this nationalism would be to build nations within the framework of states defined by its colonial borders.[3]

The territorial nationalism that took shape in Africa generated two principal rival movements that sought to advance different standards for determining national borders in Africa: continental Pan-Africanism, and ethnic nationalism. Continental territorial nationalism, or Pan-Africanism (see Chapter 4) refuted the "territorial nationalism of one state," which it viewed as perpetuating the artificial colonial entities and the many problems they had created in Africa. Instead, it proposed the establishment of a political union among all the states on the continent, or at least regional unions comprising a number of colonies. Ethnic nationalism had a completely different starting point—not a shared territorial space, but rather an existing, recognized social and cultural entity striving for self-rule. That is, it viewed the existence and political survival of an ethnic group, in the form of a state or other political framework, such as autonomy or federalism, as a means of ensuring the group's continuity and preserving its unique identity. In contrast to this aspiration of dismantling colonial borders so as to give political expression to the unique character of an ethnocultural group, the starting point for territorial nationalism was the imposed political entity that lacked a unique, shared cultural identity, and which territorial nationalism was expected to represent and defend. The common denominator of both territorial nationalism and ethnocultural nationalism was the opposition to foreign rule and the aspiration to expel it, seize control of its political apparatus, and adopt, as bases of future nations, the boundaries of the whole colony or of an administrative unit that had ethnocultural characteristics (like the Muslim Hausa-Fulani in North Nigeria, the Somali Northern Frontier District (NFD) in Kenya, or the Black African, non-Muslim population in South Sudan within a largely Arab Muslim, British-ruled Sudan).

Until the 1990s, most efforts to advance alternative forms of nationalism within colonial frameworks failed, as discussed below. The anticolonial nationalism that developed within the borders of colonial states, each state operating as a separate unit, became—despite the tremendous problems with it and the many attempts to defy and dismantle it—the dominant trend in political-territorial nationalism in Africa. The first ethnocultural breakthrough was South Sudan, which became independent in 2011. The relative resilience of colonial entities stemmed from the lack of available alternative frameworks and from fears of instability, wars, and even anarchy following the disruption of existing colonial structures and the potential disintegration into hundreds or thousands of ethnic or regional units. The colonial structures that created postcolonial structures also gave rise to collective interests: The status of political elites within the colonies, for example, depended on the continued existence of political structures within colonial borders, as they had no other basis of power. In addition, despite their artificial origins, the colonial borders had been somewhat internalized. A few examples illustrate this interesting phenomenon: Eritrea's successful struggle for independence from Ethiopia (1993) may be seen as the reemergence of a colonial entity, given Eritrea's history as a colony of Italy (1887–1941) and Britain (1941–1952) that was formally annexed to Ethiopia only in 1962. The case of Somalia also illustrates the import of colonial structures. In 1962 British Somaliland and Italian Somalia, both inhabited by the ethnocultural Somali people,[4] merged into a single political unit. Somalia, a union of two colonies, then aspired to annex French Somaliland (today Djibouti) as well as parts of Ethiopia (the Ogaden region) and northern Kenya inhabited by Somalis. Somalia failed in this endeavor, and in 1992, with the secession of northern Somalia (formerly British Somaliland), the country split into its former colonial components. Interestingly, many separatist and irredentist movements—in Cameroon, Togo, Zaire (now known as the DRC or Democratic Republic of Congo), Sudan, Uganda, and Zambia—also relied on internal and not necessarily wholly ethnocultural borders between districts or provinces within colonies. This phenomenon illustrates that even though they were artificially and randomly demarcated, colonial borders did, to some extent, become internalized. One example is the Ibo ethnocultural secession from Nigeria, which led (between 1967 and 1970) to the foundation of Biafra, which was not based on ethnic borders, but on a colonially demarcated Eastern Nigeria.

30 *From Pan-Negroism to Territorial Nationalism*

Notes

1 George Padmore (ed.), *Colonial and Coloured Unity: A Programme of Action; History of the Pan-African Congress* (London: The Hammersmith Bookshop, 1947), available at www.marxists.org/archive/padmore/1947/pan-african-congress/index.htm.
2 Only Somalia, Lesotho, Botswana, and Swaziland were ethnically and linguistically homogenous.
3 Anthony D. Smith, *Theories of Nationalism* (New York: Harper and Row, 1971), p. 216.
4 All Somalis are Muslims and speak the same language.

3 Négritude[1]

Our God is Black
by R. E. G. Armattoe

Our God is black
Black of eternal blackness
With large voluptuous lips
Matted hair and brown liquid eyes ...
For in his image we are made
Our God is black.[2]

Négritude emerged as a cultural-intellectual movement centered, in particular, in African colonies subject to French colonial rule. It was founded by black intellectuals who had moved to Paris from French colonies in West Africa and the Caribbean. Prominent among them were Léopold Senghor[3] and Aimé Césaire,[4] who evidently coined the term Négritude.[5] It was a counter-reaction to the concept of cultural assimilation associated with French colonialism and to the French effort to erase all relics of African culture and transform Africans into black French people. Négritude, as its name and the identity of its founders imply, sought to distinguish African identity and foster racial pride among blacks throughout their diasporas.

The Emergence of "Négritude"

The Négritude movement was born in Paris in the 1930s. At the time—in the aftermath of World War I—Europe was in a state of deep, ongoing crisis. Economic and social despair was accompanied by moral despair, as reflected in the reorientation of intellectual movements disappointed by European industrialization and rationalism. These movements began to focus on the importance of human emotion, downplaying the value of intellect, and exalting what was "wild" and "natural." Because such concepts accorded with European

DOI: 10.4324/9781003322818-4

Figure 3.1 Léopold Sedar Senghor.
Source: https://en.wikipedia.org/wiki/L%C3%A9opold_S%C3%A9dar_Senghor#/media/File:UNESCO_History,_Visite_de_S._Exc._M._L%C3%A9opold_Sedar_Senghor,_Pr%C3%A9sident_de_la_R%C3%A9publique_du_S%C3%A9n%C3%A9gal_-_UNESCO_-_PHOTO0000002688_0001_(cropped).tiff, CC BY-SA 3.0 IGO.

impressions of Africa, French intellectuals and writers began writing longingly about a return to nature, and some even relocated to Africa in search of a better world. Paris experienced a wave of admiration for black music, and African painting and sculpture made their mark on the work of important artists such as Matisse and Picasso. This atmosphere contributed to the quest undertaken by Senghor and his cohorts to identify what distinguished African from Western culture. During those years Europe saw the publication of numerous anthropological studies that recognized precolonial African cultures for the first time. The activism taking place within the Pan-African movement, which was aimed at fostering a distinct and proud cultural identity for blacks the world over, also left its mark on the founders of the Négritude movement.

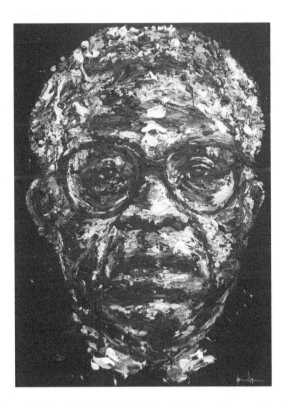

Figure 3.2 Portrait of Aimé Césaire by Hom Nguyen for the Musée de l'Homme in 2021 for the *Portraits de France* exhibition.
Source: https://en.wikipedia.org/wiki/Aim%C3%A9_C%C3%A9saire#/media/File:Aim%C3%A9_C%C3%A9saire.jpg, CC BY-SA 4.0.

Individual, People, Society, and Culture in "Négritude"

Négritude, in Léopold Senghor's eyes, represented the entirety of the Black world's values. Its role was to foster a sense of identity that would provide a counterweight to cultural colonialism, which had scorned the culture and values of the black African. The fundamental hypothesis of Négritude in effect accepted the European claim of an essential difference between Europeans and Africans, but in complete juxtaposition to the latter, the movement's founders rejected the salient European argument that Africans were inferior. In its early years the movement even entertained the counterargument—rejecting Western culture and exalting African qualities as superior—although its dominant message was "different but equal." It attributed this difference to the sensory and emotional nature of blacks, in contrast to the intellectualism that was dominant among Europeans. For the movement's adherents this difference represented the blacks' close ties to nature and harmony with it, a harmony that was completely lacking among Europeans who, instead, engaged in a struggle against nature, seeking to control it and thus destroying the environment. In contrast to the racist colonialist image, the figure of the African was that of a strong yet gentle person, vibrant and spontaneous, open and grounded, someone who lives life wholly, expressing and realizing oneself through music, art, sculpture, and poetry. The Africans' sense of harmony with their natural and social environment is evident in their hospitality, respect for elders, and assistance to others. Traditional African society was portrayed as democratic, egalitarian, and cooperative, a society without disparities in wealth or status.

Négritude theory—which emphasizes the emotional, spontaneous, and "natural" dimension in the soul of the African peoples and individuals, and exalts the simplicity and rootedness of the bond that Africans have with

Figure 3.3 African Fang mask used for the *ngil* ceremony, an inquisitorial search for sorcerers. Such art influenced modern European art, such as Picasso's cubism. See www.artdex.com/historical-influence-of-african-art-in-the-modern-art-movement/ for more information.

Source: Photographer: Marie-Lan Nguyen, Collection: Musée du quai Branly at the Louvre, https://commons.wikimedia.org/wiki/File:Fang_mask_Louvre_MH65-104-1.jpg, Public Domain.

their natural homeland, the land itself, and the working of the land—may be viewed as an expression of romantic nationalism.[6] In his essay "Negro-African Civilization,"[7] Senghor tries to delve into the depths of the negro-African soul and to trace the course of its evolution under the influence of the pastoral agricultural climate and environment of Africa. He seeks to paint a living image, warm, natural, and human, in contrast to the racist image propounded by colonialism. The following excerpts from Senghor's essay provide a stark articulation of romantic nationalism.

> How surprised the psychologists of the French army were when they discovered that Senegalese conscripts were more sensitive to the vicissitudes of the climate, and even to extreme heat, then the soldiers of "metropolitan" France; that they reacted to the least changes in the weather, and even to such barely discernible events as minute inflections of the voice. These warriors who had passed for brutes—these heroes—turned out to have the sensitivity of women. It is often said, and not without reason, that *the Negro is a man of Nature*. The African negro, whether peasant, fishermen, hunter or herdsman, lives outdoors, both off the earth and with it, on intimate terms with trees and animals and all the elements, and to the rhythm of seasons and days. He keeps his senses open, ready to receive any impulse, and even the very waves of nature, without a screen (which is not to say without relays or transformers) between subject and object. He does, of course, reflect; but what comes first is form and color, sound and rhythm, smell and touch.[8]

To illustrate the responses and character of the negro, Senghor presents "a scene from daily life: a meeting of two parents, or two friends, who have not seen each other for a long time." In his words, "The litany of greetings has initially a banal rhythm":

> Are you at peace?
> Only at peace.
> Is your father at peace?
> Only at peace.
> Is your mother at peace?
> Only at peace.
> Is everyone at home at peace?
> Only at peace.

> This is followed by an exchange of news, about parents, friends, fields and herds. Then old memories are brought up. When certain facts are recalled and dear faces evoked, the motion takes hold of their bodies. They embrace each other and hold hands for a long time. Then the litany of greetings begins again. But this time the rhythm is more pronounced; it is the very rhythm of the poem. Their breasts are distended, their throats

36   *Négritude*

constricted. The emotion is there and makes them burst into sobs and
shed heavy tears ...

For the African negro more than for anyone else, an emotion is primarily
"the subjective movement of a want"—a movement closely connected
with his physiology. Hence his sense of rhythm and the spontaneity of
his reflexes.[9]

Elsewhere Senghor states, "The African negro ... reacts more faithfully to
stimulation by the object: he espouses its rhythm. This carnal sense of *rhythm*,
that of movement, form and color, is one of the specific characteristics."[10]

Senghor's view of the common thread linking religion, communism, and
Négritude may be inferred from the following passages:

This is even truer of the African negro society. Technical activities (to
which we shall return) are always tied to cultural and religious activities: to art and magic, if not to the mystical ... We have here a society
founded essentially on human relations, and perhaps even more on
relations between men and "gods." It is an *animistic* society, I mean, a
society content with the "necessities of life," and less interested in "terres-
trial nourishment" than in spiritual nourishment ...[11] Concealed behind
them are the cosmic forces—the forces of life—which govern and animate
the appearances, endowing them with color and rhythm, life and sense.

This means that an emotion, under its initial aspect as a fall of consciousness [into the world of magic, as emotion is defined by Sartre], is
on the contrary *the rise of consciousness to a higher state of knowledge.*
It is "consciousness of the world," "a certain way of apprehending the
world." It is an integrated consciousness, for "the 'emoved'[12] subject and
the 'emoving' object are united in an indissoluble synthesis,"[13] and ... in
a dance of love ...[14]

The following excerpt expresses Senghor's view of the unique character of
blacks and their culture in relation to whites and white culture:

Let us consider first the European White in his attitude towards the
object. He is ... an *objective intelligence.* As a man of action, warrior,
bird of prey, pure vision, he first of all distinguishes himself from the
object ... Armed with precision instruments, he dissects it mercilessly
so as to arrive at the factual analysis. Learned, but moved by practical
considerations, the European White uses the Other, after slaying it, for
practical ends: He treats it as a *means.* And he *assimilates* it in a centri-
petal motion ...

The African negro is as it were locked up in his black skin. He lives in a
primordial night, and does not distinguish himself, to begin with, from

Négritude 37

the object ... The African negro is ... a pure sensory field. It is in his subjectivity and at the end of his antennae ... that he discovers the *Other* ... American psychologists have noted that the reflexes of the Negro are more natural and sure because more in agreement with the object ...

Here, then, is the subject who leaves his *I* to *sympathize* with the *Thou*, and to identify himself with it. He dies to himself to be reborn in the Other. He does not assimilate *it*, but himself ... For he lives a communal life with the Other and in *symbiosis* with it ... Subject and object are dialectically confronted in the very act of knowledge ... "I think, therefore I am," wrote Descartes, who was the European *par excellence*. The African negro could say, "I feel, I dance the Other, I am." ... Now to dance is to discover and to *re-create*, to identify oneself with the forces of life, to lead a fuller life, and in short, to *be*.[15]

Senghor's frequent assertion that "emotion is Negro" drew much criticism, and wrongly so according to him.[16] He argued that he saw no other way to describe the unique character of Africans: "It is, at any rate, this gift of emotion which explains *negrohood*, which Sartre ... defines as 'a certain affective attitude towards the world,' and which I have defined as 'the totality of the cultural values' of the African Negro."[17]

During the 1930s, the movement's leaders began dismantling the isolationist barriers within which they had nurtured the concept of cultural uniqueness, while also advancing favorable views of African-European cultural fusion—a selective fusion based on Africa's recognition of the value and uniqueness of its culture. Senghor, who viewed this as willing assimilation, adopted the slogan "Assimilate, don't be assimilated!" He argued that the two cultures need one another: African culture needs European technology, while Europe needs African qualities in order to infuse life into its cold, materialistic culture. Senghor was willing to accept Europe on the condition that it agree to enrich African culture rather than destroy it and build on its ruins. This shift stemmed, among other factors, from the Nazi rise to power in Germany. Senghor saw the dangers inherent in scorning and disparaging other cultures and races and pursuing racial and cultural isolation. The call for intercultural fusion grew stronger after World War II.

Around this time Senghor penned his poem "To New York," from which the following excerpts are taken:

To New York

New York: New York! First I have been bewildered at your beauty, these tall golden girls with long legs.
So shy at first in front of the blue steeliness of your gaze, your frozen smile.
. . .
Fifteen days without a well nor a pasture, all the birds of the air
Falling sudden and dead under the high ashes of terraces.

38   *Négritude*

Not a laugh from a child in flower, her hand in my fresh hand
Not a maternal breast, nylon legs. Legs and breasts without sweat nor smell.
. . .
New York! I say New York, let the black blood flood in your blood
Let it get the rust off your iron joints, like an oil of life
Let it give to your bridges the curve of croups and the suppleness of
    lianas.[18]

"Négritude": From Racial and Cultural Identity to Political Nationalism

Until World War II Senghor believed that the rehabilitation of Africa should begin with its cultural rehabilitation, that freedom from colonialism was not possible absent recognition of the value and uniqueness of African culture. He first expressed the link between the theory of Négritude and the sphere of politics in a 1945 article that laid out his thinking regarding intercultural fusion and the willing assimilation into a political program.[19] The essay proposed establishing "Colonial Nations" of sorts, under French rule, in which Africans would participate in governance—a concept along the lines of de Gaulle's 1958 proposal for an Afro-French community. Even after Senegal had attained independence in 1960, the principles of Négritude continued to guide Senghor's thinking. He viewed the maintenance of ties with France and its culture as one of the fundamental conditions for the development of its former colonies. It was from the theory of Négritude that the concept of *francophonie* emerged—a concept that Senghor supported and continued to develop after 1960. He ascribed great importance to the French language, which had helped shape the abstract concepts of the Négritude movement and which he viewed as a tool for spreading the movement's message throughout the world. Senghor supported the maintenance of strong cultural ties among the world's French-speaking countries, and cultivated French as the primary language of education in his own country.

Counter-Reactions to the Theory of Négritude

From its outset, Négritude sparked criticism. European intellectuals viewed it as a racist movement, given that, like white racism, it drew a link between race and cultural qualities. French philosopher Jean-Paul Sartre rejected this criticism, terming Négritude "anti-racist racism."[20]

Another critique was that Senghor idealized the image of precolonial African society. His descriptions conveyed the sense that before the beginning of colonial rule African societies had been democratic and egalitarian and had coexisted in perfect harmony. These descriptions were refuted by studies that exposed practices of slavery, despotism, and exploitation in Africa. Négritude also drew criticism from Africans, a criticism that intensified in the face of efforts to translate the theory into the political sphere. African intellectuals argued that Négritude was detached from the economic and political reality in Africa, ignored Africa's tremendous economic inferiority relative to Europe, and offered no solutions to this fundamental problem. After Senegal attained independence, criticism mounted against Senghor's views for their elitist nature and for being disconnected from the life of most Africans. A salient argument among the educated elite was that the idea of Négritude granted legitimacy to France's economic and cultural neocolonialism. One particularly critical definition of the movement emerged from a conference of the Senegalese teachers' association, where there was talk of "a doctrine of the Black who has become White and, while trying to remain White, is nevertheless termed Black."

The strong criticism leveled against the theory of Négritude does not detract from its important contribution to the cultivation of pride in African culture and values as a counterweight to the disparaging and dismissive attitude of French colonialism in particular, and of Western European culture generally. The theory of Négritude also left its mark on both the politics and the culture of French-speaking countries in Africa.

Notes

1 We are grateful to Ruth Ginio for her contribution to the preparation of this chapter.
2 Cited in Colin Legum, *Pan-Africanism: A Short Political Guide* (New York: Praeger, 1965), p. 18, www.freedomarchives.org/Documents/Finder/Black%20Liberat ion%20Disk/Black%20Power!/SugahData/Books/Legum.S.pdf.
3 Léopold Senghor, who belonged to the third largest ethnic group in Senegal (the Serer people), was born in 1906. He was a Catholic and a graduate of the Sorbonne in Paris. During the 1930s and 1940s he taught Latin, French, and French literature. He became known as a thinker, writer, and poet of the Négritude movement. Senghor embodied the fusion of African roots and Western culture and was known for his affinity for France and its culture. He served in the French Army during World War II, as a member of the French parliament during 1946–1958, and as state secretary in Edgar Faure's government (1955–1956). He became the first president of Senegal when it achieved independence in 1960 and served as head of the Francophone bloc of sub-Saharan Africa. In 1980 he resigned his position as president of Senegal, appointing Prime Minister Abdou Diouf as his successor. Senghor's works received many awards and earned him international recognition. In 1983 he became the first African to be admitted to the Académie française.
4 Aimé Césaire was born in 1913 in the Caribbean island of Martinique and attended the École normale supérieure in Paris. He was a thinker, playwright, and poet as well as one of the spiritual leaders of the Négritude movement and a cofounder, alongside his colleague Léopold Senghor of Senegal, of the quarterly *Présence Africaine*, which was dedicated to the study of black civilization and history and the cultural and spiritual revival of Black Africa. His political career included serving as a member of the French Communist Party (until 1956), acting as a delegate to the French National Assembly for Martinique for many years, and taking an active part in the political life of Martinique, where he founded the Martinican Progressive Party (Parti progressiste martiniquais, PPM).

40 *Négritude*

5 See Césaire, excerpt from *Notebook of a Return to the Native Land*, translated by Clayton Eshleman and Annette Smith, https://kboo.fm/sites/default/files/AIME%20CESAIRE--NOTEBOOK%20OF%20A%20RETURN%20TO%20A%20NATIVE%20LAND.pdf.
   Translation corrected by B.N.

6 Romantic nationalism highlights the natural aspect of the nation and its ties to the land, the landscape, and agriculture. Romantic nationalism exalts the simple, "national" individual who is rooted in the land and loyal to the country, as well as the "popular" national culture as it manifests in the vernacular and in folktales, folksongs, folk dances, and "folkloristic" arts in general. Romantic nationalism underscores what is positive in rootedness and spontaneity. It extols pluralism and national variance as akin to the beauty of a field of diverse and multicolored flowers.

7 Léopold Senghor, "On Negrohood: Psychology of the African Negro," trans. H. Kaal, *Diogenes* 10, No. 37 (1962): 1–15.

8 Ibid., pp. 1–2.

9 Ibid., pp. 11–12.

10 Ibid., p. 4.

11 The title of a work by sociologist Jules Monnerot.

12 Jean-Paul Sartre, as quoted by Senghor, *Esquisse d'une théorie des émotions* (Paris: Hermann & Cie, 1939), pp. 29–30.

13 Ibid., p. 30.

14 Ibid., pp. 14–15.

15 Senghor, "On Negrohood,", pp. 2–8.

16 Samuel W. Allen, "Negritude: Agreement and Disagreement," in *Pan-Africanism Reconsidered* (Berkeley: University of California Press, 1962), p. 314.

17 Senghor, "On Negrohood," p. 15.

18 Senghor, "To New York," trans. Anne-Charlotte Husson, *Worlds Elsewhere*, https://worldselsewhere.wordpress.com/2010/11/27/senghor-a-new-york-to-new-york/.

19 Senghor, "Vues sur l'Afrique noire ou assimiler, non être assimilés," in *La communauté impériale française* (Paris: Alsatia, 1945).

20 Sartre (1905–1980) was a French philosopher, playwright, and writer. His efforts to construct an all-encompassing theory of existentialism earned him a place of honor among the prominent philosophers of the twentieth century. He first drew public attention thanks to a collection of short stories, *The Wall*, which appeared in 1939. His first novel, considered the best of his works, was *La Nausée* [*Nausea*], published in 1938. During World War II he wrote several important plays, including *Huis Clos* [*No Exit*] (1944). After the liberation of France he took an active part in political life. In 1945 he founded the eminent journal *Les temps modernes*, and in 1964 he was awarded the Nobel Prize for literature but refused to accept it, for fear that it would "institutionalize" him and affect his writing.

4 Continental Pan-Africanism

The Background to the Emergence of Continental Pan-Africanism

The 1950s saw the emergence of a new form of Pan-Africanism. In its later incarnation Pan-Africanism sought the political unification of all states on the African continent, including the Arab states of North Africa. While the resolutions of the 1945 Congress had expressed loyalty to the racial underpinnings of African nationalism and related only to sub-Saharan Africa, the territorial framework represented by continental Pan-Africanism encompassed Africa in its entirety, not only "Black" Africa. The main driving force behind the concept of Pan-African unity was Kwame Nkrumah,[1] who in time became prime minister and president of Ghana, the first African state to liberate itself from colonial rule. Because there were only two independent sub-Saharan African states when Ghana attained independence (namely, Ethiopia and Liberia) it seemed politically expedient to unite with the five independent Arab states in Africa (Egypt, Libya, Sudan, Morocco, and Tunisia) in a Pan-African framework. During the 1950s Egypt, under Nasser's leadership, openly supported African nationalism and provided assistance to anticolonial movements in Africa, acting as a mouthpiece for African nationalism in the international arena.

The idea of Pan-African unity preserved the centrality that black nationalism had ascribed to concepts of unity since its inception in the form of Pan-Negroism. Yet it was also informed by global political trends characteristic of the post-World War II international arena. The emergence of the "Third World" as a neutral alternative to the bipolar one (that is, the world seen as divided between the Western world and the communist bloc) and the growing closeness among vastly diverse countries, some of which had just shed the shackles of colonial rule and wished to refrain from aligning themselves with either the Western or the Eastern Bloc, had a tremendous impact on Africa. In 1955, Bandung, the capital of the West Java province of Indonesia, hosted a conference aimed at promoting solidarity among states and peoples outside of Europe—Afro-Asian solidarity in particular. Despite being "white," Arabs projected a non-European image that contributed to their inclusion in the family of "colored" (non-white) peoples and made it easier to regard the

DOI: 10.4324/9781003322818-5

Figure 4.1 Kwame Nkrumah. Nkrumah strove to merge socialist ideals with traditional African values. To that end, he used to wear traditional, handwoven kente cloth wrappers.
Source: https://en.wikipedia.org/wiki/Jomo_Kenyatta#/media/File:Kwame_Nkrumah_(JFKWHP-AR6409-A).jpg, Public Domain.

Arabs of North Africa as an inseparable part of Africa. In addition, Algeria's war of independence from France (1954–1962) provided symbols of national struggle, courage, and pride with which Africans could identify, symbols that gave vital sustenance to the decolonization processes underway throughout the continent. The affinity for Africa voiced by leaders of the Algerian revolt enhanced the Pan-African sense of a shared destiny.

First Pan-African Unification Efforts

The first Pan-African organizations were founded as early as 1958, at Nkrumah's initiative. In April of that year the city of Accra, Ghana's capital, hosted the first conference of independent African countries. Ghana, Liberia,

Ethiopia, Egypt, Tunisia, Libya, Sudan, and Morocco—three African and five Arab states—participated. In December 1958 Accra hosted another gathering—the All-African People's Conference (AAPC)—attended by representatives of political parties, liberation movements, and underground movements from across the continent. These meetings were followed by routinely held conferences, both among leaders of independent states and among leaders of "emerging states." The calls for Pan-African unity found expression in a series of plans and organizational efforts pursued collectively by these political entities.

The ideological pressure to create large, inclusive political structures began to exert an influence on the political arena. The late 1950s and early 1960s saw a number of attempts at unity: the Ghana-Guinea Union, the Association of Independent African States to which Ghana and Liberia belonged, and the Union of African States, which comprised Ghana, Guinea, and Mali. None of these efforts translated into a stable political system, and each collapsed before long. Even the union between French Sudan and Senegal—the Mali Federation, a relatively far-reaching framework that included a shared government and military, and a common capital city (Dakar)—crumbled after two years into its components, namely French Sudan (which later on became Mali) and Senegal. Likewise, the attempt to form an East African Federation uniting Tanganyika, Kenya, and Uganda never bore fruit. Some unification efforts did, however, endure: the Somali Republic, a union of British Somaliland and Italian Somalia, survived from its founding in 1960 until 1992, when the former British Somaliland seceded. Other unions, on the other hand—such as that between British Southern Cameroon and French Cameroon, the merger of British Northern Cameroon with Nigeria, and that of British Togo with Ghana, and the state of Tanzania, formed in 1964 by the unification of Tanganyika and Zanzibar—all managed to last.

One cannot overlook the fact that every successful union involved special historical and social factors. The Somali union, for instance, was based on ethnic, cultural, linguistic, religious, and historical cohesion among the Somali people.[2] In Cameroon, members of the Bamileke people, across both sides of the border, urged unification. Memories of a united Cameroon also contributed to this process: the land had once been unified, as a German colony (before 1918), before Britain and France divided it as war bounty, following their victory over Germany in World War I. Northern Nigeria and Northern Cameroon, like British Togo and the Gold Coast (Ghana), had been under a common colonial administration, and their respective unions complemented a gradual process of administrative unification. The union between Tanganyika and Zanzibar (which were united under the name Tanzania) was also driven by outside considerations—in this case related to *realpolitik* (Tanganyika's concerns about the emergence of a communist "Cuba" in Zanzibar)—although the Pan-African dimension was considered important as well.

44 *Continental Pan-Africanism*

In the early 1960s, Ghana, under Nkrumah's leadership, took measures toward the establishment of a "United States of Africa." In the following passage Nkrumah explains the need for a "continental government for Africa":

> We have seen, in the example of the United States, how the dynamic elements within society understood the need for unity and fought their bitter civil war to maintain the political union that was threatened by the reactionary forces. We have also seen, in the example of the Soviet Union, how the forging of continental unity, along with the retention of national sovereignty by the federal states, has achieved a dynamism that has lifted a most backward society into a most powerful unit within a remarkably short space of time. From the examples before us, in Europe and the United States of America, it is therefore patent that we in Africa have the resources, present and potential, for creating the kind of society that we are anxious to build ... To draw the most from our existing and potential means for the achievement of abundance and a fine social order, we need to unify our efforts, our resources, our skills and intentions.
>
> Europe, by way of contrast, must be a lesson to us all. Too busy hugging its exclusive nationalisms, it has descended ... into a state of confusion ... It has taken two world wars and the break-up of empires to press home the lesson, still only partly digested, that strength lies in unity ...
>
> To us, Africa with its islands is just one Africa ... We need the strength of our combined numbers and resources to protect ourselves from the very positive dangers of returning colonialism in disguised forms. We need it to combat the entrenched forces dividing our continent and still holding back millions of our brothers. We need it to secure total African liberation. We need it to carry forward our construction of a socio-economic system that will support the great mass of our steadily rising population ... If we developed our potentialities in men and natural resources in separate isolated groups, our energies would soon be dissipated in the struggle to outbid one another ...
>
> We therefore need a common political basis for the integration of our policies in economic planning, defence, foreign and diplomatic relations.[3]

In 1963 the Organization of African Unity (OAU), a union of Africa's independent states, was established in Addis Ababa, the capital of Ethiopia. The following provisions of the OAU Charter outline its mandate and purposes:

> We, the Heads of African States and Governments assembled in the City of Addis Ababa, Ethiopia,

Continental Pan-Africanism   45

Convinced that it is the inalienable right of all people to control their own destiny,

Conscious of the fact that freedom, equality, justice and dignity are essential objectives for the achievement of the legitimate aspirations of the African peoples,

Conscious of our responsibility to harness the natural and human resources of our continent for the total advancement of our peoples in all spheres of human endeavour,

Inspired by a common determination to promote understanding among our peoples and cooperation among our states in response to the aspirations of our peoples for brotherhood and solidarity, in a larger unity transcending ethnic and national differences,

Convinced that, in order to translate this determination into a dynamic force in the cause of human progress, conditions for peace and security must be established and maintained,

Determined to safeguard and consolidate the hard-won independence as well as the sovereignty and territorial integrity of our states, and to fight against neocolonialism in all its forms,

Dedicated to the general progress of Africa,

Persuaded that the Charter of the United Nations and the Universal Declaration of Human Rights, to the Principles of which we reaffirm our adherence, provide a solid foundation for peaceful and positive cooperation among States,

Desirous that all African States should henceforth unite so that the welfare and wellbeing of their peoples can be assured,

Resolved to reinforce the links between our states by establishing and strengthening common institutions,

Have agreed to the present Charter.

ESTABLISHMENT

Article I

1. The High Contracting Parties do by the present Charter establish an Organization to be known as the ORGANIZATION OF AFRICAN UNITY.
2. The Organization shall include the Continental African States, Madagascar and other Islands surrounding Africa.

PURPOSES

Article II

1. The Organization shall have the following purposes:
   (a) To promote the unity and solidarity of the African States;
   (b) To coordinate and intensify their cooperation and efforts to achieve a better life for the peoples of Africa;
   (c) To defend their sovereignty, their territorial integrity and independence;
   (d) To eradicate all forms of colonialism from Africa; and
   (e) To promote international cooperation, having due regard to the Charter of the United Nations and the Universal Declaration of Human Rights.
2. To these ends, the Member States shall coordinate and harmonize their general policies, especially in the following fields:
   (a) Political and diplomatic cooperation;
   (b) Economic cooperation, including transport and communications;
   (c) Educational and cultural cooperation;
   (d) Health, sanitation and nutritional cooperation;
   (e) Scientific and technical cooperation; and
   (f) Cooperation for defence and security.

PRINCIPLES

Article III

The Member States, in pursuit of the purposes stated in Article II solemnly affirm and declare their adherence to the following principles:
1. The sovereign equality of all Member States.
2. Non-interference in the internal affairs of States.
3. Respect for the sovereignty and territorial integrity of each State and for its inalienable right to independent existence.
4. Peaceful settlement of disputes by negotiation, mediation, conciliation or arbitration.
5. Unreserved condemnation, in all its forms, of political assassination as well as of subversive activities on the part of neighbouring States or any other States.
6. Absolute dedication to the total emancipation of the African territories which are still dependent.
7. Affirmation of a policy of non-alignment with regard to all blocs.

MEMBERSHIP

Article IV

Each independent sovereign African State shall be entitled to become a Member of the Organization.

RIGHTS AND DUTIES OF MEMBER STATES

Article V
All Member States shall enjoy equal rights and have equal duties.

Article VI
The Member States pledge themselves to observe scrupulously the principles enumerated in Article III of the present Charter.[4]

Forces of Cohesion and Division in Africa

The driving forces behind political unification in Africa stemmed from a shared colonial past, from the desire to become an important and powerful actor in the international arena, and from the belief that a united Africa would have greater bargaining power in dealing with the superpowers. Continental Pan-Africanism represented an effort to surmount Africa's division into a multitude of states. The fact that Africa's inhabitants had yet to develop a strong sense of patriotism toward their newly formed states, that the political borders were artificial, and therefore genuine nations had yet to develop within them, would presumably have facilitated the unification of these new states into larger frameworks. At the same time, the artificiality, lack of clarity, and questionable legitimacy of the borders often generated border disputes between neighbors, sparked diverging and conflicting demands, and created tensions that impeded unification or even cooperation between states.

Colonial rule had imparted a few salient languages—English, French, and to a lesser extent Portuguese—which, on the one hand, facilitated communication between states that spoke the same language but, on the other hand, created a cultural and linguistic barrier between those that spoke different languages, particularly between Anglophone and Francophone states. The extent of cooperation among African states as a whole depended on their ability to overcome this barrier. In 1965 the Francophone states came together to form the African and Malagasy Union (Organisation commune africaine et malagache).[5] In 1967 the East African Community was founded,[6] bringing together the Anglophone countries of Kenya, Uganda, Tanganyika, and Zanzibar. The union of French Cameroon with British South Cameroon in 1961 and the formation in 1975 of the Economic Community of West African States (ECOWAS),[7] which comprised both British and French former colonies, attest to the fact that linguistic and cultural barriers are not necessarily insurmountable. On the whole, colonial languages served as both a unifying factor among states and, simultaneously, a dividing factor.

The strong emotional bond among members of the black race and the sense of a shared destiny among black African states served as unifying forces for sub-Saharan countries while creating divisions between them and the Arab countries. Even supporters of Pan-African unity were split between those who adhered to an all-inclusive African approach and others who sought to confine their political organization to sub-Saharan Africa and establish an

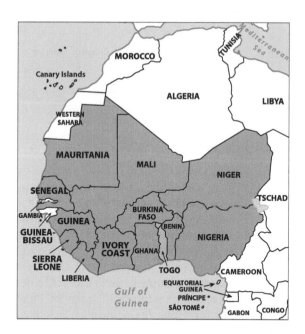

Map 4.1 West Africa. In 1967, 14 West African countries established the West African Community: Benin (or Dahomey), Gambia, Ghana, Guinea, the Ivory Coast, Liberia, Mali, Mauritania, Niger, Nigeria, Senegal, Sierra Leone, Togo, and Burkina-Fasso (or Upper Volta). The member countries agreed on economic, social, technological, and cultural cooperation.

"African League" of sorts, akin to the Arab League to which North African states belonged. Advocates of an "African League" argued that North African Arab states were loyal, first and foremost, to the Arab League and the family of Arab nations, and therefore should not be granted membership in a Pan-African organization.

Economic competition and conflicting interests among states that were often vying for the same raw-material export markets and the same sources of capital investment also played a divisive role. The tactical aspects of achieving unification were another source of dispute—between those who viewed regional alliances of neighboring countries as an interim measure on the path to complete unity and others who regarded regional alliances as an obstacle to an all-inclusive union. The division between "pro-Western" and "pro-communist" African states—in terms of their socioeconomic orientation and foreign relations—posed an additional hurdle to the formation of unions.

Other obstacles to unification stemmed from trends toward national cohesiveness that had begun under colonial rule and greatly intensified once states achieved independence. These included the cultivation of local culture and folklore, a collective historical legacy (even if invented), shared national

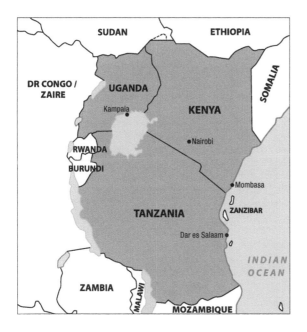

Map 4.2 East Africa. The East African Community was established in 1967 with the aim of institutionalizing and tightening the economic cooperation between Kenya, Uganda, and Tanzania. Cooperation was based mainly on shared services (mail and telegraph, seaports and railways, agricultural research, statistical analysis, etc.), as well as the fields of aviation, a common higher education system, common markets, and investment regulations. The Community dissolved in 1977 due to political conflicts between the member states.

Source: The Open University of Israel, used with permission.

symbols, and the replacement of colonial languages with African languages as official national languages: Swahili in Tanzania and Kenya, Somali in Somalia, Kirundi in Burundi, Malagasy in Madagascar, Kinyarwanda in Rwanda, and Swati in Swaziland (today's Eswatini) are prominent examples. National unification processes that highlighted territorial uniqueness tended to undermine the forces of inter-territorial unity.

Each state's sovereignty concerns were also closely tied to the interests of political, military, and bureaucratic elites, different ethnic groups, and certain economic groups, whose advantage in the internal power balance depended on preservation of the existing state format. Any change in the political framework, not to mention continental unification, could threaten the elites' position of power and privileged social standing. Accordingly, they would seek to thwart it. The element of time was also a significant factor. When Africa's political map was only beginning to take shape and its borders were still "hot"

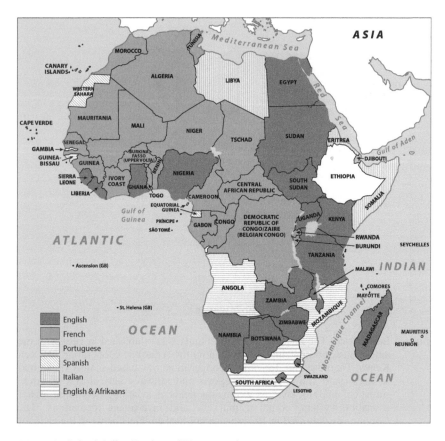

Map 4.3 Colonial distribution of European languages.
Source: The Open University of Israel, used with permission.

and malleable, the options for unity appeared more likely and feasible. Over the course of the six decades since attaining independence, the colonial political units solidified and separate networks of interests and loyalties developed in each state, posing further obstacles to the possibility of their dissolution for the sake of a continental union.

The outlook embodied in the Charter of the Organization of African Unity, which views it as a body aimed at coordinating and promoting cooperation among the states of Africa in various fields—research, aviation, transportation, economics, interstate conflict resolution, and the like—but primarily regards it as an instrument for the fortification of each separate state, accurately reflects the upper limits of unity that African states have been able to achieve in practice since having attained independence.

Notes

1 Kwame Nkrumah was born in 1909 in what was then the Gold Coast (now Ghana). He attended Catholic missionary schools and a teacher-training college in the Gold Coast. In 1935 he left for the United States to pursue university studies, during the course of which he embraced the concept of African nationalism. He took an active role in organizing the Fifth Pan-African Congress, in Manchester in 1945, and participated in drafting its resolutions, signaling the transition from Pan-Negro nationalism to political-territorial nationalism in Africa. Upon his return to the Gold Coast, in 1947, he assumed a leading role in the anticolonial struggle. Although the strategy he adopted—termed "Positive Action"—included strikes and protests but eschewed violence, he was imprisoned by the colonial rulers and released only after his party, the Convention People's Party, won the elections in 1951. Nkrumah became the first prime minister of independent Ghana. As an enthusiastic supporter of the notion of implementing Pan-Africanism (establishing a "United States of Africa"), Nkrumah participated in founding the Organization of African Unity in 1963. The radical, uncompromising African nationalism that he had advocated in his writings and speeches gave him tremendous influence in Africa during the 1950s and the first half of the 1960s. In Ghana itself, however, his status steadily deteriorated as his regime became more and more despotic. In 1960 he was appointed president, and two years later declared Ghana a one-party state, appointing himself president for life and initiating the cultivation of a personality cult. In 1966 he was overthrown in a military coup and went into exile in Guinea. He died of cancer in Romania in 1972.
2 At the same time, this cohesion did not prevent the secession of northern Somalia—formerly British Somaliland—in 1992, at the height of civil war in Somalia.
3 Kwame Nkrumah, "Continental Government for Africa," in *Africa Must Unite* (London: Heinemann, 1963), pp. 216–222.
4 Charter of the Organization of African Unity, https://au.int/sites/default/files/treat ies/7759-file-oau_charter_1963.pdf.
5 The African and Malagasy Union, founded in 1965, was created to promote economic, social, cultural, and technological cooperation among Africa's francophone states. The organization was inclined toward pro-Western conservatism. In the 1970s a number of states, including Madagascar, Cameroon, and Zaire, withdrew, thereby diminishing the organization's influence and prominence.
6 The East African Community was established in 1967 in order to support and facilitate economic cooperation between Kenya, Uganda, and Tanzania. The East African Community was based on collective services (postal and telegraph services, seaport and train services, agricultural research, statistical services, and the like), a shared airport, a single higher education system, a common market, and the allocation of investments according to the member states' needs and level of development. The organization collapsed in the 1970s because of political differences among its members.
7 In 1975, 14 West African states came together to form ECOWAS: Benin (then Dahomey), Gambia, Ghana, the Gold Coast (Ghana), Guinea, Liberia, Mali, Mauritania, Niger, Nigeria, Senegal, Sierra Leone, Togo, and Burkina Faso (then Upper Volta) for the purpose of promoting economic, social, technological, and cultural cooperation.

5 The New Nationalism and Its Historical Heritage

The new nationalism that emerged in Africa advocated political independence, economic development, social progress, cultural revival, and the implementation of equality. It sought to construct a new black man, infused with pride and free from any sense of inferiority. Most of the concepts it embraced were imported from Europe, where the nineteenth and twentieth centuries marked the golden age of modern nationalism, and from America, the birthplace of Pan-Negroism. Yet African nationalism also has roots in Africa's own historical reality. It is not a foreign transplant artificially grown in alien soil. Every form of nationalism seeks to ground its struggles and essentiality in a historical continuum. It aims to demonstrate that the new values it espouses have deep roots in earlier times. Accordingly, the new African nationalism should not be conceptualized or analyzed independently of historical events, developments, traditions, memories, or myths that originated and transpired in Africa itself. The conceptual contribution made by Europe and America is important, perhaps even decisive, but its impact must be understood against the background of Africa's own historical and cultural heritage. Just as Zionism was influenced both by liberal European nationalism and by Jewish history, culture, and religion, so too was the new African nationalism an organic product of European and American ideas, sown in African soil.

African historical scholarship, in which professional historians from Africa were now participating for the first time, evolved in parallel with the continent's political decolonization (catalyzed by World War II) and drew inspiration from it, thus forming an inseparable part of its national awakening. The process of decolonizing African history and historiography from those colonialist outlooks, which most African scholars had maintained until the mid-twentieth century, was perceived as complementing the political emancipation process. The anticolonial struggle and its culmination in independence led the pioneers of African nationalism to maintain that it was through their efforts that the present was saved and the future secured, and that what remained was to redeem the past from imperialist domination.[1]

The national missions with which writers of the new African history were tasked were numerous. Decolonization necessitated that Africans reexamine their historical and cultural image, seek sources of strength, encouragement,

DOI: 10.4324/9781003322818-6

and pride in their past, and through these develop a positive self-identity. They had to disprove the prevalent Eurocentric perceptions of barbarism, savagery, passivity, and inferiority that had been used to justify colonial domination. By documenting their past, Africans sought to return to a history whose existence colonialism had denied, but this time they would be active agents and shapers of this history rather than passive subjects. In line with the national African mission, a new historiography was enlisted for the struggle against foreign rule and in support of national consolidation. As J. F. Ade Ajayi, one of the architects of the new African historiography, explicitly stated, "That the African past must play an important part in the process of nation-building in Africa today is no longer in doubt."[2]

African historiography therefore focused its attention on Africa's precolonial kingdoms and countries. It underscored the achievements of Africans in the areas of governance, culture, and art before the arrival of the White man. Every African expression of opposition to European conquest was framed as part of the opening phase of a lengthy, continuous national struggle that would ultimately lead to Africa's liberation from colonial domination. The revolt against colonial rule, against forced labor and the mistreatment of inhabitants by colonial officials, against various types of tax (per capita taxation, hut taxes, taxes on weapons), against European arrogance and the oppression of long-standing African leaders—all these provided the heroes and the acts of heroism, the pride and the inspiration, and the historical depth and continuity that are vital for any modern national ideology.

Memories and Myths of Precolonial Africa

Until roughly the mid-twentieth century it was commonly held that Africa had no history prior to the arrival of the White man, and that its history only began when it was "discovered" by Europeans, who brought Africa into the "civilized world." The ostensibly empty map of Africa then filled up with colors—the mountains, rivers, and lakes that were "discovered" by Europeans, as well as borders and colors that demarcated the dominions of European powers. This Eurocentric worldview, which dismissed the possibility that Africa had a history and rights of its own, served the colonialist ideology. Modern African nationalism, on the other hand, rejected the portrayal of Africa as a continent that had to be discovered and conquered in order to acquire a history and culture. According to African nationalists, the Europeans who "discovered" the sources of the Nile and the Niger rivers, or Lake Victoria and Mount Kilimanjaro, merely discovered them on behalf of Europe, not on behalf of humanity as a whole. From the African point of view no discovery was involved, for Africans had been aware of their homeland and their historical heritage from time immemorial.

African nationalism holds that just as the Europeans, Arabs, Jews, Chinese, and Native Americans have a history, so too do the Africans. All peoples have a history. Admittedly, large parts of Africa lack written historical records

Figure 5.1 The Great Zimbabwe is a ruined city in the southeastern hills of Zimbabwe. It was built between the eleventh and fourteenth centuries. It is recognized by UNESCO as a World Heritage Site.
Source: https://commons.wikimedia.org/wiki/File:Great_Zimbabwe_8.jpg, CC BY 2.0.

comparable to those that exist for Europe or the Middle East, but history can also be traced by analyzing intergenerational oral traditions and archaeological findings. Moreover, as research on Africa proceeded, it became increasingly apparent that the volume of written sources exceeded initial expectations. We know of Arab resources from as early as the ninth century that discuss East Africa and areas of West Africa adjacent to the Sahara. There are also relevant European sources dating back to the fifteenth century, which were long neglected because researchers were not interested in Africa's history. Like any national movement, the African national movement too needed a historical identity. But in Africa's case there was also a special need for a history that would refute the colonial conception of the continent as savage, lacking political organization, and devoid of original culture—a "black stain" in the European Atlas—a history that would demonstrate Africans' capacity for self-governance. For this very reason African national history put the spotlight on dozens of countries and kingdoms that had existed on the continent for centuries before the first European ever set foot there. Modern historical scholarship, using sophisticated research tools, has revealed rich, diverse political cultures, sophisticated organizations and institutions, military and administrative agencies, diplomacy, and diplomatic and political entities of various sorts: traditional African kingdoms such as Congo, Buganda, Benin, Ghana, and Mali,[3] the Akan and Yoruba states, empires such as the Fulani and Oyo, and the Ashanti federation.

Many African states, upon attaining independence, adopted the names of ancient African countries so as to rid the continent's map of colonial names and grant the new states historical continuity and depth. The Gold Coast became Ghana once it achieved statehood, and French Sudan became Mali. In fact, present-day Mali is located where the ancient kingdom of Mali once existed. What was British Nyasaland is today Malawi, while Rhodesia, named after one of the fathers of British imperialism, Cecil Rhodes, became Zimbabwe after implementation of a Black-majority rule in former White settler Rhodesia. Zimbabwe was the name of the former capital and realm of King Monomotapa, where impressive archaeological ruins attest to an ancient history and glorious building tradition. The names of new states did not always correlate with their ancient geographic location: Dahomey became Benin, which had been located about 300 km to the east, in today's Nigeria, while the Gold Coast took the name of historical Ghana, once located about 1,000 km north of present-day Ghana.

The new nationalism also highlights other achievements of precolonial African civilization, such as cities, architecture, sculpture, and painting. Since

Figure 5.2 Art from Benin: Head of a king (oba).
Source: https://en.wikipedia.org/wiki/Art_of_the_Kingdom_of_Benin#/media/File:Benin_bronze_in_Bristol_Museum.jpg, CC BY-SA 2.0.

Figure 5.3 Art from Benin: One of six surviving ivory bell sculptures (egogo) used to drive away evil spirits (sixteenth century).
Source: https://en.wikipedia.org/wiki/Art_of_the_Kingdom_of_Benin#/media/File:Brooklyn_Museum_58.160_Double_Bell_Egogo.jpg, CC BY 3.0.

urbanization is considered part of the social modernization process, cities generally convey a sense of modernity. By placing emphasis on Africa's ancient cities, such as Kilwa and Mombasa in East Africa, Kano and Timbuktu in the West, and Great Zimbabwe in the South, African nationalism was better able to ascribe qualities of progress to the continent and refute its past image as zimbabwe primitive, prior to the arrival of the white man.

Nationalism generates historical myths as a means of reinforcing national claims. Such an example is the assertion that colonialism brought about the "Balkanization" of Africa by dividing it into a multitude of small, weak political entities.[4] Actually, the historical facts are quite different: before the arrival of Europeans there was far more ethnic political division in Africa, which had never been united.

Figure 5.4 Art from Benin: Leopard's head (nineteenth century).

Source: https://en.wikipedia.org/wiki/Art_of_the_Kingdom_of_Benin#/media/File:Brooklyn_Museum_56.6.31a-b_Box_in_the_Form_of_a_Leopards_Head.jpg, CC BY 3.0.

Figure 5.5 Art from Benin: Bronze head of Queen Idia (sixteenth century).

Source: https://en.wikipedia.org/wiki/Art_of_the_Kingdom_of_Benin#/media/File:Afrikaabteilung_in_Ethnological_Museum_Berlin_29.JPG, CC BY-SA 3.0.

Figure 5.6 The Great Mosque of Jenné in Mali. The first Jenné mosque dates back to the thirteenth century, the current structure to the 1910s.
Source: https://en.wikipedia.org/wiki/Great_Mosque_of_Djenn%C3%A9#/media/File:Djenne_great_mud_mosque.jpg, CC BY-SA 3.0.

Essays composed in the spirit of the new nationalism reveal a tendency to blame colonialism for all the evils that have befallen Africa: oppression, exploitation, and inequality. Some seek to convey the impression that Africa of yore was characterized by fraternity and harmony, lacking both social class and economic exploitation. On this basis they seek to construct "African democracy" and "African socialism." Indeed, African societies did have traditions and democratic and egalitarian principles, such as consultation, participation, and oversight over authority.[5] But precolonial Africa also had slavery, vast discrepancies in social status, and wars of conquest and extermination. National historians have sought to downplay the latter factors in support of efforts—characteristic of any national movement—to emphasize what was positive and appealing in its national heritage and to create a historical tradition that has educational merit and can serve as a source of pride.

The Tradition of "Primary Resistance" to the European Conquest

Some observers have argued that the conquest of Africa did not entail the use of armed force, and that the European powers simply exploited a political and military vacuum. In their view, resistance to white rule is a relatively recent

Figures 5.7 Child labor: children weaving, Cameroon, 1919.
Source: https://en.wikipedia.org/wiki/Child_labour_in_Africa#/media/File:Kamerun_children_weaving_cloth_2.jpg, Public Domain.

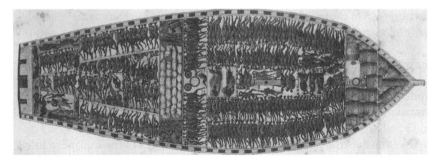

Figure 5.8 Painting of the slave deck of the ship *Marie Séraphique* of Nantes (1770), representing its "cargo" (as slaves were then viewed). Enslaved Africans were transported to the Americas. The Transatlantic slave trade and African slavery in the Americas were the major factors that shaped modern racism.
Source: https://en.wikipedia.org/wiki/Slave_ship#/media/File:Slave_deck_of_the_Marie_S%C3%A9raphique_rotated.jpg, Public Domain.

phenomenon, traceable to developments in the post-World War II era. The passages cited below, however, present a different perspective.

In a letter to the chief of the Yao ethnic group during the Maji-Maji rebellion against German rule in Tanganyika, the chief of the Ngoni ethnic group wrote in 1905:

60   *The New Nationalism and Its Historical Heritage*

> We received an order from God to the effect that all White Men had to quit the country. We are ready to fight them ... I wanted to send you cattle as a present, but I was unable to send them. This war ordered by God must come first. Send 100 men with guns. Help me in taking the Boma [a livestock enclosure] ... Let us forget now our former quarrels.[6]

A colonial official in Rhodesia had the following to say in 1915:

> Certain Mashona ethnic groups will again rebel ... The natives, although outwardly satisfied and peaceable, object to our rule ... It only requires a witch-doctor who has been fortunate in the past and has obtained a footing as a true prophet to prophesy destruction of the whites to get the majority of the tribes to rise.[7]

In 1965, Prof. D. Donald Anthony Low, discussing the history of East Africa, wrote that it was military might that brought about Kenya's surrender to British rule—adding that it had been an unequal struggle between British guns and African spears.[8]

The above passages indicate that Africa's resistance to white occupiers dates back to the very beginning of colonial rule. Indeed, to grant the anticolonial struggle legitimacy and historical depth, African historians whose publications began to appear in the 1950s stress the continuity of African resistance to white rule. The historical reality, however, is that many African territories were captured by European powers without meaningful resistance, but rather by means of "agreements" signed by local leaders, often without them being aware of the deals' significance. In pursuit of their own aims, Europeans exploited internal fighting and rivalries within Africa, employing a policy of divide and rule. Some Africans did, however, come to terms with white rule during the colonial era and cooperated with it. In general, most of the colonies knew periods of calm and stability as well as periods of resistance and revolt.

One must distinguish between "primary resistance" to the European intrusion and invasion, and the inception of colonial rule, on the one hand, and the violent rebellions that erupted against existing, established colonial European governments, on the other. There is a difference between the Swahili uprising of 1888–1891 against German rule on the shores of East Africa, a revolt that qualifies as "primary resistance" to the very entry and settlement of Germans on the Tanganyika coastline, and the Maji-Maji rebellion in South Tanganyika (1905–1907), which erupted approximately 15 years after the territory's official annexation to the German Empire.[9] "Primary resistance" was usually local and led by traditional leaders, whereas the later revolts occurred on a larger scale, often encompassing many ethnic groups led by charismatic "prophets" whose very emergence attested to the social shock waves caused by colonial domination.

The uprisings were driven not only by resistance to the occupation and foreign rule, but also by more specific causes such as opposition to religious offenses, degrading treatment, and forced labor in the service of whites (e.g., the Shona and Ndebele in Rhodesia and South Africa, 1896), taxes imposed by the colonial government (Sierra Leone, 1898), the imposition of disarmament (the Basotho in Lesotho, 1880–1881), dispossession of lands and confiscation of livestock (the Herero in German South West Africa, 1904), and cruelty on the part of colonial bureaucrats (Tanganyika, 1905). Uprisings were more frequent in those colonies where the governing authority was especially cruel and despotic, although they sometimes remained quiet for extended periods of time following a brutal crackdown. Some struggles ended very disastrously for the Africans: the suppression of the Herero revolt against the Germans in South West Africa, later Namibia, resulted in 80,000 deaths, out of a population of ca. 100,000.[10] Hostility to whites and the use of violence were common to both the "primary resistance" and the later revolts. The Ndebele and Shona wars in Rhodesia (1893, 1896–1897), the Hut Tax War in Sierra Leone (1898), the Basuto Gun War in South Africa (1880–1881), the Ashanti War in the Gold Coast (1873–1874), the Herero revolt in German South West Africa (1904), and the Barue revolt in Mozambique (1917) are characteristic examples of the "primary resistance" and rebellion in which Africans take pride.

Even though the wars usually ended in occupation and oppression, the very act of fighting and resisting was a source of pride and inspiration for African nationalism. At the same time, those cases in which Europeans suffered military losses at the hands of Africans did receive prominence. Such military victories not only highlighted the Africans' warfighting capabilities, courage, and refusal to surrender, but also helped disprove the colonialist conception of African society as "primitive." The Africans' ability to stand up to European weapons, artillery, and soldiers symbolized "modern" military and organizational proficiency and attested to the former's courage, determination, and strength. The Ethiopians' victory over Italians in Adowa in 1896, when they successfully thwarted an attempted colonial conquest of their country, received a great deal of attention in the media worldwide. Independent Ethiopia, having prevailed over the Europeans, became a symbol of African nationalism for the entire continent. Many African nationalists even used the name "Ethiopia" as a synonym for Africa.

The wars and deeds of Chief Mkwawa of the Hehe ethnic group in Tanganyika, who wiped out a German military punitive expedition, including its commanders, is a source of pride in Tanganyika/Tanzania to this day. The Basuto, in what became known as the Gun War, managed to prevent their own disarmament, avert White settlement, and thwart their annexation to South Africa. It is for this very reason that Botswana is an independent state today. Even after revolts that ended in failure and large-scale oppression, European concerns about another uprising occasionally led to reforms in colonial governance. The German policies in Tanganyika, for example, underwent significant changes after the Maji-Maji rebellion. These included efforts to cultivate African agriculture, reduce forced labor, circumscribe the power wielded by White settlers, and prevent acts of cruelty against the local population by colonial officials and soldiers.

Uprisings against White Rule and Their Place in National Ideology

The new African nationalism, which reached the height of its influence after World War II, differed completely from the "primary resistance" and revolts that took place at the start of the century. Leadership over the struggle shifted to the Westernized and educated, including Julius Nyerere;[11] Jomo Kenyatta, first president of independent Kenya from 1963 to 1987; Kwame Nkrumah, first president of independent Ghana from 1957 to 1966; Hastings Banda, first president of independent Malawi from 1964 until the early 1990s.

Figure 5.9 Julius Nyerere.
Source: https://en.wikipedia.org/wiki/Julius_Nyerere#/media/File:President_Nyerere_van_Tanzania,_koppen,_Bestanddeelnr_928-2879_(cropped).jpg, CC0.

Figure 5.10 Nelson Mandela.
Source: https://en.wikipedia.org/wiki/Nelson_Mandela#/media/File:Nelson_Mandela_1994.jpg, CC BY-SA 2.0.

They aimed not to reproduce the precolonial political map, but rather to emancipate the colonies, as delineated by their colonial borders, and transform them into modern states in accordance with Western standards: national independence, self-determination, respect and standing among the family of nations, accelerated economic development, social equality, and cultural revival. The common denominator of the new nationalism and the early twentieth-century resistance movements was their struggle against white rule.

The new nationalism generally received support from modern groups, such as workers, bureaucrats, teachers, and the educated and urbanized. To earn widespread popular support, however, national leaders also needed to recruit people from the rural areas and tribal communities that accounted for most of the African population. Toward this end, the history of warfighting against whites, through wars waged by individual ethnic groups or ethnic group alliances, became a basis for enlisting support and assistance from Africans whose worldview, sense of identity, culture, language, and symbols were of a local ethnic character. National leaders sought to "nationalize" uprisings carried out by a particular ethnic group and make them a source of pride

Map 5.1 The Maji-Maji Rebellion in German East Africa.
Source: The Open University of Israel, used with permission.

and inspiration for all the ethnic groups in the state. Such, for example, were the Zulu wars against whites, which Nelson Mandela,[12] leader of the national movement in South Africa, described as "wars fought by our ancestors in defence of the fatherland" and "the pride and glory of the entire African nation."[13]

The following passages illustrate two different perspectives on the Maji-Maji rebellion. The first presents it as a struggle driven primarily by economic motives, while the second describes it as a national struggle in every respect:

> On a morning late in July 1905 the men of Nandete [a village in eastern Tanzania] climbed a path towards a field of ripening cotton which they had cultivated. When they reached it their leaders, Ngulumbalyo Mandai and Lindimyo Machel, stepped forward and pulled three plants out of the ground. They did this in order to declare war on the German Empire.
>
> ... The rebellion began among the stateless peoples of the south-east and extended to the newly created states of the Southern Highlands. It took place at the moment of transition from the nineteenth-century economy to the colonial order and it began as a movement of highlanders and frontiersmen resisting incorporation into the colonial economy and reduction to peasant status. To uproot cotton was therefore an apt ultimatum. To the men of Nandete ... cotton symbolized the foreign penetration and

The New Nationalism and Its Historical Heritage   65

control which had followed defeat in the "war of the pumpkins"[14] seven years earlier.[15]

In 1905 in the famous Maji Maji rebellion, they ["my people"] tried again for the last time to drive the Germans out. Once again the odds were against them. The Germans, with characteristic ruthlessness, crushed the rebellion, slaughtering an estimated number of 120,000 people.

There was no nationalist movement, no nationalist agitators, no westernized demagogues, or subversive Communists who went about the country stirring up trouble against the Germans. The people fought because they did not believe in the white man's right to govern and civilize the black. They rose in a great rebellion not through fear of a terrorist movement or a superstitious oath, but in response to a natural call, a call of the spirit, ringing in the hearts of all men, and of all times, educated or uneducated, to rebel against foreign domination.[16]

Schools in Tanzania teach the Maji-Maji rebellion as a national uprising against colonial rule, and Tanzanian history books omit the fact that certain ethnic groups collaborated with the Germans. The government and ruling parties have made every effort to extol the rebellion as a national Tanzanian uprising and source of honor, pride, and inspiration for subsequent generations, and monuments erected by the government mark sites associated with the rebellion. At a convention of Tanzania's governing party, TANU, in October 1976 in Mwanza, delegates were requested to honor the memory of Maji-Maji's heroes by standing for a moment of silence.[17]

Historical figures from the past were also resurrected as part of the new African nationalism. Sékou Touré, leader of the national movement in Guinea, declared that he was a descendant of Samori Touré, founder of the short-lived Wassoulou Empire in West Africa, who had resisted French rule for many years. Presumably he believed that having an ancestor who had been part of the primary resistance would buttress his status nationally. Similarly, in Mali, leaders of the Sudanese Union claimed that they were descendants of El-Haj Omar, another historical leader of the primary resistance. At a reception for national leader Joshua Nkomo in Rhodesia in 1962, an elderly man who had participated in the revolt of 1896–1897 gifted him with an axe as a symbol of a continuing struggle. On another occasion, a grandson of one of the leaders of the 1896–1897 revolt in Rhodesia, speaking to the African masses, called on them in the name of their fathers to fight against the Whites.

Religion played an important part in fomenting unrest and enlisting support for the anticolonial struggle: The Muslims of Algeria, for example, declared a jihad against the French; in other African countries, independent Christian African churches, which played a prominent role in the national struggle, often granted sainthood to the casualties of early uprisings, thus preserving the memory of resistance and cultivating a sense of commitment to the ongoing struggle.[18] Where the anticolonial struggle was particularly

66   *The New Nationalism and Its Historical Heritage*

intense (such as in Kenya and Rhodesia) religious military squads and rituals emerged that appealed to religious sensitivities, fostered a sense of connection to historical traditions, and infused the ongoing struggle with spiritual and emotional meaning, which granted it the legitimacy of religion and tradition.

Below are descriptions of two gatherings. The first was an assembly of members of a cult led by Elijah Masinde, which was active in Kenya after World War II, and the second relates to the atmosphere in national assemblies that were held in Rhodesian villages in 1960:

> He [Masinde] wanted his followers to remember the dead in their prayers. One interesting thing about this meeting is that they were dressed as in readiness for the 1895 war. At this meeting it is alleged that he unearthed a skull in which a bullet was found buried in the mouth ... The crowd became very emotional and destructive.[19]

> Past heritage was revived through prayers and traditional singing with African instruments, ancestral spirits were evoked to guide and lead the new nation. Christian civilisation took a backseat, and new forms of worship, and new attitudes were thrust forward dramatically ... The desire was to put the twentieth century in an African context.[20]

Notes

1 Bernard Lewis, *Alei Historia* [Pages of History] (Jerusalem: Yad Ben-Zvi, 1988), p. 41 [Hebrew].
2 J. F. Ade Ajayi, "The Place of African History and Culture in the Process of Nation-Building in Africa South of the Sahara," *The Journal of Negro Education* (Summer, 1961): 206–213.
3 Israeli researcher Nehemia Levtzion provides a detailed study of the political structure, culture, history, and economy of precolonial Ghana and Mali in his book *Ancient Ghana and Mali* (London: Methuen, 1973).
4 On the concept of Balkanization, see Benyamin Neuberger, "The Concept of Balkanization," *Journal of Modern African Studies* XIII, No. 3 (1976): 523–529.
5 Larry Jay Diamond, "Roots of Failure—Seeds of Hope," in Larry Jay Diamond, Juan J. Linz, and Seymour Martin Lipset (eds.), *Democracy in Developing Countries: Africa* (Boulder, CO: Lynne Rienner, 1988), p. 14.
6 L. H. Gann and Peter Duignan, *Colonialism in Africa, 1870–1960*, Vol. 1 (Cambridge: Cambridge University Press, 1970), p. 315.
7 Ibid., p. 309.
8 D. A. Low, "British East Africa: The Establishment of British Rule, 1895–1912," in Vincent Harlow and E. M. Chilver (eds.), *History of East Africa*, Vol. II (Oxford: Clarendon Press, 1965), pp. 1–56.
9 The Maji-Maji Rebellion (1905–1907) against the forced quota of cotton growth imposed by the Germans. The name *maji-maji* (Swahili for water) derives from the insurgents' belief that the German bullets would turn into water through magic. The outcome of the rebellion was disastrous as it was followed by a German scorched-earth policy, and the ensuing widespread hunger.

The New Nationalism and Its Historical Heritage   67

10   The suppression of the Herero Revolt (1904–1907) is widely regarded as the first genocide of the twentieth century, with a connection to the Jewish Holocaust in the sense that some of its perpetrators were later active in Nazi Germany.

11   Julius Nyerere, born in 1922, served as the first president of Tanzania from its independence in 1961 until his retirement in 1985. His father was chief of the Zanaki people, a small ethnic group based along the shores of Lake Victoria. Nyerere attended missionary school and the universities of Makerere (Uganda) and Edinburgh (Scotland). A teacher by training, he founded the Tanganyika African National Union (TANU), the political party that led the struggle for independence. He was renowned for his original thinking and his efforts to create an authentic African socialism for Tanzania that centered on cooperative agriculture, prioritization of the village over the city, reduced dependence on foreign assistance through self-reliance, teaching manual labor, the nationalization of important economic sectors, and ensuring the integrity of the leadership.

12   Nelson Mandela, born in 1918, was the son of a chief. He studied law at the University of Witwatersrand in Johannesburg and in 1952 founded the first black law firm in South Africa. He became politically active in 1944, when he joined the African National Congress (ANC), and he soon assumed the leadership. In November 1962 he was sentenced to five years in prison for inciting strikes and leaving the country without permission, and in 1967 he was sentenced to life imprisonment for plotting a violent overthrow of the state. For 27 years he was imprisoned in the infamous Robben Island Maximum Security Prison. He was released by South African President Frederik de Klerk, who initiated the dismantling of apartheid and the formation of a multi-racial democracy. Upon his release he was again chosen to head the ANC and he led negotiations with the South African government to formulate a new constitution. When South Africa held its first multi-racial elections, in 1994, he was elected president.

13   Nelson Mandela's First Court Statement, 1962, www.un.org/en/events/mandela day/court_statement_1962.shtml.

14   A minor resistance war fought in 1898 against the German levying of taxes.

15   John Iliffe, *A Modern History of Tanganyika* (Cambridge: Cambridge University Press, 1979), p. 168.

16   Julius Nyerere, *Freedom and Unity* (Dar es Salaam: Oxford University Press, 1966), pp. 40–41.

17   G. C. K. Gwassa, "The German Intervention and African Resistance in Tanzania," in I. N. Kimambo and A. J. Temu (eds.), *A History of Tanzania* (Nairobi: East African Publishing House, 1969), p. 118.

18   Terrence Ranger, "Connexions between 'Primary Resistance' Movements and Modern Mass Nationalism in East and Central Africa," parts I and II, *Journal of African History* 9, No. 3 (1968): 437–453; 9, No. 4 (1968): 631–641.

19   J. D. Welime, "Dini ya Msambwa," research seminar paper (Dar es Salaam, 1965), quoted in Ranger, "Connexions," part II, p. 633.

20   Nathan Shamuyarira, *Crisis in Rhodesia* (Nairobi: East African Publishing House, 1965), pp. 68–69.

6 The Permeation of Western Liberal Concepts

During the eighteenth and nineteenth centuries, in the aftermath of bitter wars, violent uprisings, bloodshed, and periods of revolutionary terror and oppression, Western Europe began to project a different political, social, economic, and moral image. The nation-state emerged in place of empires and monarchies, the church lost some of its power, and secular democratic political systems based on the rule of law began to replace absolute monarchies. The new set of values that emerged in Europe after the French Revolution fueled social, economic, and political transformations, which in turn contributed to reshaping those values. At the center were the concepts of liberty and equality—individual and collective liberty, the rule of law, equality under the law, and equality among peoples and races—and these became bound with new values such as pluralism, tolerance, and social justice. Many thinkers contributed to shaping liberal democracy, including Locke, Rousseau, de Tocqueville, Mazzini, Mill, Burke, Paine, Jefferson, and Bentham.

The leaders of African nationalism were exposed to liberal democratic principles at universities in Britain, France, and the United States, through contact with associates in the British Labour party or the French Socialist party, and through the Western education system that developed in Africa. Western values also reached Africa through observation and reading, as well as participation in the Allied armed forces during the world wars in the name of freedom, democracy, self-determination, and equality among the nations. Leaders of the national struggle in Africa—Nkrumah in Ghana,[1] Azikiwe in Nigeria,[2] Nyerere in Tanzania,[3] Mboya and Kenyatta in Kenya,[4,5] Senghor in Senegal,[6] Lumumba and Kasavubu in the Congo (Zaire),[7,8] Banda in Malawi,[9] Obote in Uganda,[10] Kaunda in Zambia,[11] and Mondlane in Mozambique[12]— fought against the colonialist West in the name of its liberal values, demanding that the latter honor the obligation inherent in its principles of individual rights and national liberty.

The following examples illustrate African nationalism's adoption of Western concepts and terminology. Each excerpt reflects the influence of Western democratic ideas on African nationalism. Patrice Lumumba, speaking in 1960 at the ceremony for the proclamation of Congo's independence, stated:

DOI: 10.4324/9781003322818-7

Figure 6.1 Patrice Lumumba.
Source: https://mg.wikipedia.org/wiki/Patrice_Lumumba#/media/Sary:PatriceLumu mba1960.jpg, CC BY 4.0.

> Together we shall establish social justice ... We shall stop the persecution of free thought. We shall see to it that all citizens enjoy to the fullest extent the basic freedoms provided for by the Declaration of Human Rights ... We shall eradicate all discrimination ... I ask the parliamentary minority to help my Government through a constructive opposition and to limit themselves strictly to legal and democratic channels.[13]

In March 1960, Kenneth Kaunda, leader of the national movement in Zambia, wrote as follows to British Secretary of State for the Colonies Iain Macleod:

> We have already submitted our case for SELF-GOVERNMENT NOW, but I wish to sum up the case as follows:
>
> 1. THAT we do ask for the graceful transfer of power from minority groups to the majority not only because we believe it is the God-given right of any people to rule themselves but because we believe

Figure 6.2 Kenneth Kaunda.
Source: https://es.wikipedia.org/wiki/Kenneth_Kaunda#/media/Archivo:Kenneth_Kaunda_1983-03-30.jpg, Public Domain.

quite sincerely that if an atmosphere of racial harmony and peace, which we need in order to develop and exploit our abundant natural resources, is to be created, the majority must rule.
2. THAT such government minority groups need not have any fears that their interests might be jeopardized because when we say we believe that "all men are created equal and that they are endowed with certain inalienable rights, among them LIFE, LIBERTY and the PURSUIT of HAPPINESS," we mean this applies to all men on earth regardless of their race, creed, etc. We have no intention of replacing the present form of oppression with one of our own.[14]

The Emergence of New Nationalist Concepts and Modernization Processes in Africa

The concepts espoused by Western liberalism did not emerge in a vacuum. Economic and social developments prepared the ground for a conceptual shift and a change in values: urbanization, the creation of a modern transportation network, the use of mass communication, the spread of literacy, consolidation of education systems, management of commercial agriculture, and the emergence of a financial economy in place of the prevailing subsistence economy, the formation of workers', youth, students' and women's organizations and urban ethnic associations, and the creation of political parties. These were just a few of the changes that took place in Africa as part of its modernization.

Colonial Africa saw the emergence of many new cities, including Dakar in Senegal, Abidjan in the Gold Coast, Accra in Ghana, Lagos in Nigeria, Kinshasa in Zaire, Dar es Salaam in Tanzania, Kampala in Uganda, and Nairobi in Kenya. Waves of Africans migrated to the new cities, although a majority of the population remained in rural agrarian areas. Within the cities there began to emerge the first buds of a national consciousness, especially among a small echelon of elite across different ethnic groups. The transition to the city often severed individuals from the local networks that had previously provided their sense of belonging and identity. In its place they began to develop a sense of solidarity based on education and occupation, which spanned ethnic differences. The cities' newly established schools produced the first formally educated generation, and new groupings of clerks and laborers, with modern demands and needs, began to take shape. Residential segregation, with glittering white neighborhoods alongside poor black housing, created focal points of hostility and national agitation in the name of freedom and equality. Opposition to colonial rule and to the presence of Europeans helped foster a unifying national-territorial consciousness.

The growing transportation network—roads, railways, air travel—allowed leaders from different regions and ethnic groups within the colonial state to get together and form connections. Cars and trains made it possible for urban political party leaders to reach remote rural areas. The media—printed press and radio—was used to convey information and disseminate ideas. The missionary school system and Christian churches introduced Western education and the values of individualism, social justice, and peace among nations. Protestant Christianity, in particular, emphasized the autonomy of the individual, communal self-rule, and national independence. Missionaries also developed written forms of many African languages, using the Latin script, and translated the Bible into local languages. Their awareness of the difference between Christian teachings and colonial realities motivated Africans to split away from and liberate themselves from European missions and create "separatist" African churches. The new independent churches represented protest against European rule and provided spiritual and intellectual leadership as well as an organizational foundation for the nascent nationalism. This fact should not be taken as evidence that the Western Christian set of values lost its influence; rather, it attests to the depths of that influence.

The following quotes illustrate the discrepancy between the Christian churches' values and democratic concepts (individual liberty, equality, rule of law, self-determination), on the one hand, and the reality in the colonies

72 *The Permeation of Western Liberal Concepts*

Figure 6.3 African churches: The Arch Cathedral Bethel, Lagos, Nigeria.
Source: https://en.wikipedia.org/wiki/The_African_Church#/media/File:African_Ch urch_Bethel.jpg, CC BY-SA 4.0.

(racial discrimination, oppression of the majority, denial of individual liberty, administrative arbitrariness), on the other.

An African newspaper in the Belgian Congo stated in 1952:

> Certainly, racial discrimination is legally prohibited in the Belgian Congo. It nonetheless exists in fact. In cinemas, hotels, boats, trains, churches and other public places all the Africans are either excluded or clearly separated from the Europeans.[15]

Figure 6.4 African churches: A Methodist chapel in Leliefontein, Northern Cape, South Africa.
Source: https://en.wikipedia.org/wiki/Methodist_Church_of_Southern_Africa#/media/File:Methodist_Mission_Church,_Leliefontein.jpg, CC BY-SA 3.0.

According to a newspaper in Catholic Portuguese Angola:

> To tell a person he is able to interpret the Bible freely is to insinuate in him an undue autonomy and turn him into a rebel ... A Protestant native is already disposed towards—not to say an active agent in—the revolt against civilizing people.[16]

Africa's modernization produced a working class that, while initially small in number, had tremendous political impact. Workers were employed in mines, harbors, railways, and administrative services at low wages. In colonies that also employed white workers, such as Rhodesia (today's Zimbabwe) and South Africa, whites received immeasurably higher wages than blacks. In Northern Rhodesia (today's Zambia), for example, the lowest wage rate of a white worker was five times greater than the highest wage earned by a black worker. Managers and employers were exclusively white. The emergence of a working class led to the formation of trade unions that attributed the economic and social hardship of workers to colonialism and therefore played a key role in the struggle for independence.

Figure 6.5 Teaching staff and students at Liberia College, 1900. In earlier years, missionaries were the main agents for the introduction of written language into the school system.
Source: https://digitalcollections.nypl.org/items/510d47dc-951e-a3d9-e040-e00a18064a99, Public Domain.

In countries such as the Gold Coast/Ghana and Nigeria, there emerged a narrow stratum of African businessmen who adopted the capitalist values of private entrepreneurship. Farmers who grew commercial crops—coffee, cocoa, cotton, agave (sisal), peanuts—formed cooperatives. Their dependence on global supply and demand fluctuations extended their scope of interest beyond their own village and sphere of immediate subsistence and sharpened their political awareness. The relatively few educated professionals—physicians, engineers, journalists, and teachers—played a vital role in the introduction and dissemination of new ideas. They were a product of modernization as well as the driving force for its continuation. National political parties were also a direct product of modernization, for there can be no parties without an educated class, a political public, a press, transportation, and mass communications media. Indeed, the political party is a modern phenomenon, and modern products such as telephones and other technological aids are essential to its large-scale operation. The appearance of national parties that advocated Western ideas symbolized the link between modernization and the emergence of new ideas, although it is important to bear in mind that modernization can—and indeed did—exacerbate social and ethnic tensions, particularly after the disappearance of the common enemy, European colonialism.

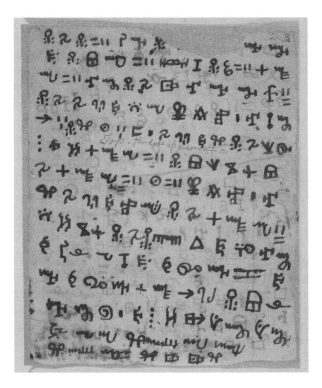

Figure 6.6 This script was created in West Africa and was one of many scripts created throughout the nineteenth and twentieth century as an alternative to the European writing that was predominantly used. The creation of the script was part of a larger endeavor to represent African languages. The origin of the image-based logograms of the Vai script is not known.

Source: https://commons.wikimedia.org/wiki/File:West_Africa_Vai_Document_Lo res.jpg, CC0 1.0.

In his essay "Afro-Asia and European Political Tradition," Prof. Shlomo Avineri summarizes the relationship between the spread of imperialism and the advent of modernization in the Afro-Asian world:

> It is clear, in any event, that the future historian, in reviewing the contribution of imperialism to global civilization, will not be able to limit his explanations to the subjective motives of the imperialist states: power, superpower competition, markets—all these will be granted the same place as that granted young Alexander's ambition of conquering the East. Just as the historian of Greece does not frame Alexander's chapter in history only in terms of his subjective motives but rather [examines] the objective fact of the East's Hellenization, which along with the Romanization of the West by Roman imperialism (again as a result, not as a motive) led to the

76 *The Permeation of Western Liberal Concepts*

creation of a single global civilization that we term Western civilization. In this sense, it was not the market competition of the late nineteenth century that was determinative, but rather the creation of an Afro-Asian world subject to the spheres [of influence] of European civilization and the transformation of the world, for the first time, into something approaching one world. No force other than imperialism would have brought the European technique, language, and ultimately, values to the ends of the earth, even though these were not its main objectives.[17]

Western Liberal Concepts—Weapons in the War against Colonial Rule

In the following two passages, representatives of the African national movement employ the terms, values, and concepts of the West while fighting against it.

The 1954 platform of the Convention People's Party in the Gold Coast stated:

> Besides the unprecedented material process, there has been a great spiritual transformation. FREEDOM IS IN THE AIR. Our people have become aware of their dignity as citizens and are burning to be free to govern themselves. They prefer *self-government with danger* to *servitude in tranquility*. They want in full measure the fundamental human freedoms of press, assembly, and speech. And above all, they want freedom from the *contempt* of foreign masters.[18]

Nelson Mandela, leader of the African National Congress, stated in 1964:

> In 1960 there was the shooting at Sharpeville, which resulted in the proclamation of a state of emergency and the declaration of the ANC as an unlawful organization.[19] My colleagues and I, after careful consideration, decided that we would not obey this decree. The African people were not part of the Government and did not make the laws by which they were governed. We believed in the words of the Universal Declaration of Human Rights, that "the will of the people shall be the basis of authority of the Government," and for us to accept the banning was equivalent to accepting the silencing of the Africans for all time. The ANC refused to dissolve, but instead went underground ... I have no doubt that no self-respecting White political organization would disband itself if declared illegal by a government in which it had no say.[20]

To illustrate the extent to which Western concepts served as weapons in the hands of educated Africans and leaders of the national movement, the following table presents such liberal democratic concepts alongside hypothetical questions by Westernized Africans who had internalized these concepts and now demanded that the Western colonial government conduct itself in accordance with the principles of its motherland.

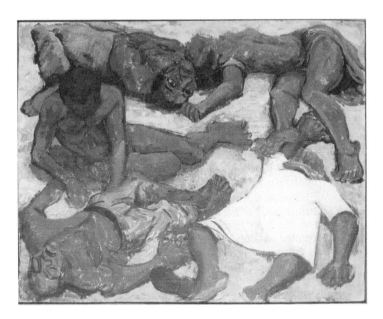

Figure 6.7 Painting depicting victims of the Sharpeville massacre (which took place on 21 March 1960, Sharpeville, Transvaal province, South Africa) by Godfrey Rubens. It is currently located in the South African Consulate in London.

Source: https://en.wikipedia.org/wiki/Sharpeville_massacre#/media/File:Murder_at_Sharpeville_21_March_1960.jpg, CC BY-SA 3.0.

Table 6.1 Westernized Africans and their struggle for independence

Western concepts	*Questions posed by Westernized Africans in their struggle for independence*
Rule of law	Is the rule of law consistent with separation of the executive branch from the judicial branch? With the judicial authorities granted to officials in British colonies and with judicial discrimination between Whites and Africans in French colonies? With the lack of protection under the law from forced labor and with the arbitrariness of employers in Portuguese colonies?
Equality under the law	Is equality under the law consistent with blatant discrimination in wages for civil servants? With the White monopoly over senior managerial positions? With the fact that investment in Black education is a small fraction of the amount invested in White education? With the meager representation of the African citizens of the French Community at the National Assembly in Paris? With election laws that grant equal representation to Whites (who are about 1% of the community), Indians (1% of the population), and Africans (98% of the population) in British Kenya in the 1950s?

(*continued*)

78   *The Permeation of Western Liberal Concepts*

Table 6.1 Cont.

Western concepts	Questions posed by Westernized Africans in their struggle for independence
Racial equality	Why does equal work not receive equal pay? Why is a discharged Italian soldier who fought against the British in Ethiopia during World War II permitted to buy land in the White Highlands of British Kenya, while an African soldier from Kenya who fought in the Kings' African Rifles, alongside the British against the Italians, is prohibited from purchasing land in his own homeland? Why is it permissible to bar Africans from neighborhoods, hotels, and clubs in their own homeland solely on the basis of skin color?
National self-determination	Why were Africans called upon to fight in World War II in the British and French armed forces on behalf of the principles embodied in Churchill and Roosevelt's Atlantic Charter, which granted self-determination to the Dutch, Yugoslavians, Danes, and Burmese, while at the same time they could not demand self-determination for themselves?
Government by consensus	What gives the colonial government the right to forcibly suppress demands for government by consensus, for a majority African government that would replace a handful of colonial officials and colonizers?
Majority rule	Every Western democratic country recognizes the principle of majority rule. Why is this principle not implemented in British Kenya or Rhodesia?
Free elections	Why is the colonial government opposed to elections based on the principle of "One Man, One Vote"—the accepted formula in all Western democracies?
Basic liberties	Why is there no freedom of expression in the Belgian Congo, no freedom of professional association in South Africa, no freedom of press in Mozambique, and no freedom of religion in Angola?
Human dignity	Why do Whites address elderly Africans with the disparaging term "boy" or speak of them as "natives" while Africans are required to address Whites respectfully?
Economic liberty	Why are Africans in South Africa barred from working in any profession they chose? Why are Africans in Tanganyika prohibited from operating bus companies? Why are Africans in Kenya prohibited from growing coffee?

Figure 6.8 Spectator segregation (apartheid) in a sports stadium, Bloemfontein, South Africa, 1969.
Source: www.flickr.com/photos/un_photo/3311468609, United Nations, CC BY-NC-ND 2.0.

Notes

1 Kwame Nkrumah (1909–1972) was the first prime minister and president of Ghana and a proponent of Pan-Africanism. He supported both socialism and nationalism, and played an active part in African international relations during the decolonization process. In 1964 Ghana became a one-party state and Nkrumah was declared president for life. Two years later, however, he was deposed in a military coup by the National Liberation Council. He lived the rest of his life in exile in Guinea (the former French Guinea, ruled by his friend Sekou Touré).
2 Nnamdi Azikiwe (1904–1996) served as the first president of Nigeria from 1963 to 1966. He was known as the "father of Nigerian nationalism." As a journalist and political leader he advocated Nigerian and African nationalism.
3 Julius Nyerere (1922–1999) was a Tanzanian politician, political philosopher, and anticolonial activist. He developed a socialist-nationalist philosophy called *Ujamaa* (Swahili for "extended family"). He governed first Tanganyika (as prime minister and president, 1961–1964) and then Tanzania (as president, 1964–1985), increasingly emphasizing national self-reliance and socialism.

80   *The Permeation of Western Liberal Concepts*

Nyerere was the son of a chief from the tiny Zanaki ethnic group on the shores of Lake Victoria. He completed his studies in mission schools and at the universities of Makerere (Uganda) and Edinburgh (Scotland). He became a teacher and founded the Tanganyika African National Union (TANU), the party that led the struggle for independence. An original thinker, he wanted to create an authentic African socialism in Tanzania, based on cooperative agriculture, an emphasis on village life in preference to city life, the reduction of dependence on foreign aid through increased reliance on internal sources, education and self-labor, nationalization of crucial parts of the economy, and integrity of the leadership.

4   Tom Mboya (1930–1969) was Pan-Africanist and trade unionist. He helped establish the Kenya National African Union (KANU), of which he was the first secretary general, and was active in the establishment of the Kenyan, Ugandan, and Tanzanian trade unions. He worked closely with John F. Kennedy and Martin Luther King in the field of education. He was 39 years old when he was assassinated.

5   Jomo Kenyatta (1897–1978) was prime minister (1963–1964) and president of Kenya from 1964 to his death. He was an African nationalist and a Pan-Africanist. In 1952 he was arrested and imprisoned by the British for allegedly initiating the Mau-Mau uprising—a "fact" later disputed by many historians—and remained in prison till 1959. Two years after his release he became president of KANU (1961–1978). He was honored with the title *Mzee* ("elder," i.e., a person respected for his age, wisdom, and experience). Nevertheless, his rule was often criticized as authoritarian and quasi-neocolonial. He was also accused of favoring his own ethnic group, the Kikuyu.

6   Lépold Senghor. For details about Senghor, see Chapter 3, note 3.

7   Patrice Lumumba (1925–1961) was the first prime minister of the Republic of Congo (today's Democratic Republic of Congo), from June 1960 to September 1960, when he was deposed by then president Kasavubu and chief-of-staff Mobutu (who himself became president in 1965 after initiating a military coup). Lumumba was assassinated by a firing squad in January 1961, both because his own growing power was feared, and because both the USSR and communism seemed to exert an increasing influence on him. In 2002, the Belgian government formally extended its apologies for Belgium's active and infamous role in the assassination (in which the CIA was also involved).

Due to the brevity of his political career, his legacy remains unclear. He is mostly remembered as an anticolonial martyr who fought for Congolese independence.

8   Joseph Kasavubu (1915–1969) was the first president of the Republic of Congo (1960–1965). His political career was overshadowed by that of Lumumba, and by his role in the latter's removal from office and eventual assassination.

9   Hastings Kamuzu Banda (ca. 1898–1997) was the first president of Malawi, serving from its independence in 1964 until his defeat in its free elections, in 1994. Born to a farming family and educated in a Scottish missionary school, he studied philosophy, political science, and medicine at universities in the United States and Britain. After receiving a medical degree in 1937 he worked as a physician in Britain and Ghana, where he lived for many years. In 1958, after more than 25 years abroad, he returned to Nyasaland (today's Malawi) to lead the national African struggle in Nyasaland (now Malawi). In 1959 he was imprisoned by the British under charges of organizing riots and inciting to insurrection. After his release he resumed leadership of the liberation movement, and in 1963 became prime minister, a position he retained after the British granted Malawi its independence in 1964. In 1996 Malawi, like

The Permeation of Western Liberal Concepts 81

many other African countries, became by law a one-party state. In 1976 a constitutional amendment made Banda president for life. In 1993 he conceded to demands for the establishment of a multiparty system, and the following year he lost the elections. He was succeeded by Bakili Muzuli, leader of the United Democratic Front. During his 30-year rule, Banda sought to develop agriculture in his country and prevent its residents from seeking employment abroad. His policies were conservative and pro-Western. He was the first African leader to establish diplomatic ties with South Africa, and in 1973 Malawi was one of the only countries in Africa that refused to sever diplomatic ties with Israel.

10 Milton Obote (1925–2005) was a leader of the anticolonial struggle in Uganda. When the country obtained independence in 1962, he became prime minister, instituted an authoritarian regime, and abolished local kingdoms. In 1972 he was deposed in a military coup that replaced him with Idi Amin. In 1980, after Amin was deposed, Obote returned from exile and resumed the presidency, until the army again deposed him in 1985.

11 Kenneth Kaunda (1924–2021) abandoned his work as a teacher in favor of anticolonial political activism, for which the British imprisoned him. In 1964 he led Zambia to independence and was elected as president. He served as leader of a two-party regime through 1990, until his defeat in the 1991 elections. Kaunda was known for his support of black majority rule in Rhodesia/Zimbabwe and South Africa.

12 Eduardo Mondlane (1920–1969) was an anthropologist and taught sociology and history at Syracuse University. He was president of the Mozambican Liberation Front (FRELIMO) from 1962 until his assassination in 1969.

13 Patrice Lumumba, June 30, 1960, "Republic of Congo, Independence Day," https:// incois.gov.in/Tutor/science+society/lectures/illustrations/lecture35/lumumbaspe ech.html.

14 Kenneth Kaunda, *Zambia Shall Be Free* (London: Heinemann, 1962), pp. 141–142.

15 Gann and Duignan, *Colonialism in Africa*, Vol. 2, p. 201.

16 Thomas Hodgkin, *Nationalism in Colonial Africa* (London: Muller, 1965), p. 98.

17 Shlomo Avineri, *Pirkei Hevra Ve-Medina* [Readings on Society and State] (Tel Aviv: Sifriyat Poalim, 1969), pp. 130–131 [Hebrew].

18 Gideon-Cyrus Mutiso and S. W. Rohio, *Readings in African Political Thought* (London: Heinemann, 1975), p. 198.

19 On March 21, 1960, the ANC held demonstrations throughout South Africa to protest "pass laws" (internal passports that black South Africans had to carry at all times). In the township of Sharpeville, in the province of Transvaal, police opened fire on demonstrators, killing 65 people. Following what became known as the Sharpeville massacre, the government of South Africa declared a state of emergency and arrested 13,000 Africans. These events radicalized Africans, who until then had hoped to achieve their aims through passive, non-violent resistance. Indeed, immediately after the Sharpeville massacre, the ANC announced that it was shifting its policy from non-violent to armed struggle.

20 Nelson Mandela, "I Am Prepared to Die," Statement at the opening of the defense case, Rivonia Trial, Pretoria Supreme Court, April 20, 1964, www.un.org/en/eve nts/mandeladay/court_statement_1964.shtml.

7   Socialist and Communist Concepts and Anticolonial African Nationalism

The following passages are taken from the writings of Lenin (*Imperialism: The Highest Stage of Capitalism*)[1] and Nkrumah (*Towards Colonial Freedom*).[2] The similarity between the remarks of the father of the Bolshevik revolution and those of the architects of African nationalism attest to the ideological influence of communism on African nationalism.

In *Imperialism: The Highest Stage of Capitalism* (1917), Lenin wrote:

> As long as capitalism remains what it is, surplus capital will be utilised not for the purpose of raising the standard of living of the masses in a given country, for this would mean a decline in profits for the capitalists ... In these backward countries profits are usually high, for capital is scarce, the price of land is relatively low, wages are low, raw materials are cheap ...

> Before the war [World War I] the capital invested abroad by the three principal countries [France, Britain, and Germany] amounted to between 175,000 million and 200,000 million francs. At the modest rate of 5 per cent, this sum should have brought in from 8,000 to 10,000 million francs a year—a sound basis for the imperialist oppression and exploitation of most of the countries and nations of the world, for the capitalist parasitism of a handful of wealthy states!

> We see plainly here how private and state monopolies are interwoven in the epoch of finance capital; how both are but separate links in the imperialist struggle between the big monopolists for the division of the world ...

> Capitalism's transition to the stage of monopoly capitalism, to finance capital, is connected with the intensification of the struggle for the partitioning of the world ...

> Cecil Rhodes ... expressed his imperialist views ... in 1895 in the following terms: "I was in the East End of London (a working-class quarter) yesterday and attended a meeting of the unemployed. I listened to the wild speeches, which were just a cry for 'bread! bread!' and on my way home I pondered over the scene and became more than ever convinced

DOI: 10.4324/9781003322818-8

of the importance of imperialism ... My cherished idea is a solution for the social problem, i.e., in order to save the 40,000,000 inhabitants of the United Kingdom from a bloodied civil war, we colonial statesmen must acquire new lands to settle the surplus population, to provide new markets for the goods produced in the factories and mines ... If you want to avoid civil war, you must become imperialists."[3]

The principal feature of the latest stage of capitalism is the domination of monopolist associations of big employers. These monopolies are most firmly established when all the sources of raw materials are captured by one group ... Colonial possession alone gives the monopolies complete guarantee against all contingencies in the struggle against competitors ...

Monopoly has grown out of colonial policy. To the numerous "old" motives of colonial policy, finance capital has added the struggle for the sources of raw materials, for the export of capital, for the spheres of influence, i.e., for spheres for profitable deals, concessions, monopoly profits and so on ...

In *Towards Colonial Freedom* (1952), Nkrumah wrote:

The aim of all colonial governments in Africa ... has been the struggle for raw materials ... The colonies have become the dumping ground, and colonial peoples the false recipients, of manufactured goods of the industrialist and capitalist of Great Britain, France, Belgium, and other colonial powers.[4]

Anticolonialism, Anticapitalism, and Anti-Westernism

In the aftermath of the 1917 October Revolution in Russia, communism became a major force of the twentieth century. An analysis of anticolonial nationalism in Africa cannot ignore its influence, both direct and indirect, and its role in accelerating Europe's withdrawal from its colonies. The generation of African intellectuals who sought the means and the path to national liberation were influenced by communist concepts about the connection between colonialism and capitalism—concepts that regarded the economically exploitative nature of colonialism as a direct outcome of the capitalist system. Many African leaders believed that the colonial situation confirmed certain communist theses, and they were therefore predisposed toward Marxist-Leninist ideas.

According to Lenin, imperialism has the following five characteristics:

1. The concentration of production and capital, leading to the creation of monopolies;
2. The merging of bank capital with industrial capital;

84 *Socialist and Communist Concepts and African Nationalism*

3. The export of capital to backward countries [please note that the term "backward" is the one used by Lenin's translators];
4. The formation of international monopolist associations that share the world among themselves; and
5. The division of the world among the capitalist powers.

Lenin thus links imperialism with capitalism. In the Soviet Union following the October Revolution, anticapitalist thinking and practice did indeed correspond with hostility toward the West—toward Western financial companies that operated in czarist Russia and toward the imperialist Western powers that intervened to thwart the Bolshevik revolution. Chinese communism, likewise, lumped the capitalist system with Western imperialism as a single driving force that sought, directly and indirectly, to control China through "spheres of influence" and the system of *capitula*.[5]

The communist revolutions in China, Cuba, and Vietnam may also be viewed as an indirect expression of anti-Western nationalism, of hostility toward an arrogant and more advanced capitalist West, and of resistance to the political and economic control exerted by powerful countries and capitalist financial associations over disadvantaged countries. These factors are important for understanding the attraction and influence of radical ideologies in Africa. African nationalism equated the capitalist economic system with foreign colonial rule, with white settlers who oppressed the local population, and with the control imposed by capitalist European financial companies. Capitalism was perceived as a global system sustained by the exploitation of cheap minerals and raw materials imported from Africa. It was linked with the West as a whole, not only with the colonial power ruling a particular colony. Thus colonialism became merged with the West and with capitalism, and anticolonialism with anti-Westernism and with hostility toward capitalism.

The communists portrayed the West as the common enemy of the Soviet Union, of communist parties throughout the world, and of nations ruled by colonialist powers. A few of the pioneers of Pan-Africanism in the United States—Du Bois, Padmore, Césaire—were members of the Communist Party for a while, until they concluded that it represented a false "deity." During their studies, African leaders such as Kenyatta and Nkrumah maintained close ties with communist circles. After World War II, French West Africa saw the emergence of cooperation between the French Communist Party and the leading national party, creating the *Rassemblement démocratique africain* (RDA),[6] headed by Felix Houphouet-Boigny,[7] Sékou Touré,[8] and Modibo Keïta,[9] the first presidents respectively of the newly independent Ivory Coast, Guinea, and Mali.

The image projected by the Soviet Union—of a country that had dismantled the capitalist system, thwarted attempted military interventions by the West, instituted revolutionary agrarian reform, and in a brief span of time transformed itself from a backward country into a global and

Socialist and Communist Concepts and African Nationalism 85

industrial superpower—appealed to the many Africans who were struggling against colonialism. Capitalism, in contrast, seemed to offer Africans a less successful model for accelerated economic development, given the slow and lengthy nature of Western Europe's industrialization process. The costs of the Soviet industrial revolution—terror, purges, forced labor camps, and millions of victims of the Stalinist regime—had not yet come to light during the years in which most leaders of the new African nationalism were developing their political consciousness. Moreover, the West, in African eyes, was associated with the capitalist companies that had imposed colonialism upon them and enjoyed its fruits.

Leaders of African national movements were inclined to accept the assistance of those willing to support their struggle against colonial rule. The Soviet Union and communist parties in the West did indeed support the anticolonial struggle because it challenged the power of the West. The ties that formed in the Far East and southeastern Asia (for example in China and Vietnam) between anti-Western communism and anticolonial nationalism catalyzed the decolonization of Africa. The relatively speedy withdrawal of the West from Africa during the late 1950s and early 1960s was intended in part to prevent the African national movement's ideological radicalization toward communism, as in fact occurred in Vietnam. Indeed, the Portuguese colonies of Africa (Angola, Mozambique, Guinea-Bissau, Cape Verde, and São Tomé and Príncipe), which waged a prolonged, violent struggle for national liberation that lasted until 1974, saw the emergence of a radical nationalism. These states also formed close ties with the Soviet Union and communist Cuba after achieving independence and maintained those relations until the dissolution of communism in the Soviet Union in the late 1980s.

During the era of colonial rule certain groups within African society tended to identify with anti-Western and anticapitalist nationalism. Farmers, who were incorporated into the global monetary economy because the crops they raised were used for export, resented their dependence on the impersonal market mechanisms that determined the prices of peanuts, coffee, cocoa, and cotton and thereby sealed their fate. Their exploitation at the hands of Europeans was tangible, given the vast gap between their own earnings and market prices in Europe and America. Consequently, they were receptive to ideas that called for changing the entire "system."

At times Africans were dependent on Indian and Arab moneylenders, whom they viewed as agents of the colonial system. The hatred directed toward them became hatred of the entire system. In some cases, colonialism also introduced the concept of private ownership over land in areas where ownership had traditionally been communal. The landowner class, introduced by colonial rule, sparked unrest among the agrarian masses.[10] National parties and movements, in turn, exploited this unrest for their own needs.

Craft workers and petty merchants turned to the national movement because of their hostility to modernization, which threatened their standing as it created modern commerce networks and promoted the import of goods

86 *Socialist and Communist Concepts and African Nationalism*

from abroad. The employer of most of the workers who labored in mines, ports, railways, and industry was the white colonial government, and the financial associations and companies owned by whites. These workers were uprooted from their villages, from the security of their family unit, and from the social order they had always known. Living in slums, under conditions of loneliness and alienation, they earned petty wages while the whites enjoyed mind-boggling wealth. They developed a fierce hatred toward white rule and the capitalism of the whites. It is no wonder, therefore, that these strata of society were the first to rise up against colonial rule, nor that they were receptive to ideas that justified their desire to change the social and economic order in the direction they sought.

African Socialism

The inclination among Africans to identify with the socialist worldview did not cause them to adopt the Soviet or Chinese formulation of Marxism-Leninism. Most of the African anticolonial movements of the 1950s and 1960s developed a socialist outlook unique to them—an African socialism.

> We must reject ... individual ownership of land, go back to the traditional African custom "where one is entitled to land if he uses it."
> (Nyerere, as quoted in Friedland and Rosberg, p. 41)

> Negro African society is collectivist, or, more exactly, communal, because it is rather a communion of souls than an aggregate of individuals ... We had already realized socialism before the coming of the Europeans ... Our duty is to renew it by helping it to regain spiritual dimensions.
> (Senghor, as quoted in Friedland and Rosberg, p. 169)

> Since there is no class struggle, African Socialism will be gradual and peaceful.
> (M. Adoum, one of the participants in the 1962
> Dakar colloquium on African Socialism, as quoted
> in Friedland and Rosberg, p. 119)[11]

African socialism sought to highlight what was unique, original, and African. As such, it should be viewed as a national ideology, a socialism aimed at authenticity rather than at replicating foreign models. African socialism rejected some of the main principles of European socialism, such as class war and hostility toward religion as the "opiate of the masses" à la Marx. Moreover, African socialists did not accept the thesis of historical materialism, that is, the conception of history and politics in terms of economics. At heart they believed strongly in the salience of political practice, which they saw as not merely a reflection of economic conditions, but as a factor that determines and shapes the economic system.

Some African nationalists argued that African society had been socialist before capitalist colonialism, with its corruptive impact, arrived. In their view there was no need to import any ideology; rather, Africans should return to their roots. The claims regarding precolonial African socialism were based on descriptions of the equality, solidarity, and communalism that had prevailed in traditional society. Indeed, in most African societies land was owned by the collective (extended family, clan, or village) and regarded as a divine gift granted for the benefit of all. There was no shortage of land in Africa, and every head of household had a right to an equivalent tract of land for his and his family's use. This system prevented the massive accumulation of land by a wealthy minority and the creation of a landowning class. Everyone benefited from mutual assistance, so that there was no neglect of the elderly, the disadvantaged, the ill, or orphans. African socialism did, indeed, view the traditional community as a large family, characterized by fraternity, a sense of organic wholeness, harmony, and a willingness to sacrifice for the collective. Nyerere referred to this "traditional" socialism as *ujamaa* (cooperative economics based on a sense of "familyhood" in Swahili).

During the years of anticolonial struggle and early statehood, there were very few African leaders who rejected socialism and did not see it as an ideological and practical alternative to capitalism, which, as noted, was associated with colonialism. Like European socialism, African socialism aspired to bring about a social and economic revolution: it sought to foster accelerated industrialization within the framework of a planned and centralized national economy, and to abolish the free market based on economic individualism. Its uniqueness lay in its national character, its aversion to adopting foreign European ideologies, and its efforts to base a future socialist national society on traditional African values of equality and communalism.

African socialism had a short lifespan. Often there was a big gap between the official ideology and the socioeconomic reality in independent states. The failure of African socialism to bring about an expeditious social and economic revolution led to its decline in the 1970s and to the adoption of capitalism-oriented economic perspectives in many African states. In those countries that underwent a violent, prolonged decolonization process, the opposite process took place: an ideological radicalization in the direction of "scientific socialism," usually following the format of Soviet communism. The next chapter addresses these radical ideologies.

The poem "Whither O Africa?" by Guinean poet Michael Francis Dei-Anang[12] reflects the cultural crossroads that Africans encountered. Dei-Anang plays with the words "backward" and "forward": backward in time, that is, a return to traditional society, actually means forward in terms of family and social values, which are ironically called "superstition," while forward in time and modernization, that is, toward "the slums, where man is dumped upon man," actually implies backwardness of these same community-based values. The poem reflects the aspirations and values at the basis of African socialism and Nyerere's concept of *ujamaa*.[13]

Notes

1 Vladimir Ilyich Lenin, *Imperialism, the Highest Stage of Capitalism: A Popular Outline* (first published in 1917 in Petrograd as a pamphlet, republished in *Lenin, Selected Works*, Moscow: Progress Publishers, 1963), available at Marxists Internet Archive, www.marxists.org/archive/lenin/works/1916/imp-hsc/imperialism.pdf.

2 Kwame Nkrumah, *Towards Colonial Freedom* (London: Heinemann, 1962), pp. XV, XVII, 3–4, 14, 16, 20, 42, 43.

3 Note that, to support his argument, Lenin is quoting Rhodes (*Die Neue Zeit*, XVI, 1, 1898, S. 304), after whom Rhodesia—today Zimbabwe—was named.

4 For this quote, see Atta Britwum, "The Lure of the Image in the Mirror: A Reading of Kwame Nkrumah's *Towards Colonial Freedom*," *Legon Journal of the Humanities* 28, No. 1 (2017): 10–19. Available online at www.academia.edu/48860926/The_Lure_of_the_Image_in_the_Mirror_A_Reading_of_Kwame_Nkrumah_s_Towards_Colonial_Freedom.

5 *Capitula* (Latin for "contractual articles") were privileges enshrined in contracts that benefited European subjects in countries of the Middle East, Eastern Africa, and the Far East. A *capitulum* would grant foreign settlers autonomy in matters of education, religion, and the administration of charities, and protect them from the local government and local law by making the latter subject to the administrative and legal systems of the European consuls, or to mixed courts that represented the European "motherland." These *capitula* undermined the sovereignty of the host country and symbolized the weakness of African and Asian states during the era of European imperialism.

6 The RDA was founded in 1946 as a national African party. It operated throughout French Africa, with main branches in the Ivory Coast, Guinea, French Sudan, and Cameroon. Between 1946 and 1950 the RDA was affiliated with the French Communist Party and adopted a radical nationalist stance. Subsequently its branches in Guinea (PDG), Cameroon (UPC), and French Sudan (US) adopted similar stances. In the 1950s its strongest branch, in the Ivory Coast (PDCI), underwent a transformation and became conservative, antinationalist, and pro-Western. In 1960, when the Ivory Coast achieved independence, the unifying framework of the RDA dissolved, and each branch became an independent national party with its own platform and approach.

7 Felix Houphouet-Boigny, born in 1905, was president of the Ivory Coast from its independence until his death in 1993. He was among the founders and leaders of the RDA. In the 1950s Houphouet-Boigny represented the conservative pro-Western approach. He called not for independence for the French colonies in Africa, but rather for equal rights and the inclusion of Africans in the French-African community. During 1958–1960 he served as a minister in the French government. It was only the pressure of national movements in other African colonies that forced him to accept the principle of independence. In the 1960s and 1970s the Ivory Coast became the wealthiest state in West Africa—a model of development based on a capitalist economy, Western investment, and the engagement of thousands of French experts and advisors. The 1980s saw a deterioration in the state's economy and Houphouet-Boigny lost much of his prestige as a result of massive unnecessary expenditures—transfer of the capital city to Yamoussoukro, construction of the largest cathedral in the world, and government corruption. Houphouet-Boigny was known for his close ties with the State of Israel and its leaders.

Socialist and Communist Concepts and African Nationalism 89

8 Sékou Touré (1922–1984), who began his political career as a leader of trade unions, maintained a radical national outlook. From 1952 he served as the head of Democratic Party of Guinea (Parti démocratique de Guinée, PDG), founded in 1947. In 1958, under his leadership and by referendum, Guinea became the only French colony in Africa to reject French President Charles de Gaulle's proposal of relinquishing independence and joining the French African community. Touré's stance and the outcome of the referendum in Guinea led to a rupture with France, which employed a scorched-earth policy when withdrawing from its colonies (removing teachers, technicians, and advisors, dismantling telephone lines, instituting an economic boycott, and so forth). This policy drove Guinea into the arms of the Soviet bloc. Touré, the first president of Guinea, turned the country into a socialist state, nationalized its economy, and instituted an oppressive one-party regime. During 1958–1977 Guinea was considered the "Cuba" of West Africa. In the late 1970s Guinea began gradually to draw closer to the West. After Touré's death, and following a military coup, Guinea adopted a more liberal economic policy and strengthened its ties with France and other Western countries.

9 Modibo Keïta (1915–1975) was the first president of Mali (formerly French Sudan), serving from 1960 to 1968. He was a founder of the RDA and head of its Sudanese branch, the Sudanese Union (Union soudanaise, US). Keïta served as a vice president in the National Assembly of France and as secretary of state in the French office of the president, but after Mali attained independence, he adopted a socialist-nationalist and anti-French position.

10 For example, in 1900 in the kingdom of Buganda, Uganda, the British divided most of the fertile lands among traditional leaders in order to earn their trust and support. Thus, there emerged a class of estate owners and landed gentry whose economic interests compelled them to cooperate with the colonial government. The agrarian unrest that was directed against these landowners took a popular-national form.

11 William H. Friedland and Carl J. Rosberg Jr. (eds.), *African Socialism* (Stanford, CA: Stanford University Press, 1967), pp. 41, 119, 169.

12 Michael Francis Dei-Anang was born in the Gold Coast (today's Ghana) and attended the University of London. From 1943 he worked for the colonial government of the Gold Coast. After independence he served as director general of the country's Foreign Ministry. Dei-Anang was representative of the narrow echelon of intellectual elite that emerged in Africa during the colonial era, led the anticolonial struggle, and integrated into the political and administrative leadership of the state after attaining independence.

13 The entire poem is available in *The New African* 1, No. 6 (1962): 14, https://disa.ukzn.ac.za/sites/default/files/pdf_files/nafv1n6.jun62_10.pdf.

8 Radical Ideologies of National, Economic, Social, and Cultural Liberation

The Origins of Radical Nationalism in Africa

In the final quarter of the nineteenth century, when the architects of colonialism arrived in Africa seeking to impose colonial order, and as they worked to fortify it during the first quarter of the twentieth century, their belief was that they would long rule over the land. Yet, in the immediate aftermath of World War II, the end of colonial rule already appeared to be near at hand. Many Africans—and the colonial powers themselves, foremost among them Britain—felt a need to institute fundamental change in the colonial relationship. Intellectually and organizationally, these were vibrant years in Africa, a time of constitutional reform and the growth of popular political parties under charismatic leadership, which, for the first time, gave a legitimate voice to Africans, enabling them to openly express their desire for liberty and equality. Years of relative economic prosperity, following numerous European investments alongside accelerated economic development, contributed to the general impression that relations between Africans and Europeans had reached a turning point, and that the end of the colonial era—whether via statehood or as part of a federation with France—inevitably meant the end of all the economic, political, and social hardship resulting from colonial rule.

However, not all the colonies in Africa were able to experience the joys of decolonization. The optimism and excitement that accompanied the effects of decolonization in some colonies differed dramatically from the atmosphere of stagnation, despair, and protest prevalent in colonies that found themselves excluded from the decolonization process. In Mozambique, for instance, NESAM[1]—a high-school student organization that engaged in national-cultural activities and whose members came from the narrow echelon of intellectual elite—was banned and its leaders arrested or exiled.[2] Budding political movements and anticolonial parties were outlawed, driving their activists underground. Demands that received redress in many colonies, including requests that were perceived as moderate, such as the call for broader African representation in colonial institutions, were categorically rejected in other colonies.

Consequently, the political map of 1950s Africa reveals a vast gap between those colonies that were striding toward the goals Africans sought—namely, a

DOI: 10.4324/9781003322818-9

National, Economic, Social, and Cultural Liberation 91

genuine transformation of colonial relations leading to liberation from colonial rule—and those in which the demands themselves met with fierce resistance on the part of the colonial powers. The early decolonization processes bypassed Portugal's colonies: Angola, Mozambique, Guinea-Bissau, and the Cape Verde islands, as well as São Tomé and Príncipe near the coast of West Africa. The same is true for a few Spanish territories in Africa (Equatorial Guinea and Mauritania). Another category of colonies that decolonization bypassed was White-settler colonies such as Namibia, Algeria, Kenya, Zimbabwe, and South Africa. Despite decolonization being their declared policy after World War II, White settlers thwarted decolonization even in colonies that were subject to British rule. To understand anticolonial ideology, it is essential to take into account the brutal and overtly oppressive nature of governance in these colonies, which inflicted suffering on local inhabitants on a larger scale and far more harshly than in colonies without White settlers, among other reasons because it entailed dispossessing many Africans of their lands. The colonial rulers' continuing commitment to prioritizing the interests of settlers, who staunchly opposed any change that would dilute their colonial privileges, was the main obstacle to decolonization, the very essence of which was to foster such change.

Racial discrimination is a cornerstone of every colonial government. The following passage attests to the role of White settlement in racial discrimination and to the implications for the struggle against colonialism:

> There is a great difference between a White and a Black. The White, because he is white, finds a job easily, earns a good living, can support his family and cover his expenses, including the education of his children. While the African obtains work with difficulty, and as a result earns miserably little, not being able to satisfy even his minimum needs ... Why is it that the African, owner of the land, must suffer and the White enrich himself at the cost of the African? ... We Mozambicans cannot continue to accept such humiliations ... No, we have all had enough of so much oppression. The torture is coming to an end. It is time to demand our rights. But if the Portuguese do not want to leave, what are we going to do? ONLY FIGHT. It is only through struggle that they will be convinced we want freedom, that we want to take back our land. Mozambique is only for Mozambicans and we do not accept the intervention of any outsider. Many promise us their assistance, but it is we who must take the initiative. We are going to expel the Portuguese! Let us shout at the top of our lungs: FREEDOM! FREEDOM! FREEDOM![3]

The Aims of Radical Ideologies

What were the ramifications of the colonial powers' refusal to implement change in these colonies, in terms of the historical development of national ideologies and the struggle against colonial rule? Compared with the

92 *National, Economic, Social, and Cultural Liberation*

anticolonial ideologies that emerged in the 1940s and 1950s in colonies that saw progress toward liberation and independence, the ideologies that emerged in colonies where decolonization was delayed, especially from the 1960s onwards, were more radical, revolutionary, and militant in nature. Indeed, the colonial rulers themselves helped cultivate this radical image as a way of undermining the legitimacy of those ideologies. However, the reputation for radicalism that these ideologies acquired stemmed from the belligerence of their stance toward colonialism and its effects on African societies, and of course from the operational implications of their views regarding the modes of struggle (guerilla warfare) against colonial rule.

The radical ideologies regarded colonialism as a devious and duplicitous enemy that necessitated a comprehensive critical analysis in order to assess the damage it had caused to African societies and to formulate solutions and approaches to rehabilitation. The following passage critiques key aspects of colonialism:

> A social system based on the exploitation of man by man in its most extreme form, seen as a whole, colonialism means the economic plunder of the land of the politico-social servitude of man. But it is not only this … Firearms and the whip not being sufficient, colonialism resorts to the destruction of the African … making him lose his identity with himself through the destruction of his culture … To avoid uprisings, the ideal conditions for enslavement had to be created … making the slave accept being a slave. How? … There was only one way to proceed: to destroy the colonial's culture and make him either submit or be alienated by the "superior culture" of his oppressor.

> In the initial phase, they start by denigrating the values of the colonized–cultural racism is the beginning of cultural assassination and its manifestation … Then they loudly proclaim that the values of the black man (or of any other colonial) are immoral and un-aesthetic, or insignificant, that his is an "inferior culture" … The deification of the allegedly superior European culture is the most characteristic feature of the alienated colonial … Then comes the next phase of the process, that of getting the "superior culture" of the master accepted in the present. It is here that the problem of the effects of colonialism on culture becomes most critical. In fact this is the culminating moment when the colonial moves away from himself, i.e., from his people, to adopt the culture which is alien to him.

> The independent African countries need to display a will of iron in reviving African culture. This task of restoring the African to himself is now one of the most crucial problems in the construction of the new independent African states … if they wish to free Africa more rapidly from the effects of colonialism and to struggle more effectively against the economic and political dependence to which many African countries are still subjected.[4]

National, Economic, Social, and Cultural Liberation 93

The liberation movements that operated in the 1940s and 1950s explicitly identified colonial officialdom as an enemy of the Africans and sought to replace it. But by the early 1960s, after only a few years of independence, many in Africa could already sense the very real and continuing presence of colonialism, and they realized that political independence was only a preliminary stage in an inestimably long and ongoing struggle for full liberation. The radical nationalists were not satisfied with merely ousting the colonial government itself, and even before officially attaining independence they identified neocolonialism as one of their enemies and targets of struggle. FRELIMO,[5] the Mozambique liberation movement, framed this struggle as follows:

> Today we fight against Portuguese colonialism. We create, at the same time, the conditions which will prevent neo-colonialism from establishing itself in our country. But we must know exactly what colonialism and neo-colonialism are in order to be able to fight them ... Actually, colonialism and neo-colonialism are the same thing; it is only in their form and in the way they exhibit themselves that they differ. Neo-colonialism is more disguised, more "modernized". It appears as a consequence of the liberation struggle of the colonized peoples ... The colonial countries are ... forced to spend a great deal of money on the army ... In addition, the nationalists seem to threaten the economic structure created by the colonizers ... All this causes a great loss for the colonizing countries. They invent, then, a way of eliminating this difficulty and of exploiting the territory, as before ... This is what we call neo-colonialism. Its main difference in relation to colonialism is that, in the former, there is no territorial occupation; there is only economic control. The Portuguese would no longer need to have an army or administrators in Mozambique. It would be the puppet government itself which would open all the doors to the Portuguese, forcing us to work for them. This is the danger of which every Mozambican must be aware. We are fighting in order that in Mozambique there may exist a government chosen by the people, representing the will of the people and working for the good of the people of Mozambique. We fight so that we may destroy colonialism in every one of its forms. Down with colonialism! Down with neocolonialism![6]

The lurking dangers that posed a threat to independence even after official political independence, such as identified above, had a deep impact on the goals of liberation movements active in the 1960s and 1970s. As noted, they were not satisfied with merely removing colonial rule, seeking instead to destroy the existing social order and establish a new order free of colonial influence—that is, they wanted to instigate a revolution. The powerful need to abolish the old order and build a new one, besides contributing to the image of an independent state, also dictated modes of thought and action even during the course of the struggle and blurred the lines between liberation movements and states that had already attained independence. In 1972

94 *National, Economic, Social, and Cultural Liberation*

Amilcar Cabral,[7] leader of the liberation movement in Guinea-Bissau and Cape Verde,[8] stated that "as long as imperialism exists, an independent state in Africa must be a liberation movement in power—or else it will not be."[9] A liberation movement, accordingly, was seen as a state in the making, or even as a fully independent state: "We can say that our country is like a state of which a part of the national territory is yet [*sic*] occupied by the colonial force."[10]

The following excerpts outline the radical ideologies' vision for the future and their image of African society in the era of independence.

> Our people ... under the enlightened leadership of its founder and No. 1 militant, Amilcar Cabral, has, in the course of 17 years of political and armed struggle, constructed a new life and now possesses a constantly evolving administrative organization, social and cultural services, a judicial system, a steadily developing economy and national armed forces ... [This attests to] the self-determination of our people and the *de facto* existence of an efficiently functioning State structure ... The People's National Assembly, expressing the sovereign will of the people, solemnly proclaims the State of Guinea-Bissau. The State of Guinea-Bissau is a sovereign, republican, democratic, anti-colonialist and anti-imperialist State whose primary objectives are the complete liberation of the people of Guinea-Bissau and Cape Verde and the forging of a union between those two territories for the purpose of building a strong African homeland dedicated to progress.[11]

> After independence it will be necessary to organise a popular State. By popular, I mean democratic, where the people can participate fully ... About the organisation of the economy we say that the Angolan people must have the riches of our country, we must give fair wages to avoid exploitation of the workers, and so on. This is what is normally called the socialist way ... We think that ideologically we follow not necessarily the Communist or Marxist line but we follow the socialist line, with justice for everyone.[12]

> The objectives of FRELIMO are very clear: the total and complete independence of the Mozambican people and the liquidation of Portuguese colonialism. The Mozambican people are an entity quite distinct from the Portuguese people, and they have their own political, cultural and social personality which can only be realized through the independence of Mozambique. We are not fighting to become Portuguese with black skins ... Freedom and independence, the affirmation of our own personality—these then are the objectives of our struggle.[13]

The following excerpts point to the revolutionary roles attributed to education, indicating the centrality of education in radical nationalism.

National, Economic, Social, and Cultural Liberation 95

What is the objective of our education? In what way does it distinguish itself from the two other forms of education prevailing in our society, i.e., traditional and colonial education? ... Our education ... must give us a Mozambican personality which assumes our reality and assimilates critically and without servility the ideas and experiences of other people of the world ... In traditional society, given the low level of knowledge which characterises it, superstition takes the place of science and blocks any scientific analysis of the physical and social milieu in favour of the supernatural ... Traditional education aims at creating in the new generations passivity and respect towards acquired ideas; it encourages the belief in the infallible wisdom of the older generations ... Colonial education is concerned with teaching only to the extent that it facilitates further exploitation. It aims at reinforcing division within the colonised society by separating those who are educated and those who are not. Among the former it encourages a feeling of shame and later a despising of their culture and traditions ... Today a new culture is being developed based on traditional forms with a new content dictated by our new reality. This reality is constituted first of all by the liberation struggle itself, but also, by the common effort of Mozambicans originating from different places and ethnic groups who are united in the struggle for the construction of a new Mozambique. From this point of view, culture plays an important role in the reinforcement of national unity ... Revolutionary education must aim at destroying the corrupt ideas and habits inherited from the past; develop the scientific spirit in order to eliminate superstition; promote the emergence of a national culture; liquidate individualism and elitism.[14]

We believe that the revolution will create [a] "new man" ... There are two aspects of our struggle: on the one hand, our aim is to destroy the colonial structure, on the other it is to build our country ... The programme of our movement includes an educational stage designed to alter the mentality of our people. However, when dealing with cultural aspects rooted in our people for centuries, these cannot be erased from their life overnight. Certain popular habits are good, some are not. We are concerned with keeping and reviving those Angolan cultural practices which have been despised or destroyed through centuries of colonization ... There are also some habits which are not positive. Our people is very religious. Certain religious practices are not adapted to modern life ... The creation of the "new man" is the greatest and the most difficult task to be accomplished by us.[15]

Ideological Sources of Influence

The previous chapter addressed the influence of socialism on the anticolonial ideologies that emerged in Africa. If the earlier anticolonial ideologies, of the 1940s and 1950s, sought to formulate a unique socialist outlook—"African

96 *National, Economic, Social, and Cultural Liberation*

Figure 8.1 Makonde woodcarvers at work in a FRELIMO production camp. The Makonde are famous for their ebony carvings. Other crafts, such as weaving and pottery, are also practised in the production camps. Some of the finished products are exported to Tanzania in exchange for needed domestic and military supplies.

Figure 8.2 FRELIMO hospital for combatants in a military camp.

Figure 8.3 A young student at one of the schools set up by FRELIMO. Most of the schools are outdoors. Various UN funds and programmes have been established to help meet the urgent needs of the indigenous peoples of Southern Africa in education.

Source: www.flickr.com/photos/un_photo/14542497636; www.flickr.com/photos/un_photo/14378906070/in/album-72157645441072806/; www.flickr.com/photos/un_photo/14563917304/in/album-72157645441072806/, United Nations, CC BY-NC-ND 2.0.

socialism"—the aim of which was to reinstate authentic African values rather than adopt a foreign ideology, to distill from "classical" socialism those elements suited to Africa and its needs while rejecting those unsuited, then what stands out in the radical anticolonial ideologies is the imprint of a stricter and more dogmatic socialist outlook—"scientific socialism"—in its Marxist-Leninist version as inspired by the Soviet communism. The later ideologies were not characteristically radical at the outset, but they became increasingly radicalized in parallel with the escalating struggle and transition to armed conflict in the early 1960s. Arguably, therefore, the process of radicalization provided the necessary ideological accompaniment to a fierce and continuous struggle.

Eduardo Mondlane, the first leader of Mozambique's liberation movement, explicitly described this trend in a 1986 interview: "FRELIMO is now really

98 *National, Economic, Social, and Cultural Liberation*

far more socialist, revolutionary, and progressive than ever before, and now tends more and more in the direction of socialism of the Marxist-Leninist variety."[16]

Marxism's influence on radical African ideologies is evident in the latter's analysis of colonial relations—the parties involved, their motives, and the historical context of their activities. The issue of class struggle, one of the cornerstones of the Marxist worldview they did adopt, posed an interesting challenge because the objective of the struggle in Africa was *national* liberation. Indeed, these ideologies do not refute the existence of social strata in African societies or deny their political implications. When Cabral called for "class-national" unity he was also directing his words at those Africans who, because of class interests, were betraying the national struggle.[17] Yet the fundamental clash underscored by these radical ideologies was the clash between rulers and subjects, between occupiers and occupied. Cabral proposed that the class struggle be integrated with the national struggle in the following way:

> This revolt [against colonial rule] is not the product of a class as such. Rather it is a whole society acting as a nation-class that carries it out. This nation-class is dominated not by people from the colonized country but rather by the ruling class of the colonized country ... Hence our struggle is essentially based not on a class struggle but rather on the struggle led by our nation-class against the Portuguese ruling class. It is precisely here that we find the link between our struggle and that of the Portuguese people ... against the same ruling class. Naturally, the consequences are: firstly, through this fight we are shaping our African Nation which, as you know, was not yet very well defined, with all the problems of many ethnic groups, of the divisions created by the colonialist power itself ... We are building our African Nation which is becoming more and more conscious of itself. But at the same time we must be alert to the development of classes within this new nation ... In this way, not only do we strengthen our political and moral unity as a nation, but we also strengthen our vigilance so as to keep the class struggle from taking on aspects which could be detrimental to the progress of our own people.[18]

The use of a foreign European ideology to break the chains of European bondage and establish an authentic African identity posed another fundamental contradiction for anticolonial movements. Leading ideologues of the radical movements tried to resolve it in various ways:

> We believe that a struggle like ours is impossible without ideology. But what kind of ideology? I will perhaps disappoint many people here when I say that we do not think ideology is a religion ... I confess that we didn't know these great theorists [Marx and Lenin] terribly well when we began. We didn't know them half as well as we do now! We needed to know them, as I've said, in order to judge in what measure we could

National, Economic, Social, and Cultural Liberation 99

borrow from their experience to help our situation—but not necessarily to apply the ideology blindly just because it's a very good ideology ... But ideology is important in Guinea. As I've said, never again do we want our people to be exploited. Our desire to develop our country with social justice and power in the hands of the people is our ideological basis. Never again do we want to see a group or a class of people exploiting or dominating the work of our people ... If you want to call it Marxism, you may call it Marxism ... But the labels are your affair; we don't like those kind of labels ... This doesn't mean that we have no respect for all that Marxism and Leninism have contributed to the transformation of struggles throughout the world.[19]

Other leaders stressed that the movements were not directly adopting any particular European ideology, and thus there was no cause for concern that one form of dependence would be substituted for another:

FRELIMO wishes to create an economic system where there will be no exploitation of man by man, an economic system in which man works and benefits from his work, where men are united in a nation but cooperate freely with other nations of their choice. We mean by freedom the right to live, to work, to think, to speak, and above all the right to choose the way in which we want to live, to choose our friends ... We support socialism as a means of development which brings man towards dignity ... But we do not believe that the development of our country, its independence and socialism, can be copied from other countries. This is why we believe in the adaptation of these scientific ideas to local conditions. I would like to make it clear that when we say that we support socialism, it does not mean that we thereby lose our independence.[20]

However, the ideological effort invested in downplaying the importance of external sources of influence, and the effort to present them instead as sources of inspiration and support in constructing essentially African systems, did not correspond with the official ideology of these states. After attaining independence, states such as Angola and Mozambique pledged their allegiance to Soviet-style Marxism-Leninism. The organizational structures they adopted as well as their economic-political policy accorded with the systems of communist countries. This communist influence was explicitly evident in the long-term presence of Cuban military units. Only in the early 1990s, with the collapse of Soviet communism, did they officially renounce Marxism-Leninism.

From Political Struggle to Armed Struggle

The most overt manifestation of militancy on the part of liberation movements in those colonies where decolonization was delayed was the resort to armed struggle against colonialism—in Algeria, Kenya, and Cameroon in the 1950s,

100 *National, Economic, Social, and Cultural Liberation*

in the Portuguese colonies of Angola, Mozambique, and Guinea-Bissau from the 1960s until their liberation in the mid-1970s, and in the outbreaks of violence in Rhodesia (Zimbabwe), South West Africa (Namibia), and South Africa in the 1960s and 1970s. The reason their struggle shifted from the political arena to the battlefield stemmed from the colonial authorities' persistent refusal to view African movements and organizations as legitimate political players and to hold talks with them. The Africans' decision to use force in order to oust colonialism in all its obstinance reflected their recognition that, given the circumstances, no external factor would bring about the change for which they longed, and that they must take charge of their own fate:

> We must not expect that independence will fall from the sky, or that others may come to free our land for us. It is all of us, through a day by day, constant, continuous struggle, who will build [the] independence of Mozambique, fighting as long as we have to.[21]

By directly confronting the military might of colonialism, Africans were able to shatter colonialism's image of them as passive, lazy, and weak, and instead to project such qualities as proactiveness, courage, and determination, thereby fostering a positive change in their own sense of identity and self-worth.

Beginning in the 1960s, those liberation movements that had decided to confront colonialism on the battlefield also came under the influence of Frantz Fanon,[22] the first intellectual to formulate a systematic and reasoned ideology of anticolonial armed struggle, inspired by the struggle to liberate Algeria in which he had been involved. Fanon, who served as the guiding spirit for decolonization efforts characterized by militant fervor, became the most enthusiastic advocate of armed struggle and violence.

Shortly before he died of cancer, Fanon published *The Wretched of the Earth*, which later became one of the pillars of modern revolutionary theory. In the following passages he explains why in his view a gradual and peaceful process of decolonization is not possible:

> Colonialism is not a thinking machine, nor a body endowed with reasoning faculties. It is violence in its natural state, and it will only yield when confronted with greater violence.[23]

> The colonial world is a world cut in two. The dividing line, the frontiers are shown by barracks and police stations. In the colonies it is the policeman and the soldier who are the official, instituted go-betweens, the spokesmen of the settler and his rule of oppression ... The intermediary does not lighten the oppression, nor seek to hide the domination; he shows them up and puts them into practice with the clear conscience of an upholder of the peace; yet he is the bringer of violence into the home and into the mind of the native ... To break up the colonial world does not mean that after the frontiers have been abolished lines of communication will be set

Figure 8.4 Frantz Fanon.
Source: https://en.wikipedia.org/wiki/File:Frantz_Fanon.jpg, Fair Use.

up between the two zones. The destruction of the colonial world is no more and no less than the abolition of one zone, its burial in the depths of the earth or its expulsion from the country.[24]

Decolonization, which sets out to change the order of the world, is, obviously, a program of complete disorder … Decolonization is the meeting of two forces, opposed to each other by their very nature … For if the last shall be first, this will only come to pass after a murderous and decisive struggle between the two protagonists … That affirmed intention to place the last at the head of things … can only triumph if we use all means to turn the scale, including, of course, that of violence.[25]

The violence of the colonial regime and the counter-violence of the native balance each other and respond to each other in an extraordinary reciprocal homogeneity. This reign of violence will be the more terrible in proportion to the size of the implantation from the mother country.[26]

102 National, Economic, Social, and Cultural Liberation

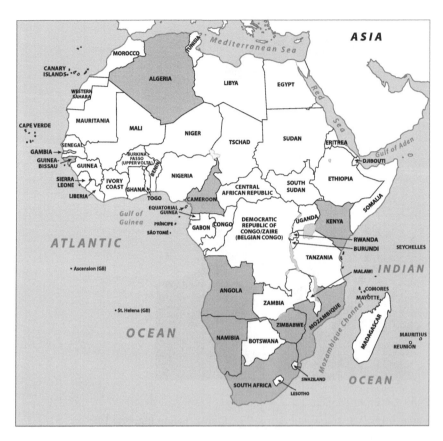

Map 8.1 Areas in which the decolonization struggle was violent.
Source: The Open University of Israel, used with permission.

Fanon regarded the notion of decolonization based on compromise and free of struggle as a colonial invention. Anticolonial movements that eschewed violent struggle were not seeking, in his view, to fundamentally change the colonial order and therefore were not on the path to true liberation:

> In the colonial countries where a real struggle for freedom has taken place, where the blood of the people has flowed and where the length of the period of armed warfare has favored the backward surge of intellectuals toward bases grounded in the people, we can observe a genuine eradication of the superstructure built by these intellectuals from the bourgeois colonialist environment ... But it so happens sometimes that decolonization occurs in areas which have not been sufficiently shaken by the struggle for liberation, and there may be found those same know-all, smart, wily intellectuals. We find intact in them the

manners and forms of thought picked up during their association with the colonialist bourgeoisie. Spoilt children of yesterday's colonialism and of today's national governments, they organize the loot of whatever national resources exist.[27]

To illustrate the outcome of such illusory decolonization, Fanon quotes the first president of the Republic of Gabon, Léon M'ba, who during an official visit to Paris stated, "Gabon is independent, but between Gabon and France nothing has changed; everything goes on as before."[28]

Because he saw violence as a fundamental, inherent characteristic of colonial relations, Fanon believed that it was a necessary element in the process of liberation. The following passages point to the functions of violence as envisioned by Fanon:

Decolonization never takes place unnoticed, for it influences individuals and modifies them fundamentally ... It brings a natural rhythm into existence, introduced by new men, and with it a new language and a new humanity. Decolonization is the veritable creation of new men ... The "thing" which has been colonized becomes man during the same process by which it frees itself.[29]

For the colonized people ... violence, because it constitutes their only work, invests their characters with positive and creative qualities. The practice of violence binds them together as a whole, since each individual forms a violent link in the great chain ... The groups recognize each other and the future nation is already indivisible. The armed struggle mobilizes the people, that is to say, it throws them in one way and in one direction ... [It] introduces into each man's consciousness the ideas of a common cause, of a national destiny, and of a collective history ... The building-up of the nation is helped on by the existence of this cement which has been mixed with blood and anger ... We have said that the native's violence unifies the people. By its very structure, colonialism is separatist and regionalist. Colonialism does not simply state the existence of tribes; it also reinforces it and separates them ... Violence is in action all-inclusive and national ... It follows that it is closely involved in the liquidation of regionalism and of tribalism.[30]

At the level of individuals, violence is a cleansing force. It frees the native from his inferiority complex and from his despair and inaction; it makes him fearless and restores his self-respect.[31]

Despite Fanon's influence as radical prophet of the apocalypse, radical liberation movements actually adopted a more cautious and reserved approach to the use of armed struggle, at times even conveying a tone of self-justification and apology. All the African liberation movements initially tried to negotiate with the colonial authorities, but some discovered that the political horizon

104 *National, Economic, Social, and Cultural Liberation*

was blocked and that the political and social protests they voiced were met with even greater oppression.

All the anticolonial movements have histories that include at least one massacre of activists in the course of a demonstration or strike: for example, a series of mass killings in Sétif, Algeria, in May 1945, and the massacres in Mueda in 1960 and in Xinavane in 1961, both in Mozambique. Similarly, the Sharpeville massacre in South Africa in 1960 was a turning point in its struggle for the African National Congress, which until then had advocated non-violence. In his account of the evolution of the struggle in Guinea-Bissau following the 1959 Pijiguiti massacre at the Port of Bissau, Cabral related:

> We tried during the years of 1950, 1953, 1954, 1955 and 1956 to convince the Portuguese Government that it was necessary to change. In that moment, even we didn't think about independence ... We received, as answer, only repression, imprisonment, torture and in 1959 [the Pijiguiti massacre] ... This massacre showed us that it was not well, it was not good, it was not intelligent to fight against the Portuguese with empty hands. We didn't want, absolutely not, to resort to violence, but we realized that the colonial Portuguese domination was a situation of permanent violence. Against our aspirations they systematically answered with violence, with crimes, and we decided in that moment to prepare ourselves to fight ... We saw Africa beginning with independence, in many African states, and we decided to do our best also to get our right to self-determination and independence.[32]

Resort to violence was therefore the inevitable choice for African nationalists in the face of colonial authorities' refusal to address their demands for freedom and independence. In the 1950s violent struggle took the form of localized attacks and acts of sabotage, with some elements of guerrilla warfare—whether limited in scope as in Kenya and Cameroon or widespread as in Algeria—and acts of terrorism, both against representations of colonial presence and against African collaborators. The 1960s, on the other hand, saw the institutionalization of violent struggle and its management. The following political movements established genuine liberation armies: UNITA, FNLA, and MPLA in Angola;[33] FRELIMO in Mozambique; PAIGC in Guinea-Bissau; ZAPU and ZANU in Rhodesia [today's Zimbabwe];[34] SWAPO in South West Africa [today's Namibia];[35] and PAC and ANC in South Africa.

The liberation movements saw themselves as "the people's army" whose duty it was to promote national unity and,[36] within the military framework itself, contribute to civic missions in the areas of education and healthcare in liberated regions.[37] In doing so they presented themselves as an alternative to colonial authorities, provided moral justification for their armed struggle, and mobilized popular support.

Ultimately all the anticolonial movements were successful in their struggles. Notwithstanding the tremendous power discrepancies and difficulties entailed

National, Economic, Social, and Cultural Liberation   105

in a prolonged armed struggle against colonialism, the radical ideologies managed to imbue these movements and their members with a fighting spirit that led them to the finish line: toppling colonial rule and attaining independence. Guinea-Bissau achieved statehood in 1974, Angola and Mozambique in 1975, "white" Rhodesia became Zimbabwe under majority African rule in 1980, Namibia seceded from South Africa in 1990, and in South Africa itself blacks achieved democratic majority rule in 1994. Although there were additional reasons behind the colonial authorities' decision to reverse their refusal regarding the liberation of these colonies, the determined struggle waged by Africans themselves was a very important factor.

The discussion of postcolonial ideologies and their implementation strays somewhat from the subject of this study, the stated focus of which is anticolonial nationalism. Nonetheless, to satisfy the reader's natural curiosity regarding the fate of these radical movements after liberation, let us take a brief look at the era of independence. Compared with the relative success of their struggle against an external enemy, the postindependence achievements of these radical liberation movements were quite modest and their failures, in terms of realizing their ideological vision, quite momentous. Their ideological revolutionary spirit did not facilitate African states' capacity to address the many challenges posed by independence, even when their leadership consisted of the radical liberation movements themselves ... FRELIMO in Mozambique, MPLA in Angola, PAIGC in Guinea-Bissau, or ZANU in Zimbabwe. Any hopes that a difficult and prolonged anticolonial struggle would foster internal unity were dashed. As it turned out, the struggle actually politicized the various ethno-cultural groups and deepened the divisions among them. Likewise, the mission of bridging between urbanites and villagers, between intellectuals and the uneducated, met with failure. Even within the relatively narrow strata of urban intellectuals there were ideological and political, as well as personal, differences that prevented internal cooperation. In Angola and Mozambique these divisions deepened after independence, escalating into fierce and long-lasting civil wars.

Their adoption of Marxist-Leninist socialism as a means of ensuring equality also proved ineffectual in terms of changing the nature of relations between independent African states and states that are seen as developed. At best, the radical states shifted their dependence on external players—a dependence that had characterized all African states—from the former colonial authorities and the capitalist West to the communist bloc, which they saw as an ideological model and important source of support during their years of struggle. The patronage that characterized relations between African communist states and the Soviet bloc countries indicates that the liberation movements' concerns surrounding neocolonialism—which they feared and against which they sought to fortify themselves even in the course of their struggle—had not immunized them against becoming similarly dependent on powers such as the Soviet Union and China, notwithstanding those two countries' lack of a colonial past in Africa or their collective ideological critique

106 *National, Economic, Social, and Cultural Liberation*

of the phenomenon. Moreover, the ever-increasing economic hardship in Africa of the 1980s and the growing weakness of communist countries gradually led the communist African states to reinforce their ties with the West. In the early 1990s the revolutionary African states renounced their ideological commitment to Marxist-Leninist socialism and officially closed this chapter in their history.

Notes

1 Portuguese acronym for Núcleo dos Estudantes Africanos Secundários de Moçambique, i.e., Nucleus of Mozambican Secondary-School African Students.
2 Eduardo Mondlane, *The Struggle for Mozambique* (London: Zed Press, 1982), pp. 113–114.
3 FRELIMO, "Why We Fight," 1963, in de Braganca and Wallerstein, *African Liberation Reader*, Vol. 1, pp. 12–13, https://libcom.org/library/african-liberation-reader-vols-1-3.
4 MPLA, "The Effects of Colonialism on the Colonized African Peoples," August 2, 1971, ibid., pp. 139–142.
5 FRELIMO (Portuguese: Frente de Libertação de Moçambique, i.e., Liberation Front of Mozambique) was founded in 1962. In 1964 it adopted a policy of violent struggle, in which it engaged for about a decade. Its first leader was Eduardo Mondlane, who like most of his fellow leaders of anticolonial movements, was an intellectual. Following his assassination in 1969, the presidency of the movement was transferred to Samora Machel, who led Mozambique to independence in 1975 and headed its Marxist one-party regime until his presidential aircraft crashed in 1986.
6 FRELIMO, "Colonialism and Neo-Colonialism," 1965, ibid., pp. 4–5.
7 Amilcar Cabral was born in Guinea-Bissau in 1924 and assassinated in 1973. An agronomist, poet, and revolutionary, he lived and studied for many years in Cape Verde, located near Guinea-Bissau. While working as an agronomist in the service of the Portuguese, he conducted extensive field studies in Guinea, examining the system of agricultural production and the colonial economy, and these studies shaped his political outlook. As a political revolutionary, Cabral was at the forefront of the anticolonial vanguard party that led Guinea to independence. Cabral embodied an interesting set of contradictions: an African of mixed heritage with Portuguese citizenship, and an intellectual who oversaw coordination of the prolonged struggle for Guinea-Bissau's independence. His biography reflects the developmental stages of radical movements—from social-cultural activities in the 1950s to political resistance within the framework of the PAIGC, the liberation movement of Guinea and Cape Verde, founded in 1960, which is regarded as the most organized and successful among the liberation movements in Portuguese colonies. Through an armed struggle launched in the early 1960s, the movement took over a substantial portion of the colony, and in 1973 Cabral announced the establishment of an independent state within a year. Shortly after this declaration he was assassinated, apparently by agents of the Portuguese secret service.
8 PAIGC (Portuguese: Partido Africano para a Independência da Guiné e Cabo Verde, i.e., the African Party for Independence of Guinea and Cape Verde) fought for the liberation of Guinea-Bissau and Cape Verde but split after achieving independence, when the two became separate independent states.

National, Economic, Social, and Cultural Liberation   107

9 Amilcar Cabral, "Homage to Nkrumah," May 13, 1972, ibid., Vol. II, p. 109.

10 Ibid., p. 74.

11 Guinea Bissau People's National Assembly, Proclamation of Independence, September 24, 1973, ibid., Vol. III, pp. 207–208.

12 Agostinho Neto, "MPLA's Ideology," August 20, 1972, ibid., Vol. II, p. 100.

13 FRELIMO, "The Coup d'État of April 25," statement of April 27, 1974, ibid., Vol. I, pp. 35–36.

14 FRELIMO, "Shaping the Political Line," June 25, 1972, ibid., Vol. III, pp. 104–196.

15 Agostinho Neto, "Our Culture and the New Man," April 1972, ibid. p. 190.

16 Eduardo Mondlane, "The Evolution of FRELIMO," 1968, ibid., Vol. II, p. 121.

17 Amilcar Cabral, cited in ibid., p. 79.

18 Amilcar Cabral, "The Nation-Class," October 28, 1971, ibid., Vol. I, pp. 69–70.

19 Amilcar Cabral "The Relevance of Marxism-Leninism," October 22, 1971, ibid., Vol. II, pp. 107–108.

20 Joaquim Chissano, "FRELIMO's Ideology," November 27, 1970, ibid., p. 103.

21 FRELIMO, "On the Necessity of a Prolonged War," May 8, 1968, ibid., Vol. III, p. 149.

22 Frantz Fanon (1925–1961) was born in Martinique, at the time a French colony in the West Indies. He studied medicine in France, specializing in psychiatry. During the Algerian uprising he was stationed at a hospital in Algeria, where he became an enthusiastic supporter of the FLN (French: Front de libération nationale, i.e., National Liberation Front). In 1956 he officially joined the movement. A radical socialist, he advocated economic and social revolution in the Third World so as to bring progress to the masses of peasants living in poverty and ignorance. Fanon believed in the cleansing power of violence by the oppressed in rising up against colonial role. He rejected illusory independence, "black colonialism," and the idea of a ruling African oligarchy that would replace White rule but not change the "system." In his first book *Black Skin, White Masks* (French: *Peau noire, masques blancs*, 1952), he analyzed the psychological characteristics of racism and colonial rule. Among his other well-known works are *The Wretched of the Earth* (*Les damnés de la terre*) and *Toward the African Revolution* (*Pour la révolution africaine*).

23 Frantz Fanon, "Concerning Violence," in *The Wretched of the Earth* (New York: Grove Press, 1963), p. 61, www.campusincamps.ps/wp-content/uploads/2015/10/Frantz-Fanon-Concerning-Violence-trans_-Farrington.pdf.

24 Ibid., pp. 38–39, 41.

25 Ibid., pp. 36–37.

26 Ibid., p. 88.

27 Ibid., pp. 46, 48.

28 Ibid., p. 67.

29 Ibid., pp. 36–37.

30 Ibid., pp. 93–94.

31 Ibid., p. 94.

32 Amilcar Cabral, "A Situation of Permanent Violence," Febraury 26, 1970, in de Braganca and Wallerstein, *African Liberation Reader*, Vol. II, pp. 63–64.

33 MPLA (Portuguese: Movimento Popular de Libertação de Angola, i.e., the People's Movement for the Liberation of Angola) was founded in 1956. In 1961 a protest initially organized in the capital city of Luanda spread throughout Angola, turning into a violent struggle that the Portuguese army then suppressed. The rebels continued fighting from guerrilla bases established in neighboring

108 *National, Economic, Social, and Cultural Liberation*

countries. Under the leadership of Agostinho Neto, the movement adopted a Marxist-Leninist ideology and enjoyed the support of the Soviet Union and Cuba. Ethno-cultural as well as politico-ideological differences split the anticolonial struggle into three separate movements. MPLA was active primarily among the Kimbundu people concentrated in central Angola. FNLA (Portuguese: Frente Nacional de Libertação de Angola, i.e., the National Front for the Liberation of Angola), established in 1962, primarily represented the Bankongo people of northern Angola and was supported by the United States and Zaire. The movement, led by Holden Roberto, disintegrated after Angola achieved independence. The third underground movement, founded by Jonas Savimbi in 1966 in southern Angola among the Ovimbundu people, was UNITA (Portuguese: União Nacional para a Independência Total de Angola, i.e., National Union for the Total Independence of Angola), which was supported by China, the United States, South Africa, and a few African states. The bitter disputes between MPLA and UNITA continued even after Angola achieved independence in 1975, escalating into a fierce civil war that lasted about 20 years.

34 ZANU (the Zimbabwe African National Union) and ZAPU (the Zimbabwe African Peoples Union) were the two main anticolonial movements operating in the 1960s in Rhodesia, which was governed by white settlers. During the 1970s they led a guerrilla war against white rule. In 1979 the parties agreed to hold general elections that would, for the first time, include blacks, who accounted for 98 percent of the population. The basis for division between the two movements was ethnic, personal, and ideological. The elections resulted in a major victory for ZANU, under the leadership of Robert Mugabe. ZANU was the more radical party, supported by the Shona people, who constituted a majority of the population. Its victory over ZAPU, led by Joshua Nkomo, led in the early 1980s to violent escalation of inter-ethnic rivalry. (ZAPU drew support from the Ndebele people.) In 1989 the two parties were merged under the authoritarian leadership of Robert Mugabe.

35 SWAPO (the South West Africa People's Organisation), was founded in 1960 as a political movement for the liberation of South West Africa (later Namibia) from South Africa, which had governed it since 1915. (During 1884–1915 it was subject to the rule of Germany.) In the mid-1960s the movement launched a guerrilla war that lasted until 1989. In 1990, after SWAPO's victory in the general elections under the leadership of Sam Nujoma, South West Africa achieved independence and changed its name to Namibia.

36 MPLA, "The Generalization of the Armed Struggle," February 4, 1969, ibid., Vol. III, p. 146; FRELIMO, "The First Steps," 1972, ibid., pp. 150–151; FRELIMO, "On the Necessity of a Prolonged War," pp. 147–149.

37 Cabral, "A Situation of Permanent Violence," p. 64.

9 Opponents of National Independence

The preceding chapters may have created the impression that a consensus existed in Africa in favor of liberation from the yoke of colonialism. In fact, however, not all Africans sought national independence, and some even explicitly opposed it. Prominent among the latter were Léopold Senghor of Senegal and Félix Houphouët-Boigny of the Ivory Coast, both of whom, ironically, inherited the rule of power from the colonial authorities in their respective countries.

In the postcolonial era, once Africa's liberation from foreign rule had been completed and political independence was—at least in principle—established, it became difficult to reconcile opposition to independence with the myth, cultivated both in Africa and in research on Africa, that the anticolonial movement essentially enjoyed unanimous support. As early as 1971, African historian Bethwell Ogot dared to defy the prevailing view that all Africans were "nationalists." He argued that it was actually "loyalists"—opponents of independence—who continued to set the tone in Kenya after independence.[1] Ogot believed that history should not be based on popular myths, and we too will adopt his approach.

The opponents of national independence comprised leaders, groups, and parties that, during the 1940s and 1950s (and in Portuguese colonies the 1960s and 1970s as well), when anticolonial nationalism was at its height, opposed the withdrawal of European authorities and the granting of independence to their territories, as defined by colonial borders, or at least sought to postpone independence for some time. This does not apply to the leaders, groups, and kingdoms that cooperated with the European powers during the era of primary resistance to the colonial invasion. Nor does it apply to the interwar period, when foreign rule was to a large extent seen as acceptable and the demand for self-determination and independence was not yet fully fledged.

Resistance to independence stemmed from a variety of reasons, and opponents to the nationalist independence movements could accordingly be classified into four categories: 1) supporters of a plan for a French-African union; 2) "ethnic" opponents to an independence movement dominated by a rival ethnic group; 3) "traditional" leaders opposed to "modern nationalists"; and 4) "opportunists" who opposed independence for practical reasons (such

DOI: 10.4324/9781003322818-10

110   *Opponents of National Independence*

as jobs, status, income). The first two groups represent a more principled resistance to a political independence based on colonial boundaries and to a newly established nationalism within the colonial border. The latter two groups, in contrast, did not object to independence as the ultimate objective or to its legitimacy. Yet, as liberation from colonial rule seemed increasingly near at hand, the internal rivalry within each colony and among various social groups vying for better governing and representative positions in the context of independence increased as well. These groups preferred colonial rule to the possibility of a rival group seizing power.

We will now take a closer look at each of these four groups of opponents to national independence.

1) Supporters of the French-African Union

Supporters of the French-African union rejected the option of severing ties with the colonial power and aspired instead to establish a common French-African community. They were not "collaborators" as they did not support the continuation of colonial rule under its standard definition, namely, European rule over Africans. Decolonization, in their view, meant emancipation and full equality of rights for Africans in the context of a French-African "community" or "union." Their aspiration to have African subjects become French citizens in every sense accorded with the worldview of liberal and socialist circles in France, who similarly wished to see the colonies become an inseparable part of France (hence the phrase *La France d'outre-mer*, i.e., "Overseas France").[2]

The black African representatives in the French National Assembly during the years 1946–1958 generally supported what the nationalists regarded as the "colonialist" government. Nevertheless, prominent African leaders such as Senghor, Houphouët-Boigny, Amadou Lamine-Guèye, and Fily Dabo Sissoko served as ministers in French governments in these years. Following the Brazzaville Conference of 1944, and until de Gaulle returned to power in 1958, most African leaders in Africa's French colonies opposed any call for independence. Opponents of the pro-French-African establishment included Sékou Touré of French Guinea and Modibo Keïta of French Sudan (the later Mali), who became radical nationalists in the late 1950s. Similarly, a referendum on immediate independence versus autonomy as part of the French community was conducted in all the French colonies at the initiative of President de Gaulle in July 1958. By and large, all the colonies (aside from Guinea) preferred to follow their leaders and remain part of the French community. Another indication of the extent to which African leaders identified with France was the close ties between African political parties and their French "mother" parties, from the communists on the left to the Gaullists on the right.

While before World War II, African Francophone supporters of France had supported the complete assimilation of African colonies with France, after the war they backed a different model of relations—that of association. Assimilation adherents aspired to be French Black citizens, rejecting the notion of African (or, in North Africa, Arab) independence. Until World War II the call for assimilation drew strong support among Muslim intellectual circles in Algeria. Ferhat Abbas, who headed Algeria's government in exile during the 1950s and led an armed struggle against the French presence in the country, had—a mere 20 years earlier—disclaimed the existence of an Algerian nation and regarded himself as a Frenchman in every respect.[3] In Senegal too, conservative circles such as the PSS (French acronym for Parti socialiste sénégalais, i.e., Senegalese Socialist Party) advocated full assimilation with France and the transformation of Senegal into a French *département* (i.e., territorial administrative division) in all respects.

After 1945, supporters of a union shifted their stance in favor of a looser association by a French-African federation. Senghor and Houphouët-Boigny, future respective presidents of Senegal and the Ivory Coast, were most prominent among the leaders who fiercely opposed independence for their countries and instead advocated the vision of a federation with France. Interestingly, Senghor's opposition to political independence for Senegal did not, in his view, contradict his advocacy of racial-cultural nationalism as embodied by the négritude movement.[4] He saw no clash between cultivation of the African culture and heritage and loyalty to and affiliation with France, between cultural uniqueness and a political French-African bond. Houphouët-Boigny, for his part, adopted the phrase *"oui" à la communauté et "non" à la sécession* (community yes, secession no), countering what he coined *le mythe de l'indépendance* (the myth of independence) with the concept of *fraternité républicaine*.[5] In 1957, just three years before the Ivory Coast achieved independence, Houphouët-Boigny stated at the UN General assembly that it would be possible to realize liberty, equality, and fraternity within the framework of the French community.[6]

What was the ideological rationale of the union advocates? In light of the outcome of World War II, Houphouët-Boigny, Senghor, and their associates regarded nationalism as a factional ideology that promoted war and violence, arguing that its time had passed. As such, the loftiest objective, in their view, was equality rather than independence. They were strongly influenced by Mahatma Gandhi's theory of non-violence,[7] and by theories of universal humanism that presented an antithesis to nationalism. Senghor and Houphouët-Boigny believed that for small, impoverished countries, independence was no more than an illusion in any case, as these countries did not have the capacity to provide for their own security, development and welfare, or to ensure their sovereignty.[8] Sékou Touré, leader and then president of Guinea, stated in 1958 that "Il n'y a pas de dignité sans liberté: nous préférons la liberté dans la pauvreté à la richesse dans l'esclavage" (We prefer poverty in freedom to riches in slavery).[9]

Houphouët-Boigny's response was that liberty and poverty cannot coexist. When Nkrumah asserted that the struggle for independence should come first

112 *Opponents of National Independence*

("Seek ye first the political kingdom"), Houphouët-Boigny appealed to his compatriots, "If you don't want to vegetate in bamboo huts, concentrate your efforts on growing cocoa and coffee. They will fetch a good price and you will become rich."[10]

2) Ethnic Opposition

Ethnic opposition to anticolonial nationalism was relatively widespread in Africa toward the end of the colonial era. Political parties, or regional organizations that represented ethnic groups, feared the rise to power of rival ethnic groups. It was not rare for such groups to prefer the continuation of colonial rule, regarding it as the lesser evil, and therefore to oppose national movements that strove for independence. While at times they explicitly declared their support for the continuation of colonial rule, in other instances they refrained from openly expressing opposition to decolonization, but took measures at the practical level against their ethnic rivals rather than the colonial enemy. As these parties usually proposed that independence be postponed for several years, national movements that demanded "freedom now" consequently condemned them as "collaborators" and "traitors." There were numerous examples of ethnic groups, including large, dominant ones, that opposed the termination of colonial rule for fear of the fate that would befall them in an independent state. We will present only a few.

In Rwanda a small minority, the Tutsi, had ruled tyrannically for centuries over the Hutu, who constituted a majority of the population. The Hutu came to see the Belgian colonial authorities as their protectors, particularly throughout the 1950s, and therefore when the Tutsi demanded rapid decolonization that would ensure their rule once independent statehood was achieved, the Hutu conditioned their assent to independence on the abolition of the Tutsi monarchy. In 1959, when a UN delegation visited Rwanda, at the time a UN-mandated trusteeship under Belgian rule, they were met by Hutu demonstrators carrying signs that protested Tutsi rule and praised Belgium's trusteeship.[11] There thus emerged a paradoxical situation in which Rwanda's ethnic minority, under an elite leadership, represented the radical anticolonial stance, whereas the majority continued to support colonial rule despite being labeled "reactionary" collaborators.

A similar situation prevailed in Zanzibar, where the majority viewed colonial rule as the lesser evil. While an Arab oligarchy, which had maintained supremacy over the African majority even after slavery was abolished on the island, led the anticolonial struggle, the African majority opposed any form of independence that would not also entail a fundamental restructuring to reflect its numeric proportionality in relation to the Arab elite.[12] In South Sudan, too, the population feared the consequences of a British withdrawal that would leave them at the mercy of the Arab north. The governor of Equatoria, a province in southern Sudan, stated in 1963 that the south was shocked by the British intention of withdrawing within three years and abandoning it to authorities who were despised by a majority of the population.[13]

In the early 1950s in Nigeria, the Muslim north, led by Nigeria's largest ethnic group, the Hausa-Fulani, and their party, the Northern People's Congress (NPC), opposed southern calls for independence for fear that groups from the south, particularly the Ibo and Yoruba, regarded as more modern and educated, would dominate the public administration, economy, and government. Northern leader Ahmadu Bello argued that acquiescence to the southern demands for early independence would amount to suicide.[14]

In the Gold Coast (later Ghana), inhabitants of the north and of the Ashanti Region in the south feared that independence under the leadership of Nkrumah and his party would result in the southern Fanti people dominating the entire state. For this reason, in the early 1950s, northern leaders fought against the call for "self-governance now," which they viewed as extreme. Because of the Ashanti people's National Liberation Movement's efforts to thwart negotiations on independence with the British, its members were accused of sabotaging the struggle for freedom and independence. In point of fact, their position was diametrically opposed to the fierce, prolonged struggle waged by the Ashanti people against the British colonial invasion in the nineteenth century.

In Kenya several ethnic groups feared a dictatorship of the Kikuyu, the largest population group, particularly if the Mau Mau rebels were successful in ousting the British. Indeed, many members of the Abaluhya, Kalenjin, Maasai, and Giriama ethnic groups helped the British suppress the rebellion.[15] In the French colony of Cameroon and the Portuguese colony of Mozambique, as well, the anticolonial struggle relied on the support of several ethnic groups in the colony, while other groups refrained from becoming involved or even assisted the colonial forces in suppressing the rebellion.[16]

3) Opposition by the Traditional Leadership

A third base of opposition to independence comprised traditional leaders who regarded the new national ideology as a threat to the traditional relations they represented and over which they reigned. These traditional leaders feared the accelerated erosion of local African cultures and the destabilization of social order, which in turn would undermine their position vis-à-vis a new, young, and Westernized nationalist leadership that, once it seized the reins of power, could curtail their authority and wealth.

In the French colonies the colonial government helped organize "administrative parties" (*partis d'administration*) that granted substantial representation to traditional leaders, whose role it was to impede nationalist organizations and efforts and to help the French maintain their rule. Examples include the Cameroonian Union (Union camerounaise, or UC), led by Ahmadou Ahidjo and the traditional leaders of North Cameroon. In Guinea, Fulani leaders in the region of Fouta Djallon resisted anticolonial efforts by the Democratic

Figure 9.1 Photograph of Queen Elizabeth II and Commonwealth leaders, taken at the 1960 Commonwealth Conference, Windsor Castle. Front row: (left to right) E. J. Cooray (Sri Lanka), Walter Nash (New Zealand), Jawaharlal Nehru (India), Elizabeth II (UK), John Diefenbaker (Canada), Robert Menzies (Australia), Eric Louw Back (Australia). Back row (left to right): Tunku Abdul Rahman, Roy Welensky (Rhodesia and Nyasaland), Harold Macmillan (UK), Mohammed Ayub Khan (Pakistan), Kwame Nkrumah (Ghana). In Ghana there was internal conflict between people who demonstrated for immediate independence, and people who demonstrated for the gradual discontinuity of colonial rule.

Source: https://en.wikipedia.org/wiki/Kwame_Nkrumah#/media/File:Queen_Elizabeth_II_and_the_Prime_Ministers_of_the_Commonwealth_Nations,_at_Windsor_Castle_(1960_Commonwealth_Prime_Minister's_Conference).jpg, Public Domain.

Party of Guinea (Parti démocratique de Guinée, or PDG) led by Sékou Touré.[17] In Upper Volta (today's Burkina Faso), the traditional leader of the Mossi people founded the governing party, the Union for the Defense of the Interests of Upper Volta (Union pour la défense des interêts de la Haute Volta, or UDIHV).[18] Likewise, in Tanganyika, traditional leaders, assisted by the colonial government, formed the United Tanganyika Party (UTP), which in alliance with white settlers aimed to undermine the momentum of the Tanganyika African National Union (TANU). In juxtaposition to TANU's demand for "one man, one vote" in a colony where Africans constituted

98 percent of the population, UTP members advocated a multiracial state with equal representation for Africans, Indians, and Europeans. This was an indirect effort to preserve the colonial system at a time when it was already quite difficult to express straightforward support for maintenance of the colonial status quo.[19]

Opposition of a different sort, which may be termed traditional, was evident in Kenya. The loyalists, who opposed the Mau Mau rebels, included traditional leaders as well as devout Christians who saw violence and hatred of Whites as a violation of Christian principles and a blow to Christian fraternity. Some of them, while aspiring to achieve independence in the future, refused to support violent struggle and sought to preserve the existing "law and order." The Mau Mau rebels knew precisely who their main enemies were, and most of their victims were hence Kikuyu loyalists. Interestingly, even though the Mau Mau rebellion ultimately became part of the national pantheon, those who benefited from its struggle were in fact the loyalist rivals who, since independence, have held the key positions in Kenya's political establishment, public administration, economy, and society.

Figure 9.2 Troops of the King's African Rifles carrying supplies while on watch for Mau Mau fighters.
Source: https://en.wikipedia.org/wiki/Mau_Mau_rebellion#/media/File:KAR_Mau_Mau.jpg, Public Domain.

116　*Opponents of National Independence*

4) The "Opportunists"

Among the traditional leadership and the new middle class there were, as noted, quite a few whose opposition to ending foreign rule in favor of self-rule stemmed from narrow interests—they owed their status, income, and employment to the colonial system. Such opportunists included, for example, African soldiers who served in colonial armies, as illustrated by the case of Mozambique: the Portuguese army managed to rule over the country during 1962–1974 thanks only to the tens of thousands of Africans who served among its ranks and accounted for 60 percent of its soldiers. Military service made it possible for them to earn a relatively decent wage, learn a trade, and establish their social standing; consequently, they did not rebel against their commanders or practice mass desertion. In some instances, members of the same family fought one another: Joaquim Chissano, for example, a leader of armed struggle against the Portuguese and Mozambique's second president, had a brother who served in the Portuguese army.[20]

The above classification of opponents of national independence into four categories is not unequivocal. Certain forms of opposition may be ascribable to two categories. Traditional leaders who feared loss of status, and perhaps loss of income as well, might also be classifiable as opportunists. In other cases, ethnically based opposition correlated with the resistance of traditional leaders. Likewise, soldiers in colonial armies who came from certain areas or belonged to certain population groups may be classifiable as representing both ethnic opposition and opportunistic opposition to decolonization.

The loyalism that existed in Kenya illustrates, above all, the difficulty of making definitive distinctions: loyalists included "ethnic" opponents who feared Kikuyu predominance alongside internal opponents from among the Kikuyu people; "traditionalists" alongside members of the Westernized middle class; Africans who supported the British for selfish financial reasons; and Africans motivated by Christian idealism. It is therefore important to bear in mind that the reality was inestimably more complicated than it is possible to convey through the above classifications.

Notes

1 Bethwell Ogot, "Revolt of the Elders: An Anatomy of the Loyalist Crowd in the Mau Mau Uprising, 1952–1956," *Politics and Nationalism in Colonial Kenya* (Nairobi: East African Publishing House, 1972), p. 135.
2 In Africa, Arab North Africa excluded, *La France d'outre-mer* included eight territories in West Africa (Senegal, Ivory Coast, French Sudan [today's Mali], Dahomey [today's Benin], Upper Volta [today's Burkina Fasso], Niger, French Guinea [today's Guinea-Conakry]); four territories in Central Africa (Congo Brazzaville [today's Republic of Congo], Gabon, Ubangi-Shari [today's Central African Republic], Chad); Madagascar; French Somaliland [today's Djibouti]; UN Trusteeship territories (French Togo [today's Togo] and French Cameroon [today's Cameroon]).

Opponents of National Independence   117

3 Guy Pervillé, *Les étudiants algériens de l'université française 1880–1962* (Paris: Éditions du centre national de la recherche scientifique, 1984), p. 227.

4 Léopold Senghor, "On Negrohood: Psychology of the African Negro," (trans. H. Kaal, *Diogenes* 10, No. 37 (1962): 1–15.

5 Félix Houphouët-Boigny, quoted in Crawford Young, "Decolonization in Africa," in Gann and Duignan, *Colonialism in Africa*, Vol. II, p. 470.

For Houphouët-Boigny's "mythe de l'indépendance," see Jean Lacouture, "Premières reactions favorable," in *Le Monde*, August 26, 1958.

www.lemonde.fr/archives/article/1958/08/26/premieres-reactions-favorab les_2301701_1819218.html.

For his "fraternité républicaine," see Jean-Pierre Dozon, *Frères et sujets. La France et l'Afrique en perspective*, Paris, Flammarion, 2003, 350 pages. Dans Politique africaine 2005/2 (N° 98), pp. 181–196.

www.cairn.info/revue-politique-africaine-2005-2-page-181.htm   [last viewed July 14, 2021].

6 Félix Houphouët-Boigny, "French Africa and the French Mission," in Rupert Emerson and Martin Kilson (eds.), *The Political Awakening of Africa* (Englewood Cliffs, NJ: Prentice-Hall, 1968), pp. 73–82.

7 Mahatma Gandhi (1869–1948) studied law in London. The racial discrimination he experienced during the 20 years he worked as a lawyer in South Africa convinced him to become politically active on behalf of the Indian community. Upon his return to India, in 1915, he became one of the leaders of the Indian National Congress party, which demanded independence from the British. Gandhi was renowned for his strong opposition to violence and became a worldwide model for non-violent national struggle. An advocate of coexistence between the Hindu majority and Muslims in India, he was assassinated by a Hindu extremist who objected to his compromising approach toward Muslims.

8 Jacques Louis Hymans, *Leopold Sedar Senghor: An Intellectual Biography* (Edinburgh: Edinburgh University Press, 1971), p. 159; Aristide Zolberg, *One-Party Government in the Ivory Coast* (Princeton, NJ: Princeton University Press, 1964), p. 157.

9 Sékou Touré, as quoted in "Le 2 octobre 1958, la Guinée de Sékou Touré proclame son indépendance," *Jeune Afrique* Archive, October 2, 2006. www.jeuneafrique. com/132294/archives-thematique/la-guin-e-proclame-son-ind-pendance-2/   [Last viewed July 13, 2021].

10 Zolberg, *Onechives-Party Government*, p. 151.

11 Richard F. Nyrop, *Area Handbook for Rwanda* (Washington: American University Press, 1969), p. 18.

12 Michael F. Lofchie, *Zanzibar: Background to Revolution* (Princeton, NJ: Princeton University Press, 1965), pp. 150–174.

13 Peter Woodward, *Condominium and Sudanese Nationalism* (London: Collings, 1979), p. 148.

14 James S. Coleman, *Nigeria: Background to Nationalism* (Berkeley: University of California Press, 1963), pp. 398–399; Olajide Aluko, "Politics of Decolonization in British West Africa," in J. F. A. Ajayi and Michael Crowder (eds.), *History of West Africa*, Vol. II (London: Longman, 1974), p. 640.

15 George Bennett, *Kenya: A Political History, the Colonial Period* (London: Oxford University Press, 1963), passim.

118 *Opponents of National Independence*

16 Richard A. Joseph, *Radical Nationalism in Cameroun: Social Origins of the UPC Rebellion* (Oxford: Oxford University press, 1977), pp. 8–13; Thomas H. Henriksen, *Revolution and Counterrevolution: Mozambique's War of Independence, 1964–1974* (Westport, CT: Greenwood Press, 1983), pp. 8, 60–62, 79, 95, 98.

17 L. Gray Cowan, "Decolonization in Africa," "Guinea," in Gwendolyn M. Carter (ed.), *African One-Party States* (Ithaca, NY: Cornell University Press, 1962), pp. 149–236.

18 Young, "Decolonization in Africa," p. 481.

19 J. Clagett Taylor, *The Political Development of Tanganyika* (Stanford, CA: Stanford University Press, 1963), pp. 45, 137, 145, 156, 158, 169; John Iliffe, *A Modern History of Tanganyika* (Cambridge: Cambridge University Press, 1979), pp. 522–535.

20 Thomas Henriksen, *Mozambique: A History* (London: Collings, 1978).

10 The Organization of African Unity and the African Union

Pan-African Unification

The Organization of African Unity (OAU), like its successor, the African Union (AU), was an intergovernmental organization whose membership comprised all states on the African continent. The OAU was founded in 1963 as a response to two opposing trends that prevailed in 1950s Africa, and even more so in the early 1960s, as many states achieved independence. The first of these was Pan-Africanism, which underscored the continent's unity, its shared colonial history, African brotherhood, and the need for states to be large and strong. The spokesperson for this trend, as noted, was Kwame Nkrumah, who aspired to establish the "United States of Africa" in order to overcome artificial, colonial borders. The second, and opposing, trend underscored the sovereignty of the new states, the "sanctity" of their borders, and the need for "nation-building" within existing borders. This trend indirectly highlighted the contrasts between African countries—Arab vs African states, Anglophone vs Francophone states, and radical vs conservative states.

Indeed, the impression in the early 1960s was that Africa was divided not only into sovereign states, but also into rival blocs. Conservative Francophones formed the African and Malagasy Union (Organisation commune africaine et malgache, OCAM), which included the Ivory Coast, Benin, Upper Volta, Cameroon, the Central African Republic, Congo/Brazzaville, Gabon, the Malagasy Republic, Mauritania, Niger, and Senegal. It was juxtaposed by the radical Casablanca Bloc, founded in 1961, which comprised Morocco, the Algerian government-in-exile, Libya, Egypt, Ghana, Mali, and Guinea. To counter the latter there emerged the Monrovia Bloc, formed through a union of OCAM's Francophone states and conservative Anglophone states (Nigeria, Liberia, and Sierra Leone) as well as Ethiopia and Tunisia. Libya, under the leadership of King Idris Senussi, belonged at that time to both blocs.

The Organization of African Unity

The OAU was founded in 1963 in Addis Ababa, which also served as its seat and organizational headquarters, and disbanded in 2002. The organization

DOI: 10.4324/9781003322818-11

120   *The Organization of African Unity and the African Union*

recognized the sovereignty of all its member states and declared that it opposed any border changes. In so doing it took a stance against maximalist Pan-Africanism (the United States of Africa) as well as any form of ethnic separatism. Its charter defined it as an organization for cooperation among sovereign states, effectively framing it more along the lines of the United Nations than the United States. The OAU Charter emphasized jurisdictional sovereignty even more than the United Nations Charter underscores this principle, as the following examples illustrate:

- Only the Assembly of Heads of State and Government had the authority to make binding decisions;
- *All* resolutions of the Assembly had to be determined by a two-thirds majority of the Members of the Organization (in contrast to the UN General Assembly, which only requires a two-thirds majority for "important questions" and allows for a simple majority on all other matters, BN);
- There was no equivalent of the Security Council—i.e., a subset of the Assembly that could make implementable decisions (such as military intervention, adoption of a position in the international arena, recognition or non-recognition of a government). Bodies such as the Commission of Mediation, Conciliation, and Arbitration or the Liberation Committee had no real authority;
- The Organization's resolutions were not enforceable by sanctions (e.g., its resolution to sever relations with the UK following Rhodesia's unilateral declaration of independence in 1965);
- It lacked a permanent secretariat with wide-ranging authorities.

In addition to the states' sovereignty, independence, and territorial integrity, the OAU placed emphasis on its commitment to non-interference in the internal affairs of states, peaceful relations among states, unity of the continent, and African solutions to African problems (in accordance with the UN Charter, which promotes regional resolution of regional problems).

One may safely say that the OAU's main achievements during 1963–1990 related to the issue of liberation from colonial rule. Although its Liberation Committee was unable to provide significant military assistance to the liberation movements in Angola, Mozambique, Guinea-Bissau, Rhodesia, South West Africa, or South Africa, and in the cases of Angola and Rhodesia also failed to unite the movements, it is still safe to say that the political and diplomatic struggle waged by the OAU in the international arena played an important part in tightening political, economic, and cultural sanctions against South Africa and Rhodesia and in exerting pressure on Portugal. However, even in this area the Organization sometimes failed to achieve its aims. Its resolution on the severing of diplomatic relations with the UK following Rhodesia's declaration of independence, for example, went unheeded even by members of the Organization itself (with the exception of Tanzania).

The Organization of African Unity and the African Union 121

Scholars are divided on the OAU's significance and the impact of its activities. Some view it as an organization of states with virtually no import as a collective body, whereas others argue that it had value as an institution, beyond its role as a meeting place for sovereign states. The following statements reflect these differing approaches:

> There is no OAU; there are only members and their interests come first.[1]
> The OAU provides an institutionalized forum that facilitates the mutual adjustment of member states' policies and actions within an evolving framework of general norms and operation practices.[2]

Over the course of 20 years (1963–1983), the OAU, seeking to uphold the principle of "African solutions," refrained from referring African conflicts to the UN (although the territorial dispute between Libya and Chad split the OAU into two camps and therefore did result in a referral to the UN in 1983). The Organization's stance stemmed from concerns about foreign intervention in African affairs, the possibility of setting a precedent by "inviting" such intervention, the presumption that referral to the UN would project weakness on Africa's part, and concerns that given the bipolar nature of their relations, intervention by the UN's major powers could impede conflict resolution. Some observers view the prioritization of African solutions as an OAU achievement, but considering the Organization's failure to resolve the conflicts and stem the bloodshed of those years, this seems a questionable achievement.

The Organization of African Unity did successfully mediate the Sands War between Algeria and Morocco (1963–1964), bringing it to an end, but most of its efforts to prevent or resolve wars, mediate, and address violent internal disputes failed. Salient examples include the wars between Somalia and Ethiopia, and Chad and Libya, the separatist wars in Biafra (1967–1970), South Sudan (1955–1972, 1983–2005), and Eritrea (1962–1991), the war in Western Sahara (1976–2002), and the civil wars in Angola (1975–2002), Mozambique (1975–1992), Somalia (1991–), Chad (1979–1982, 2005–2008), Liberia (1989–1996, 1999–2003), the Ivory Coast (2002–2007), Ethiopia (1974–1991), Zimbabwe (1980–1986), Rwanda (1990–1994), Burundi (1993–2005), and the Democratic Republic of the Congo (1996–1997, 1998–2003, 2007–2009). A striking example is the failure of the Neutral Military Observers Group (NMOG) to prevent the civil war in Rwanda from escalating to genocide in 1994.

The principles of jurisdictional sovereignty and non-interference in domestic affairs prevented the Organization from taking action against despots who personally initiated the slaughter of hundreds of thousands in their own countries (Idi Amin in Uganda, Jean-Bédel Bokassa in the Central African Republic, Francisco Macías Nguema in Equatorial Guinea, Mengistu Haile Mariam in Ethiopia,[3] Robert Mugabe[4] in Zimbabwe), or against governments that committed atrocities—from ethnic cleansing to genocide

122 *The Organization of African Unity and the African Union*

(Sudan in South Sudan during 1955–1972 and 1983–2005 and in Darfur during 2003–2008, Rwanda in 1994). Among the OAU's low points was its election of prominent dictators as chairmen (Idi Amin, Mobutu, Mengistu, and Ibrahim Babangida). Generally speaking, the Organization of African Unity operated on the assumptions that it lacked the authority or desire to intervene in internal affairs, that it had to work with the government in power (even if the regime was despotic and violently brutal), that it could not recognize separatist movements or governments, and that whenever a member state was engaged in hostilities, it had to support whoever controlled the capital (as it repeatedly demonstrated in Angola, Chad, and Congo/Zaire).

The Organization failed to ensure African solutions to African problems. It did not prevent Cuban-Soviet intervention in Angola (in the 1970s and 1980s) or in the Horn of Africa (1978–1979), nor French military intervention in Chad, Djibouti, the Ivory Coast, Congo-Brazzaville, Congo/Zaire, and other states. Moreover, it lacked the power to offer an alternative to UN forces in the Democratic Republic of the Congo, Angola, Mozambique, Namibia, Ethiopia-Eritrea, Somalia, and the Central African Republic. The OAU recognized the right of sovereign states to "invite" external, non-African, assistance against rebels, even though this amounted to an admission of failure to find an African solution to an African problem. On the other hand, a request for African assistance (for example, Senegalese forces in Gambia; Namibian, Zimbabwean, and Angolan forces in Congo/Zaire) was seen as more legitimate because it did not contradict the principle of African solutions to African problems. The organization also failed to realize its plans for economic unification of the continent, and the 1980 Lagos Plan of Action, intended to establish an African common market by 2025 and serve as a counterweight to International Monetary Fund and World Bank structural adjustment programs, remained on paper only.

The OAU played a significant part in issues surrounding the Arab-Israeli conflict when it adopted a collective stance in favor of severing diplomatic relations with Israel after the 1973 war. Its position prompted pro-Israel states, including Ethiopia, Kenya, and the Ivory Coast, to cut ties with Israel. In the 1980s and 1990s, however, the Organization refrained from adopting a position either favoring or opposing the renewal of relations with Israel. In 1999, in the aftermath of large-scale terrorist attacks in Kenya and Tanzania in 1998, the Assembly of Heads of State and Government adopted the OAU Convention on the Prevention and Combating of Terrorism (the Algiers Convention), although by this time it was already evident that the OAU's days were numbered.

The African Union

The AU was established in 2002, replacing the Organization of African Unity. The aspirations that served as guiding principles for the AU's founders were more far-reaching than those of its predecessor's founders. In effect, they

The Organization of African Unity and the African Union   123

sought to reproduce the European Union's success—hence the similarity in name and in some of its institutions. In contrast to the OAU, which exalted non-interference, the AU committed itself to the principles embodied in the concept of "Responsibility to Protect" (R2P), which includes protecting citizens of African states from dictators and despots who are slaughtering their own people. This approach was a reaction of sorts to the harsh criticism leveled against the OAU following the genocide in Rwanda (1994) and the atrocities committed in the 1970s in Burundi and Uganda, and in the 1980s and 1990s in Sudan and Ethiopia.

"Responsibility to Protect" includes a responsibility to prevent, a responsibility to react, and a responsibility to rebuild. Indeed, at least at the legal, normative, and declarative levels, the principle reflects a transition from a "culture of non-intervention" (per the OAU) to a "culture of non-indifference" (per the AU).[5] To implement R2P, the AU established observer missions in places and regions of unrest, such as the Central African Republic, Chad, the Comoros, the Ivory Coast, the Democratic Republic of Congo, Ethiopia, Eritrea, the Great Lakes region (Rwanda and Burundi), Liberia, Mauritania, Somalia, and Western Sahara.

Moreover, the AU established a Peace and Security Council (PSC), which, like the UN Security Council, consists of 15 states and has the authority to impose sanctions (e.g., against a state that underwent a military coup). In instances of "war crimes, genocide, and crimes against humanity," the Assembly of the Union (composed of heads of state and government) has the authority to decide on military intervention (Article 4(h) of the AU Constitutive Act). This inclination toward intervention also lay behind the creation of the African Human Rights Court and the Pan-African Parliament, a body with advisory and consultative powers that, once again, brings to mind the European Parliament. A schematic of the AU's organizational structure and excerpts from its Constitutive Act (charter) appear next.

Constitutive Act of the African Union[6]

Following is the text of the Constitutive Act of the AU, signed by the heads of state of all 53 African countries:

We, Heads of State and Government of the Member States of the OAU:

1. The President of the People's Democratic Republic of Algeria
2. The President of the Republic of Angola
3. The President of the Republic of Benin
4. The President of the Republic of Botswana
5. The President of Burkina Faso
6. The President of the Republic of Burundi
7. The President of the Republic of Cameroon
8. The President of the Republic of Cape Verde
9. The President of the Central African Republic

124 *The Organization of African Unity and the African Union*

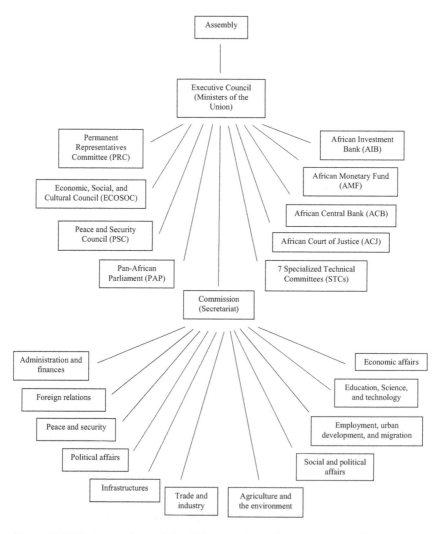

Figure 10.1 The Institutions of the African Union at its inception.

10. The President of the Republic of Chad
11. The President of the Islamic Federal Republic of the Comoros
12. The President of the Republic of the Congo
13. The President of the Republic of Côte d'Ivoire
14. The President of the Democratic Republic of Congo
15. The President of the Republic of Djibouti
16. The President of the Arab Republic of Egypt
17. The President of the State of Eritrea
18. The Prime Minister of the Federal Democratic Republic of Ethiopia

The Organization of African Unity and the African Union   125

19. The President of the Republic of Equatorial Guinea
20. The President of the Gabonese Republic
21. The President of the Republic of The Gambia
22. The President of the Republic of Ghana
23. The President of the Republic of Guinea
24. The President of the Republic of Guinea-Bissau
25. The President of the Republic of Kenya
26. The Prime Minister of Lesotho
27. The President of the Republic of Liberia
28. The Leader of the 1st of September Revolution of the Great Socialist People's Libyan Arab Jamahiriya
29. The President of the Republic of Madagascar
30. The President of the Republic of Malawi
31. The President of the Republic of Mali
32. The President of the Islamic Republic of Mauritania
33. The Prime Minister of the Republic of Mauritius
34. The President of the Republic of Mozambique
35. The President of the Republic of Namibia
36. The President of the Republic of Niger
37. The President of the Federal Republic of Nigeria
38. The President of the Republic of Rwanda
39. The President of the Sahrawi Arab Democratic Republic
40. The President of the Republic of Sao Tome and Principe
41. The President of the Republic of Senegal
42. The President of the Republic of Seychelles
43. The President of the Republic of Sierra Leone
44. The President of the Republic of Somalia
45. The President of the Republic of South Africa
46. The President of the Republic of Sudan
47. The King of Swaziland
48. The President of the United Republic of Tanzania
49. The President of the Togolese Republic
50. The President of the Republic of Tunisia
51. The President of the Republic of Uganda
52. The President of the Republic of Zambia
53. The President of the Republic of Zimbabwe

INSPIRED by the noble ideals which guided the founding fathers of our Continental Organization and generations of Pan-Africanists in their determination to promote unity, solidarity, cohesion and cooperation among the peoples of Africa and African States;

CONSIDERING the principles and objectives stated in the Charter of the Organization of African Unity and the Treaty establishing the African Economic Community;

126 *The Organization of African Unity and the African Union*

RECALLING the heroic struggles waged by our peoples and our countries for political independence, human dignity and economic emancipation;

CONSIDERING that since its inception, the Organization of African Unity has played a determining and invaluable role in the liberation of attainment of the unity of our continent and has provided a unique framework for our collective action in Africa and in our relations with the rest of the world.

DETERMINED to take up the multifaceted challenges that confront our continent and peoples in the light of the social, economic and political changes taking place in the world;

CONVINCED of the need to accelerate the process of implementing the Treaty establishing the African Economic Community in order to promote the socio-economic development of Africa and to face more effectively the challenges posed by globalization;

GUIDED by our common vision of a united and strong Africa and by the need to build a partnership between governments and all segments of civil society, in particular women, youth and the private sector, in order to strengthen solidarity and cohesion among our peoples;

CONSCIOUS of the fact that the scourge of conflicts in Africa constitutes a major impediment to the socio-economic development of the continent and of the need to promote peace, security and stability as a prerequisite for the implementation of our development and integration agenda;

DETERMINED to promote and protect human and peoples' rights, consolidate democratic institutions and culture, and to ensure good governance and the rule of law;

FURTHER DETERMINED to take all necessary measures to strengthen our common institutions and provide them with the necessary powers and resources to enable them discharge their respective mandates effectively;

RECALLING the Declaration which we adopted at the Fourth Extraordinary Session of our Assembly in Sirte, the Great Socialist People's Libyan Arab Jamahiriya, on 9.9. 99, in which we decided to establish an African Union, in conformity with the ultimate objectives of the Charter of our Continental Organization and the Treaty establishing the African Economic Community;

HAVE AGREED AS FOLLOWS:

. . .

Article 2

Establishment

The African Union is hereby established in accordance with the provisions of this Act.

Article 3

Objectives

The objectives of the Union shall be to:

(a) achieve greater unity and solidarity between the African countries and the peoples of Africa;
(b) defend the sovereignty, territorial integrity and independence of its Member States;
(c) accelerate the political and socio-economic integration of the continent;
(d) promote and defend African common positions on issues of interest to the continent and its peoples;
(e) encourage international cooperation, taking due account of the Charter of the United Nations and the Universal Declaration of Human Rights;
(f) promote peace, security, and stability on the continent;
(g) promote democratic principles and institutions, popular participation and good governance;
(h) promote and protect human and peoples' rights in accordance with the African Charter on Human and Peoples' Rights and other relevant human rights instruments;
(i) establish the necessary conditions which enable the continent to play its rightful role in the global economy and in international negotiations;
(j) promote sustainable development at the economic, social and cultural levels as well as the integration of African economies;
(k) promote cooperation in all fields of human activity to raise the living standards of African peoples;
(l) coordinate and harmonize the policies between the existing and future Regional Economic Communities for the gradual attainment of the objectives of the Union;
(m) advance the development of the continent by promoting research in all fields, in particular in science and technology;
(n) work with relevant international partners in the eradication of preventable diseases and the promotion of good health on the continent.

Article 4
Principles
The Union shall function in accordance with the following principles:

(a) sovereign equality and interdependence among Member States of the Union;
(b) respect of borders existing on achievement of independence;
(c) participation of the African peoples in the activities of the Union;
(d) establishment of a common defence policy for the African Continent;
(e) peaceful resolution of conflicts among Member States of the Union through such appropriate means as may be decided upon by the Assembly;

128   *The Organization of African Unity and the African Union*

(f)   prohibition of the use of force or threat to use force among Member States of the Union;

(g)   non-interference by any Member State in the internal affairs of another;

(h)   the right of the Union to intervene in a Member State pursuant to a decision of the Assembly in respect of grave circumstances, namely: war crimes, genocide and crimes against humanity;

(i)   peaceful co-existence of Member States and their right to live in peace and security;

(j)   the right of Member States to request intervention from the Union in order to restore peace and security;

(k)   promotion of self-reliance within the framework of the Union;

(l)   promotion of gender equality;

(m) respect for democratic principles, human rights, the rule of law and good governance;

(n)   promotion of social justice to ensure balanced economic development;

(o)   respect for the sanctity of human life, condemnation and rejection of impunity and political assassination, acts of terrorism and subversive activities;

(p)   condemnation and rejection of unconstitutional changes of governments.

In accordance with the new charter, during the years 2003–2009 the African Union deployed peacekeeping forces to Burundi, Sudan, and Somalia. Sometimes the mission was successful (e.g., the AU Mission in Burundi—AMIB), while at other times it failed completely (e.g., the AU Mission in Sudan—AMIS). In the case of Burundi, the AU took part in pursuing a peace agreement, consolidating it, and implementing it through AMIB. The Mission's role was to ensure the safety of underground leaders who joined the national unity government, assist in the disarmament of underground movements, and support the reintegration of ex-combatants into society. In 2007 the AU also deployed a mission to Somalia, composed mainly of soldiers from the Ugandan army, but it was unable to put an end to the country's civil war.

Case Study: The African Union and Darfur

Since 2003 the Darfur region in western Sudan has been a battleground for violent clashes between the government and rebel forces (the Sudan Liberation Movement/Army—SLM/A, and the Justice and Equality Movement—JEM). During 2003–2008, Arab-Muslim government forces, with the assistance of brutal Janjaweed militias, engaged in the genocide of African groups (who were Muslim as well). Hundreds of thousands were killed, and about 2.7 million Africans, facing the threat of death, became internally displaced persons. The AU's efforts to secure an agreement between the sides were unsuccessful; a ceasefire achieved in April 2004 and a peace agreement reached in May 2005 both collapsed.

The Organization of African Unity and the African Union   129

Although the AU had the authority to intervene, it lacked the political will to do so. It provided military support in the form of the African Mission in Sudan (AMIS), which numbered 7,000 troops whose mandate necessitated that they remain neutral and impartial, acting only with the consent of both sides (the perpetrators as well as the victims of slaughter). Sudan, a member of the AU's Peace and Security Council, blocked any efforts to make this mission less "toothless." The mission utterly failed to protect the population because its troops lacked authority, equipment, training, and the will to put themselves at risk, as well as operational guidelines. It even failed to disarm the militias, despite this being a specific demand of UN Security Council Resolution 1556 (July 30, 2004). Sudan did everything in its power to thwart AMIS's efforts to fulfill its mandate.[7]

In 2007 the UN and AU decided to form a hybrid mission—the United Nations African Mission in Darfur (UNAMID). In its early years the mission failed to better the situation, and because of its powerlessness the residents of Darfur began viewing it dismissively.[8] However, the mission remained in Darfur for 13 years, through the end of 2020. By the time of its departure the situation had changed: a three-year power-sharing transitional government was formed after President Omar al-Bashir was deposed in April 2019, and the Security Council established a political mission to assist Sudan in its political transition. UNAMID's departure drew protests from many Darfuri residents, who argued that even though it had not effectively protected them, its departure would leave them even more vulnerable.[9] Acting Foreign Minister Omar Qamareddine said that UNAMID had "contributed to achieving peace," adding, "It's true that its tenure was marred by some obstacles but it was, overall, good."[10]

The AU has also attempted to resolve some of its member states' internal conflicts. In 2005 it launched mediation efforts between Mugabe's government and the opposition in Zimbabwe. This violent conflict, which claimed hundreds of deaths, was "resolved" at least temporarily in 2008 through the establishment of a national unity government that divided political power between President Mugabe and opposition leader Morgan Tsvangirai, who was appointed as prime minister.

The Union reached a similar solution in Kenya, where elections to the parliament and presidency in December 2007 were followed by rioting and bloodshed. President Mwai Kibaki's election had entailed violence and fraud, and many believed that if the elections had been free and fair, opposition leader Raila Odinga would have been chosen. Large-scale violence between members and allies of the Kikuyu people (Kibaki's ethnic group) and members and allies of the Luo people (Odinga's ethnic group) resulted in the death of about 1,300 people and displacement of 300,000 who lost their homes when they fled or were forcibly dispossessed. Mediation efforts by the African Union Panel of Eminent Personalities, headed by former UN Secretary-General Kofi Annan, helped secure an agreement to end the conflict in 2008. The arrangement they reached was very similar to the one

130　*The Organization of African Unity and the African Union*

achieved in Zimbabwe: a division of power between the ruling party and the opposition. Kibaki remained president and Odinga was appointed as head of a national unity government numbering 92 ministers!

Notes

1　I. William Zartman, "The OAU in the Africa State System," in Y. E. Ayouty and I. William Zartman (eds.), *The OAU after Twenty Years* (Westport, CT: Praeger, 1984).
2　William J. Foltz, "The Organization of African Unity and the Resolution of Africa's Conflicts," in Francis M. Deng and I. William Zartman (eds.), *Conflict Resolution in Africa* (Washington: Brookings Institution, 1991), pp. 350–351.
3　Mengistu Haile Mariam (1937–) came to power following a military coup and established a brutal pro-communist regime in Ethiopia. He was deposed in 1991, after a protracted civil war, and received asylum in Zimbabwe.
4　Robert Mugabe (1924–2019) served as prime minister (1980–1987) then president (1987–2017) of Zimbabwe from the time of its independence in 1980. He established an oppressive regime that blatantly violated human rights and brought the country to economic ruin.
5　Tim Murithi, "The African Union Transition from Non-Intervention to Non-Indifference: An Ad Hoc Approach to the Responsibility to Protect," *Internationale Politik und Gesellschaft* (January 2009): 90–106.
6　Constitutive Act of the African Union, https://au.int/sites/default/files/pages/34873-file-constitutiveact_en.pdf.
7　Samuel Makinda and Wafula Okumu, *The African Union—Challenges of Globalization, Security and Governance* (London: Routledge, 2008).
8　"Briefing: Sudan," *The Economist*, November 11, 2008, pp. 30–33; Irit Back, "The ICC Arrest Warrant against Omar al-Bashir: Darfur and the Non-Intervention Discourse," *Tel Aviv Notes*, June 1, 2009.
9　"UN-AU Mission in Sudan's Darfur Ends Mandate after 13 Years," *Al-Jazeera*, December 31, 2020, www.aljazeera.com/news/2020/12/31/un-au-mission-in-sudans-darfur-ends-mandate-after-13-years.
10　"UN, African Union Peacekeeping Mission in Sudan's Darfur Ends," *France24*, December 31, 2020, www.france24.com/en/africa/20201231-un-african-union-peacekeeping-mission-in-sudan-s-darfur-ends.

11 Black Zionism

The Return to Africa in Theory and Practice[1]

> Oh I'm bound to go to Africa,
> I'm bound to go there soon.
> I'm bound to go to Africa,
> To wear those golden shoes.
> > Traditional song adopted as hymn, ca. 1900, by Southern Negroes
> > who followed Bishop Henry Turner[2] (Jenkins 1975: 8)

The Idea of Black Zionism

The ideology of a "return to Africa" from the African diaspora was called Black Zionism in the first half of the twentieth century, indicating an affinity with Jewish Zionism. Sundquist defines Afro-Zionism as "a mode of pan-Africanism that took its inspiration in significant part from modern Zionism's goal of restoring the Jewish State ... by repopulating the land of Palestine" (Sundquist 2005: 120). As in the Jewish case, in the African-American case, too, a praxis of return existed for centuries, well before the development of a well-thought-out ideology. As in the Jewish case, Black Zionism was a reaction to persecution, racism, degradation, and discrimination, particularly a reaction to slavery. Black Zionism was the black reaction to the race theories of Gobineau, Carlyle, and Robert Knox. Again, as in Jewish Zionism, Black Zionism reflects profound disappointment with emancipation, with the results of the American Civil War, with Lincoln's Emancipation Proclamation. After a short period of hope for the achievement of equality and human dignity, Reconstruction in the American South was followed by segregation, disenfranchisement, the rise of the Ku Klux Klan, and lynchings, all of which lasted till the 1960s. Black Zionist ideology contained a variety of ingredients—the idea of salvation, a claim for racial unity, longing for the "African homeland," pride in African civilization, the rejection of assimilation, and "return to the roots," and the aspiration not only for self-determination and liberty, but also for black statehood and power.

DOI: 10.4324/9781003322818-12

132 *Black Zionism: The Return to Africa in Theory and Practice*

The idea of salvation was grounded in religious or quasi-religious longing. It was deeply imbedded in slave songs not only in the US but also in Brazil and the Caribbean Islands. The slaves saw themselves in bondage and exile, and hoped for deliverance, for a return to their beloved Africa. Africa was frequently identified with heaven, a heaven that could be reached only after death. There was widespread belief in the return of the soul to Africa. Belief in return was very intense, as was reflected in numerous slave songs.

> Lord I want to cross over into
> camp ground
> Oh, when I get to heaven, I'll walk
> all about.
> There's nobody there for to turn me out
> Go down, Moses,
> way down in Egypt's land
> tell ol' Pharaoh,
> to let my people go.
>
> (Geiss 1974: 28)

Religious longing was for the Promised Land, for Zion and Canaan, and for the Jordan River—the Atlantic Ocean—which had to be crossed.

Unity of race is another basic Black Zionist idea. As Jewish Zionism first had to establish the idea that Jews are a nation, one nation, and that the Jewish Question is a "national problem," in Black Zionist ideology, too, the starting point was that all blacks are unified by race. Africans in Africa and Africans in Mississippi and Alabama, Jamaica, and Cuba, in England and France are all one Black Nation. Pan-Negroism and Pan-Africanism were the names given to this idea, which gained ground in the early twentieth century.

Already in 1919, W.E.B. Du Bois, the black American Harvard sociologist who for decades was the leading intellectual of black cultural nationalism, asserted that the problem of the twentieth century is the problem of the color line. The Zionist-inspired solution to this was the idea of a return to Africa. Indeed, a deep emotional and intellectual connection to Africa is part of Black Zionism. Edward W. Blyden, who was born on the Caribbean island of St. Thomas, was the "father" of black nationalism, and became Liberia's secretary of state in 1864. He described his links to Africa in the following words:

> Africa! There is no heart beating under a covering of sable hue, which does not throb with emotion at the sound of this word. To the exile from these shores labouring under the burning, though congenial, sun of South America, or shivering under the influence of Northern snows, it brings comfort, consolation and hope. It tells him of a country, a home given to him by that Almighty Being…
>
> (Blyden 1856)

Black Zionism: The Return to Africa in Theory and Practice 133

The writer Richard Wright formulated it differently: "One does not react to Africa as Africa is ... One reacts to Africa as one is, as one lives one's reaction to Africa in one's life." Blyden and Wright formulated their attachment to Africa in similar words, but this still leaves open the question whether one should "return" to Africa, or not. Blyden did, Wright did not.

Africa is often depicted—both in Black Nationalism and in Black Zionism—as a Garden of Eden, a place where man is in harmony with nature. Three poems by American poets Countee Cullen (1903–1946) and Langston Hughes (1902–1967), and by the Haitian Jacques Roumain reflect this theme:

> What is Africa to me:
> Copper sun or scarlet sea,
> Jungle star or jungle track,
> Strong bronzed men, or regal Black
> Women from whose loins I sprang
> When the birds of Eden sang?
> One three centuries removed
> From the scenes his fathers loved.
> Spicy grove, cinnamon tree,
> What is Africa to me?
> ...
>
> (Countee Cullen, "Heritage," in Jenkins 1975: 24)
>
> ...
> It's the long road to Guinea
> No bright welcome will be made for you
> In the dark land of dark men:
> Under a smoky sky pierced by the cry of birds
> Around the eye of the river
> the eyelashes of the trees open on decaying light
> There, there awaits you beside the water a quiet village
> And the hut of your fathers, and the hard ancestral stone
> where your head will rest at last.
>
> (Jacques Roumain, "Guinea," in Jenkins 1975: 45)
>
> ...
> I built my hut near the Congo and it lulled me to sleep.
>
> ...
> I've known rivers:
> Ancient, dusky rivers.
> My soul has grown deep like the rivers.
>
> (Langston Hughes, "The Negro Speaks of Rivers," in *Crisis*, June 1921, in Hughes 1959: 4)

Another basic feature of Black Zionism is pride in the achievements of African civilization—a reaction to white racism, which saw Africa as "primitive," without history, culture or heritage:

134 *Black Zionism: The Return to Africa in Theory and Practice*

When Europe was inhabited by a race of cannibals, a race of savages, naked men, heathens, and pagans, Africa was peopled with a race of cultured Black men, who were masters in art, science, and literature; men who were cultured and refined; men, who, it is said, were like the gods.

(Garvey 1967 Vol. I: 77)

This, thought I, is the work of my African progenitors ... Feelings came over me far different from those which I have felt when looking at the mighty works of European genius. I felt that I had a peculiar "heritage in the Great Pyramid" built [by] ... the enterprising sons of Ham, from whom I am descended. The blood seemed to flow faster through my veins. I seemed to hear the echo of those illustrious Africans. I seemed to feel the impulse from those stirring characters who sent civilization into Greece ... I felt lifted out of the commonplace grandeur of modern times; and, could my voice have reached every African in the world, I would have earnestly addressed him in the words of the Liberian poet Hillary Teague: "From Pyramidal Hall; From Thebes, they loudly call; Retake your Fame."

(Blyden 1873: 55)

As in the Jewish case, the Black Zionists rejected national assimilation to the host nations. They propagated a return to the roots, to their African culture. They thought not only about political liberation, but also about cultural-psychological liberation. In rejecting assimilation, they opted for black liberation. Blyden mocks all those who want to vanish as blacks:

"Let us do away with the sentiment of Race. Let us do away with our African personality and be lost, if possible, in another Race." This is as wise or as philosophical as to say, let us do away with gravitation, with heat and cold and sunshine and rain. Of course the Race in which these persons would be absorbed is the dominant race, before which, in cringing self-surrender and ignoble self-suppression they lie in prostrate admiration.

(Blyden, in *Sierra Leone Weekly News*, 27 May 1893:
in Esedebe 1982: 36)

And indeed, the Zionists cultivated black or African folklore, poetry, sculpture, arts, and dance, and hailed the "African" values of spontaneity, harmony, nature, simplicity, and closeness to the soil. Countee Cullen and Langston Hughes of the 1920s Harlem Renaissance, also known as Black Literary Renaissance or New Negro Movement, were outstanding examples of this cultural Zionism, which wanted to see a New Black Man who is free from all imposed and self-inflicted sense of inferiority. While touring Africa in 1891, another Black Zionist, Bishop Henry Turner, said that Africa was "full of proud-walking sons," and that "what the Black Man had in Africa was his manhood" (in Jenkins 1975: 99). Blyden himself admonished his fellow-Blacks, urging them to "honor and love your Race. Be yourselves … If you are not yourself, if you surrender your personality you have nothing left to give the world" (*A Voice from Bleeding Africa*, in Jenkins 1975: 39).

Race was central: Black Zionism was based on black identity, black unity, black solidarity, black pride, and an aspiration for black revival. It was seen as an antithesis to white racism, black slavery, black degradation, and black oppression. It strove for the equality of the black race in a worldwide sense. In most cases it was not racism that strove for black superiority and for hostility towards whites. It was, in Sartre's classical phrase, "an antiracist racism." In this, too, there are striking similarities to Jewish Zionism, which wanted to create a new and strong Jewish nation in its historic homeland.

The notion of homecoming is central to Black Zionism, as it was to Jewish Zionism. Without the aspiration to return to the homeland, there is no Zionism. By way of caution we should mention that not all return to Africa was Zionist-inspired. In the eighteenth and nineteenth centuries white European abolitionists (like the British abolitionist Granville Sharp) and even "enlightened" racists (like the white men of the American Society for Colonizing the Free People of Color) advocated the resettlement of freed slaves in Africa as a human solution to the "negro problem." Again, we notice a striking similarity to Jewish Zionism, which was often supported by anti-Semites who wanted to encourage a Jewish exodus from Europe.

The motif of return has been evident ever since the slaves were taken to the New World. The metaphors—Egypt, Exodus, Moses, Promised Land—were all borrowed from the Old Testament. A few examples will suffice to illustrate this:

> I asked my Lord, shall I ever be the one
> (I asked my Lord) shall I ever be the one,
> shall I ever be the one, (I asked my Lord I be),
> To go sailin', sailin', sailin', sailin',
> Gwine over to the Promised Land?
>
> (*Slave Song*, in Jenkins 1975: 34)

> America to which our fathers were carried by violence, where we lived and still live by sufferance as unwelcome strangers, is not the rock whence we were hewn. Our residence there was and is transitional, like that of the Hebrews in Egypt, or Babylon, looking to an exodus. That exodus may never come for all; but the feeling and aspiration on the part of the exile must ever be towards the Fatherland, as the Jew, wherever he is, looks to Palestine, and in the depths of his soul continually exclaims, "If I forget thee O Jerusalem, let my right hand forget her cunning."
>
> (Blyden, in Drachler 1975: 56)

136 *Black Zionism: The Return to Africa in Theory and Practice*

We know where we're going, we know where we're from,
We're leaving Babylon, we're going to our fatherland.
Exodus, movement of Jah people,[3]
Movement of Jah people.
Send us another Brother Moses gonna cross the Red Sea ...
Jah come to break down oppression, rule equality,
Wipe away transgression, set the captives free.

(Bob Marley, *Exodus*, 1977: in Sundquist 2005: 127)

Black Zionism aimed to put an end to the suffering and oppression in exile by achieving black self-determination, black government, and black power in a liberated homeland. Excerpts from Blyden's and Garvey's writings speak for themselves:

If Europe is for the Europeans, then Africa shall be for the Black peoples of the world. We say it; we mean it... The other races have countries of their own and it is time for the four hundred million Negroes to claim Africa for themselves.

(Garvey, in Cronon 1955: 65)

Wake up Ethiopia! Wake up Africa! Let us work towards the one glorious end of a free, redeemed and mighty nation. Let Africa be a bright star among the constellations.

(Garvey 1967, Vol. I: 5–6)

The Negroes of the world say, we are striving towards Africa to make her the big Black republic.

(Garvey, in Jenkins 1975: 89)

Reacting to Booker Washington's integrationist book *The Story of the Negro*, which advocates the gradual integration of blacks into American society through professional advancement, Garvey asks:

Where is the Black man's Government? Where is his King and his kingdom? Where is his President, his country, and his ambassador, his army, his navy, his men of big affairs?

(Garvey 1967, Vol. II: 126)

Blyden, who greatly emphasized the importance of culture and roots, did not hide his view that Black Zionism was also about power and politics:

So long as we remain thus divided, we may expect impositions. So long as we live simply by the sufference of the nations, we must expect to be subject to their caprices ... We must build up negro states; we must establish

Black Zionism: The Return to Africa in Theory and Practice 137

and maintain the various institutions; we must make and administer laws, erect and preserve churches, and support the worship of God; we must have governments; we must have legislation of our own; we must build ships and navigate them; we must ply the trades, instruct the schools, control the press, and thus aid in shaping the opinions and guiding the destinies of mankind.

(Blyden "Liberia's Offering," 1862: in Esedebe 1982: 40)

The Praxis of Return

Very few blacks did return to Africa from the Americas, but throughout the nineteenth and twentieth centuries there were movements of return. The returnees came not only from North America (Canada and the US), but also from the Caribbeans (St. Thomas, Jamaica, Barbados, Cuba) and South America (Guyana, Brazil). They were known in West Africa by their countries of origin—Americans, Cubans, Brazilians. The best-known projects of return were to Sierra Leone (and its capital Freetown, the Town of the Free), which was a British colony until the 1960s, and Liberia (the so-called Land of the Free), which became independent in 1847. The "homecoming" to Sierra Leone started in 1786, and to Liberia in 1787. Between 1817 and 1857, approximately 13,000 African Americans made their home in Liberia. Monrovia, the capital of Liberia, is named after the American president James Monroe. Both projects were strongly supported by Whites— the British government and colonial authorities, in the case of Sierra Leone, and the American Colonization Society, a mix of white philanthropists and racists, in the case of Liberia. While the Afroo-Americans came mostly from the US, the Sierra Leonians came from captured slave ships on the high seas, and from Nova Scotia in Canada—many of them were Maroons from Jamaica. Many other groups did also support the Black cause—e.g., a group from Jamaica, which settled in today's Cameroon in 1842 and founded the colony of Victoria; a group from St. Kitts, which landed in Guinea in 1855; and groups of Afro-Cubans and Afro-Brazilians, which reached Nigeria (Lagos), Dahomey (today's Benin), and Togo in the nineteenth century (Geiss 1974: 24).

Paul Cuffee (1759–1817), an early Black Zionist and Quaker, born to a Black father and an American-Indian mother, propagated a return to Africa in the early nineteenth century. In 1815 he led a group of 40 Blacks from Boston, New York, and Philadelphia to Sierra Leone (Esedebe 1982: 9–10, Geiss 1974: 84). Another early Zionist and Harvard-trained Black physician, Martin Delany (1812–1885), was deeply influenced by Nat Turner's slave revolt in 1831. He came to the conclusion that blacks must be proud of their race, but could do so only if they were free in their African homeland. In 1854 he founded the National Emigration Convention in Ohio; and in 1859 he led the Niger Valley Exploration Party, and signed agreements with the chiefs of

138 *Black Zionism: The Return to Africa in Theory and Practice*

Abeokuta, allowing the foundation of colonies by returnees. His legacy was ideological rather than practical, since the Abeokuta agreements were never put into practice. His Zionist writings, however, were strong and forceful.

> Our policy must be ... Africa for the African race and Black men to rule over them.
>
> (Geiss 1974: 65)

> I had only one object in view—the moral, social and political elevation of ourselves and the regeneration of Africa.
>
> (Jenkins 1975: 93)

> Africa is our fatherland and we are its legitimate descendants ... Africa, to become regenerated, must have a national character, and her position among the existing nations of the earth will depend mainly upon the high standard she may gain compared with them in all her relations, morally, religiously, politically and commercially ... I have determined to leave to my children the inheritance of a country, the possession of territorial domain, the blessings of a national education, and the indisputable rights of self-government, that they may not succeed to the servility and degradation bequeathed to as by our fathers.
>
> (Jenkins 1975: 165)

As in Jewish Zionism, not all Zionists actually returned to Africa. Some simply did not make it, and others propagated Zionism while remaining in "exile." Alexander Crummell, a missionary, propagated a "return to the land of our fathers" (Jenkins 1975: 97) and went to Liberia in 1855. Together with Blyden, he founded the Liberia College of Social Sciences and Humanities in Monrovia, but he returned to the US in 1873. An additional important figure is Bishop Henry McNeal Turner, who was profoundly disappointed that the American Constitution did not protect the American blacks. He called the constitution a "dirty rag." From 1890 onwards, he arranged for ships to bring African Americans to Liberia, and personally made the trip in 1891. Three years later, in 1894, he founded the International Migration Society. Turner was also one of the organizers of the 1893 Chicago Congress on Africa. More important in the Zionist context is the foundation of a black-only Zionist Church, the African Methodist Episcopalian Church, which aimed to disentangle the movement of return from white patronage and philanthropy. It played a crucial role in the Zionist Garveyite mass-movement in the first half of the twentieth century. Turner regarded Africa as a "land of true wisdom, full of proud walking sons of Nature." For him, return to Africa was also a return to "nature" and "manhood" (Jenkins 1975: 99). Another colorful Zionist is Chief Alfred Sam, an African-born native of the Gold Coast (today's Ghana), who migrated to the US in 1911. He introduced himself as an Ashanti Chief and founded the Akim Trading Company in Oklahoma in

Black Zionism: The Return to Africa in Theory and Practice   139

1913. The idea behind the company was to export rubber and palm oil from Africa to the US and bring blacks from the US to Africa, so that ships would be usefully employed on both routes. Chief Sam's ideas were a mixture of business and politics.

> Our plan is to establish a government in which our race will be supreme. When our colony is established and the people of our race see that we are successful this boat will be crowded on every trip she makes to Africa.
> (Jenkins 1975: 105)

Chief Sam stressed the economic dimension of return. His "economic Pan-Africanism" was to lead to the development of an Africa ruled by a black government (Stein 1986: 110)

Other leading Zionists are the intellectual Edward W. Blyden (1832–1912) from St. Thomas, and the Jamaica-born agitator Marcus Garvey. Blyden was born in Charlotte-Amalie, the capital of the Danish-ruled island in 1832, well before slavery was abolished there in 1848. As a youth he went to America to study at the Rutgers Theological Seminary. He was not admitted because of his skin color, which led to his disgust with racist America, and his return (in 1850) to West Africa, where he built a splendid career, combining education, administration, diplomacy, and politics. He served, amongst others, as head of a secondary school, professor of Classics and Islamic studies at Liberia College, president of Liberia College, and director of Islamic education in Sierra Leone. In addition, he also was Liberia's consul for education in the US, his task being "to invite Negroes back to the Fatherland" (Neuberger 1985: 152), special envoy in Paris, ambassador in the UK, secretary of the interior, secretary of state, and candidate for the presidency.

All major ideas of twentieth century Black and African nationalism—Garvey's Black Zionism, Senghor's and Césaire's Négritude, Nkrumah's African Personality and Padmore's Pan-Africanism—had their roots in Blyden's late nineteenth-century writings. His Zionism represented a personal, ideological, intellectual, and emotional reaction to slavery, racism, discrimination, and exploitation of blacks by whites. His nationalism and Zionism called for black solidarity and authenticity, for a Black African culture based on music, art, and poetry—essentially, for a return to the roots. Blyden was not opposed to progress; he objected to blind imitation and assimilation:

> The African must advance by methods of his own ... he must show that we are able to go alone, to curve our own way.
> (Blyden, in Lynch 1970: 151)

The most prominent Black Zionist of the 1920s and 1930s is Marcus Garvey (1887–1940). Born in Jamaica and descendent of the Maroons (runaway slaves who had rebelled against slaveholders in the hills of Jamaica), he lacked any formal education, but became leader of an American mass movement that

140 *Black Zionism: The Return to Africa in Theory and Practice*

attracted millions of followers. He coined the phrase Black Zionism. In 1912–1914 he collaborated in London with the Egyptian-African Duse Muhammed Ali in publishing the *African Times and Orient Review*. Later on, he founded his organizational base in the US, the Universal Negro Improvement Association (UNIA), whose aims were as follows:

- to establish a universal confraternity among the race
- to promote the spirit of race pride and love
- to reclaim the fallen of the race
- to administer and assist the needy
- to assist in civilizing the backward tribes of Africa
- to strengthen the imperialism of independent African states
- to establish commissaries or agencies in the principal countries of the world for the protection of all Negroes, irrespective of nationality
- to promote a conscientious Christian worship among the native tribes of Africa
- to establish universities, colleges and secondary schools for the further education and culture of the boys and girls of the race
- to conduct a worldwide commercial and industrial intercourse. (Garvey, in Stein 1986: 30)

Garvey's goals were far-reaching: return to Africa by a black shipping line (the Black Star Line), liberation of Africa from white, colonial rule, and establishment of a black empire to represent black power and black independence. In fact, he established an "African Republic" (in New York), and an African government in exile, and an army, the Universal African Legion, which would reconquer Africa (Kinfe 2003: 106–107).[4] He was also active in establishing a black-only church, the African Orthodox Church.

UNIA's anthem—the "Negro Hatikvah" (Sundquist 2005: 126)—reflects its aims and explains its appeal to millions of American blacks in the American South and in the slums of the North:

I
Ethiopia, thou land of our fathers,
Thou land where the gods loved to be,
As storm cloud at night suddenly gathers
Our armies come rushing to thee.
We must in the fight be victorious When swords are thrust outward
    to gleam.
For us will the vict'ry be glorious
When led by the red, Black and green.

CHORUS
Advance, advance to victory,
Let Africa be free;

Black Zionism: The Return to Africa in Theory and Practice 141

Advance to meet the foe
With the might
Of the red, the Black and the green.

II
Ethiopia, the tyrant's falling,
Who smote thee upon thy knees,
And thy children are lustily callin
From over the distant seas.
Jehovah, the Great One has heard us,
Has noted our sighs and our tears,
With His spirit of Love he has stirred us
To be One through the coming years.

CHORUS
Advance, advance, etc.

III
O Jehovah, though God of ages
Grant unto our sons that lead
The wisdom Thou gave to Thy Sages
When Israel was sore in need.
Thy voice thro' the dim past has spoken,
Ethiopia shall stretch forth her hand
By thee shall all fetters be broken,
And Heav'n bless our dear Motherland.

CHORUS
Advance, advance, etc.

(Garvey 1970: 31–32)[5]

Garvey's Zionism was militant:

We are striking homewards towards Africa to make her the big Black republic. And in the making of Africa a big Black republic, what is the barrier? The barrier is the white man; and we say to the white man who now dominates Africa that it is to his interest to clear out of Africa now, because we are coming not as in the time of Father Abraham, 200,000 strong, but we are coming 400,000,000 strong, and we mean to retake every square inch of the 12,000,000 square miles of African territory belonging to us by right Divine… We are out to get what has belonged to us politically, socially, economically, and in every way. And what 15,000,000 of us cannot get we will call in 400,000,000 to help us get.

(Garvey, September 1920: in Jenkins 1975: 89)

142 *Black Zionism: The Return to Africa in Theory and Practice*

Garvey was in fact a right-wing Black Zionist. The emphasis he put on race was not merely defensive, compensatory, and egalitarian. He spoke of black superiority and purity, and hated lighter-skinned coloreds of "mixed" race. Garvey spoke of "African fundamentalism." For him God is black, Jesus is Black. He supported capitalism but thought business ought to be black. He also thanked white racists for having "lynched race pride into the Negroes" (Stein 1986: 154). Some of his opponents even called his racial messages, populism, and demagogy "black fascism."

The Garveyites were not only active in America. UNIA also had branches in West Africa. The Lagos branch was founded and headed by the Jamaican Amos Shackleford (1887–1954), who had "returned" to Africa in 1913 and became a leading businessman, intellectual, and politician. He was vice-president of the Nigerian National Democratic Party (NNDP), and leading member of NCNC, the Nigerian Council of Nigeria and the Cameroons (Falola 2004: 60).

After World War II, anticolonial nationalism expanded rapidly all over Africa.

In 1957 the Gold Coast (today's Ghana) became the first British colony to gain independence—to be followed by Guinea, the first French colony to claim its sovereignty. Over the course of the following decade, most other British and French colonies and protectorates, and Belgian-ruled Congo, Rwanda, and Burundi, and Italian Somalia followed suit. It did not happen the Garveyist way. No Afro-American army "liberated" Africa. Decolonization was a result of internal changes in Africa and in the Western colonial countries, in which Black Zionism hardly played a role. Nevertheless, the 1950s saw leading Black Zionists return to Africa. Nkrumah's Ghana attracted major Black Zionist leaders. William E.B. Du Bois, though already in his nineties, settled in Ghana in 1961 to become the editor of the planned Encyclopedia Africana, but his death at the age of 95 put an end to the project. Three major Pan-African leaders from the Caribbeans—George Padmore from Jamaica (author of *Pan-Africanism or Communism*), Ras Makonnen from British Guyana, and Frantz Fanon, the world-famous psychoanalyst and radical nationalist ideologue from Martinique—became Nkrumah's advisors on nation-building and international affairs. The African scholar Ali Mazrui saw Du Bois's and Padmore's death "as citizens of Ghana ... as a Back to Africa event of unique symbolism" (Mazrui 1975: 234). Later on, the American Black Power leader Stokely Carmichael settled in Sekou Touré's Guinea. Carmichael later changed his name to Kwame Touré. Another Black Zionist group that settled in Liberia in the 1960s, and later in Israel, are the Black Hebrews, who consider Israel as part of Africa, and the Suez Canal as an artificial barrier of little significance.

Black Zionism and Zionism

The term Black Zionism is not fortuitous. It reflects the impact of Jewish Zionism on Black Zionism. The Jewish Question was compared to the Negro

Black Zionism: The Return to Africa in Theory and Practice   143

Question, the Jewish diaspora to the African diaspora, persecution of Jews to persecution of Blacks. These analogies eventually led to the pursuit of similar solutions—Jewish Zionism and Black Zionism. This raises the obvious question as to what Black Zionism had to say about Jewish Zionism.

From an early age Blyden became interested in the Jewish situation. He grew up on so-called Jew Hill, and amongst Jews, in Danish St. Thomas. He learned Hebrew, and in 1866 even visited Palestine. An account of this trip was published in *From West Africa to Palestine*. Later on, he wrote a booklet *On the Jewish Question* (1898). In his writings he referred to Palestine as the Land of Israel, and to the period of independence and glory of the Jewish people as a period of "wonderful prosperity as a Jewish nation in Canaan" (Blyden 1873: 121). He spoke about the return of the Jews to their historic homeland.

> There is one subject however upon which there seems to be remarkable unanimity among the principal sects—Jews, Christians and Muslims— with regard to the final destiny of Jerusalem: that is to be the scene of latter day glories, that the Jews are to be restored to the Land of their Fathers and the Messiah to "be enthroned."
>
> (Blyden 1873: 199)

A year after the First Zionist Congress, he wrote:

> There is hardly a man in the civilized world—Christian, Mohamedan or Jew—who does not recognize the claim and the right of the Jew to the Holy Land and there are few who, if conditions were favorable, would not be glad to see them return in a body and take their place in the Land of their Fathers as a great, leading secular power.
>
> (Blyden 1898: 8)

For Blyden, Herzl was "a new Moses, dedicated to the liberation of his oppressed people." When Herzl died in 1904, Blyden held a eulogy in Monrovia for the man who strove "for the repatriation of the Jews to the ancient homeland" (Blyden, in Holden 1966: 784). He clearly saw Zionism as a model for the African diaspora.

> I have taken and do take the deepest possible interest in the current history of the Jews, especially in that marvelous movement called Zionism. The question in some of its aspects is similar to that which at this moment agitates thousands of descendants of Africa in America anxious to return to the Land of their Fathers.
>
> (Blyden 1898: 7)

As noted before, Garvey was in a sense a fascist Black Zionist—just as there were, especially in the 1920s, fascist Jewish Zionists. Indeed, his hatred of whites

144 *Black Zionism: The Return to Africa in Theory and Practice*

also implied hatred of Jews. What interests us in the context of this chapter, however, is the analogy between both kinds of Zionism, Black and Jewish. For Garvey, "Africa is for the Africans [which includes Afro-Americans, B.N.] like Palestine [is] for the Jews." He aimed to establish "another [Black, B.N.] Palestine in Africa." His reference to Zionism also had an instrumental character: He thought that "the recognition of the Jew may help the Negro to force his argument for his free state."

Du Bois's Black Zionism was more cultural, less power oriented. Sundquist calls it "a model of race-based diasporic consciousness" (Sundquist 2005: 123). Nevertheless, his analogy is not very different from Garvey's. At the First Pan-African Conference (in fact, Pan-Black Conference, B.N.) in 1919, he exclaimed:

> The African movement means to us what the Zionist movement must mean to the Jews, the centralization of race effort and the recognition of the racial fount.
>
> (Du Bois, *Crisis,* February 1919: 166)

His Zionism was deeply moral. It was less the actual return to Africa than the aspiration for dignity, equality, roots, and opposition to assimilation. As to Jewish Zionism, its moral dimension had become even more self-evident to him after the Holocaust.

> [The] theoretical demand for a Zion now became a necessity for more than a million displaced and homeless Jews. There was actually no other place on earth for them to go.
>
> (Chicago Star, 1948)

> The Jew wandering through Europe has for two thousand years been fighting for a place.
>
> (ibid.)

The million Jewish survivors of the Holocaust had a human right to go to the Jewish homeland where there is room for them, where there is work for them to do, "where what Jews have already done is for the advantage, not simply of the Jews but of the Arabs" (ibid.)

Du Bois even accused the British of being at least partly responsible for the Holocaust because they closed the gates of Palestine for the Jews who wanted to escape from Nazi Europe, although for the Jews Palestine was "the country of their origin." For Du Bois, Jewish migration to Palestine/Israel is not "colonial" settlement of a foreign land. It is, on the contrary, a return: The Jews simply "go back to Zion and refound a state which they have lost" (ibid.).

The similarities of Jewish and Black Zionism are indeed striking, although Jewish Zionism was a success story while Black Zionism was a failure in the sense that there was no massive exodus from the diaspora.

Black Zionism: The Return to Africa in Theory and Practice   145

Both Zionisms defined the Jewish problem and the Negro question as national or racial questions. For Du Bois the problem of the twentieth century is the problem of the color line—the relation of the darker to the lighter races of men in Asia, in Africa, in America and the islands of the seas (Du Bois 1903: 13).

The similarity between Jewish and Black Zionist terminology is indeed striking: diaspora, exile, historic homeland, return, persecution, statehood, cultural roots, new man. The Zionist idea of "normalization," so central in Socialist Zionism, also emerges in Black Zionism.

> "Black cops, Black customs men, Black pilots, Black guys refuelling the plane, Black managers of airports, Black, Black, Black, man," said an American. But you know, you get this funny feeling too. You've been so long indoctrinated that these jobs, well they're so skillful that no Black guy can do them. You honestly feel Christ! what's a Black guy doing around that plane? It's all gotten so far inside you that you too, just for a moment, wonder if they're really competent. How about that? You hear yourself thinking that, and by God you laugh, and I remember laughing, why of course they're competent, I'm home! It's *them* that runs it all, it's *us*! How can you explain that to anybody who has never felt the discrimination of the United States? You are just so happy, and man, you just want to shout, hell, Black can do it ... Black guys *do* it!
>
> (Jenkins 1975: 141–142)

Black Zionists, well aware that not all blacks would return to the homeland, talked about the significant contribution a rebuilt Africa would make to the identity, pride, and security of those who stayed behind in exile. Indeed, while black America inspired African nationalism until the Second World War, in the 1950s and 1960s, many blacks in the diaspora took deep pride in the African struggle for independence.

There are also similarities between the Pan-African and the Zionist conferences and congresses—between the 1942 Zionist Biltmore Conference (where a clear demand for a Jewish state was voiced for the first time) and the 1945 Manchester Pan-African Congress (where black leaders of Africa, together with American blacks such as Du Bois, Padmore, Makonnen, and Amy Garvey, called for the first time for self-determination and complete independence). In fact, a major slogan of the Manchester Conference was "Down with anti-Semitism."

The Black Zionist dream of a new Egypt, Ethiopia, Ghana, Mali, or Zimbabwe—all African kingdoms—was not very different from the Zionist dream of a new Judea. On the Black Zionist right wing, Garvey's dream of a black army that would conquer Africa was similar to dreams of the Jewish Zionist right wing. So was the readiness of both Jewish and black right-wing Zionists to enlist the support of their worst enemies, who in fact wanted to get rid of both Jews and blacks. Just as Jabotinsky negotiated with the Ukrainian

146 *Black Zionism: The Return to Africa in Theory and Practice*

nationalist and anti-Semite Petliura, Garvey established contacts with the Ku Klux Klan.

Another interesting similarity is the importance both movements attached to culture. Black Zionists saw the establishment of a reputable university—the returnees' Fourah Bay College in Sierra Leone was founded in 1827—as crucially important. A similar act of spiritual, intellectual, and emotional revival was the foundation in 1925 of the Hebrew University of Jerusalem.

From almost any perspective, it is not only justifiable, but almost unavoidable, to speak about Black Zionism and its similarity to Jewish Zionism. Further research on Black Zionism and its relationship to Jewish Zionism may help to heal the deepening rift that has developed between blacks and Jews in the last decades.

Notes

1 This chapter was originally published as "Chapter Thirty. Black Zionism—The Return to Africa in Theory and Practice" pp. 595–611 in *Transnationalism: Diasporas and the Advent of a New (Dis)Order*, edited by Eliezer Ben-Rafael and Yitzhak Sternberg, originally published in 2009 by Brill.
2 To avoid anachronism in this chapter, I do use the terms "Negro" and "Black," which were prevalent in the nineteenth and twentieth centuries, and routinely used by African Americans at the time.
3 Jah = Yahweh, from Eli-jah.
4 The intention to build an army was declared, but never realized.
5 https://en.wikisource.org/wiki/The_Universal_Ethiopian_Anthem_and_How_it_Came_to_be_Written.

Bibliography

Blyden, E.W. (1856). *A Voice from Bleeding Africa on Behalf of her Exiled Children*. Liberia: G. Killian, Printer.
——. (1873). *From West Africa to Palestine*. Freetown: T.J. Sawyer Publishers.
——. (1898). *On the Jewish Question*. Liverpool: Lionel Hart and Co.
Cronon, E. (1955). *Black Moses: The Study of Marcus Garvey and the Universal Negro Improve–ment Association*. Madison: University of Wisconsin Press.
Drachler, J. (ed.). (1975). *Black Homeland, Black Diaspora*. Port Washington, NY: National University Publications.
Du Bois, W.E.B. (1903). *The Souls of Black Folk*. Chicago: A.C. McClure.
——. February 1919, June 1921. *Crisis*.
Esedebe, P.O. (1982). *Pan-Africanism: The Idea and the Movement, 1776–1963*. Washington: Howard University Press.
Falola, T. (2004). *Nationalism and African Intellectuals*. Rochester, NY: University of Rochester Press.
Garvey, A.J. (1970). *Garvey and Garveyism*. London: Collier-Macmillan.
Garvey, M.M. (compiled by A.J. Garvey, vol. I, II). (1967). *Philosophy and Opinions*. London: F. Cass.
Geiss, I. (1974/1968). *The Pan-African Movement*. London: Methuen.

Holden, E. (1966). *Blyden of Liberia*. New York: Vantage Press.

Hughes, L. (1959). *Selected Poems*. New York: Knopf.

Jenkins, D. (1975). *Black Zion: The Return of Afro-Americans and West Indians to Africa*. London: Wildwood House.

Kinfe, A. (2003/1991). *Politics of Black Nationalism: From Harlem to Soweto*. Trenton, NJ: Africa World Press.

Lynch, H.R. (1970/1967). *Edward Wilmot Blyden: Pan-Negro Patriot*. Oxford: Oxford University Press.

Mazrui, A. (1975). "New World Roots of Pan-Africanism," pp. 228–236 in J. Drachler (ed.), *Black Homeland, Black Diaspora*. Port Washington, NY: National University Publications.

Neuberger, B. (1985). "Early African Nationalism, Judaism and Zionism: Edward Wilmot Blyden," *Jewish Social Studies* XLVII(2): 151–166.

Stein, J. (1986). *The World of Marcus Garvey: Race and Class in Modern Society*. Baton Rouge: Louisiana State University Press.

Sundquist, E.J. (2005). *Blacks, Jews, Post-Holocaust America*. Cambridge, MA: Harvard University Press.

12 Conclusion

National ideologies began to emerge in Africa before political decolonization actually commenced. Once decolonization processes were underway, these ideologies supplemented them and subsequently continued to develop in different directions even after African states achieved independence. National ideologies, which emphasized cultural and racial qualities and represented all blacks in all diasporas, characterized the initial phase of awakening and subsequently dissipated gradually. Racial-cultural nationalism, which one researcher viewed as "a determined effort on the part of black peoples to rediscover their shrines from the wreckage of history [and] a revolt against the white man's ideological suzerainty in culture, politics and historiography,"[1] underwent an important phase in coping with white racism, the cornerstone of European colonialism, and in endeavoring to revive African culture. After World War II there emerged national ideologies that emphasized politics and territory and focused on the African inhabitants of Africa. The main demand posed by the new African nationalism was to oust colonial rule as a condition for the liberation and welfare of the African peoples.

Once the goal of African states' independence from foreign rule was established, the national ideologies shifted their focus to disputes over the borders of the anticipated national entities: continental Pan-Africanism, which sought the unification of all the independent states on the one hand, ethnic nationalism on the other, and in-between, a territorial nationalism based on the colonial borders. At the conclusion of the decolonization process it was the colonial format that received political validation and survived, despite the many attempts to derail it. In those colonies where the colonial authorities refused to loosen their grip and prevented Africans from pursuing legitimate courses of action, decolonization took the form of prolonged violence and often generated radical, revolutionary anticolonial ideologies. These ideologies sought not only the official removal of foreign rule, but also the creation of a new social order free of any colonial imprint, and they rejected future relations with the colonial power specifically and with the West generally.

One of the interesting questions in the evolution of African nationalism is its attitude toward the legacy of colonialism and former colonial powers. One of the common denominators shared by all the national ideologies that

DOI: 10.4324/9781003322818-13

Conclusion 149

emerged in Africa was the tension inherent in the combination of a unique, "authentic" African identity and the influence of European ideas through which this uniqueness was to be expressed. The fact that African nationalism in all its forms used European languages, ideas, and values, whether liberal or socialist, to identify and express its uniqueness reflects the depth of Europe's influence on Africa. The ideologies continued to develop, as noted, even after independence, which in turn gives rise to interesting questions: What were the roles assigned to ideology in the transition from anticolonial struggle to independence, when it became necessary to cope with political, social, and economic challenges? How were ideologies translated into political action? Which ideas were infused into the newly attained independence? Addressing these ideological aspects will require further in-depth examination of the political system in independent African states.

Note

1 Bernard Magubane, *The Ties That Bind: African-American Consciousness of Africa* (Trenton: Africa World Press, 1987), p. 230.

Appendix 1: Albert Memmi

Albert Memmi, "Mythical Portrait of the Colonized," in *The Colonizer and the Colonized* (Boston: Beacon Press, 1965), 79–86.

Just as the bourgeoisie proposes an image of the proletariat, the existence of the colonizer requires that an image of the colonized be suggested. These images become excuses without which the presence and conduct of a colonizer, and that of a bourgeois, would seem shocking. But the favored image becomes a myth precisely because it suits them too well.

Let us imagine, for the sake of this portrait and accusation, the often-cited trait of laziness. It seems to receive unanimous approval of colonizers from Liberia to Laos, via the Maghreb. It is easy to see to what extent this description is useful. It occupies an important place in the dialectics exalting the colonizer and humbling the colonized. Furthermore, it is economically fruitful.

Nothing could better justify the colonizer's privileged position than his industry, and nothing could better justify the colonized's destitution than his indolence. The mythical portrait of the colonized therefore includes an unbelievable laziness, and that of the colonizer, a virtuous taste for action. At the same time the colonizer suggests that employing the colonized is not very profitable, thereby authorizing his unreasonable wages.

It may seem that colonization would profit by employing experienced personnel. Nothing is less true. A qualified worker existing among the colonizers earns three or four times more than does the colonized, while he does not produce three or four times as much, either in quantity or in quality. It is more advantageous to use three of the colonized than one European. Every firm needs specialists, of course, but only a minimum of them, and the colonizer imports or recruits experts among his own kind. In addition, there is the matter of the special attention and legal protection required by a European worker. The colonized, however, is only asked for his muscles; he is so poorly evaluated that three or four can be taken on for the price of one European.

From listening to him, on the other hand, one finds that the colonizer is not so displeased with that laziness, whether supposed or real. He talks of it

Appendix 1: Albert Memmi 151

with amused affability, he jokes about it, he takes up all the usual expressions, perfects them, and invents others. Nothing can describe well enough the extraordinary deficiency of the colonized. He becomes lyrical about it, in a negative way. The colonized does not let grass grow under his feet, but a tree, and what a tree! A eucalyptus, an American centenarian oak! A tree? No, a forest!

But, one will insist, is the colonized truly lazy? To tell the truth, the question is poorly stated. Besides having to define a point of reference, a norm, varying from one people to another, can one accuse an entire people of laziness? It can be suspected of individuals, even many of them in a single group. One can wonder if their output is mediocre, whether malnutrition, low wages, a closed future, a ridiculous conception of a role in society, does not make the colonized uninterested in his work. What is suspect is that the accusation is not directed solely at the farm laborer or slum resident, but also at the professor, engineer or physician who does the same number of hours of work as his colonizer colleagues; indeed, all individuals of the colonized group are accused. Essentially, the independence of the accusation from any sociological or historical conditions makes it suspect.

… By his accusation the colonizer establishes the colonized as being lazy. He decides that laziness is constitutional in the very nature of the colonized. It becomes obvious that the colonized, whatever he may undertake, whatever zeal he may apply, could never be anything but lazy. This always brings us back to racism, which is the substantive expression, to the accuser's benefit, of a real or imaginary trait of the accused.

It is possible to proceed with the same analysis for each of the features found in the colonized.

Whenever the colonizer states, in his language, that the colonized is a weakling, he suggests thereby that this deficiency requires protection. From this comes the concept of a protectorate. It is in the colonized's own interest that he be excluded from management functions, and that those heavy responsibilities be reserved for the colonizer. Whenever the colonizer adds, in order not to fall prey to anxiety, that the colonized is a wicked, backward person with evil, thievish, somewhat sadistic instincts, he thus justifies his police [*sic* policy] and his legitimate severity. After all, he must defend himself against the dangerous foolish acts of the irresponsible, and at the same time—what meritorious concern!—protect him against himself! It is the same for the colonized's lack of desires, his ineptitude for comfort, science, progress, his astonishing familiarity with poverty. Why should the colonizer worry about things that hardly trouble the interested party? It would be, he adds with dark and insolent philosophy, doing him a bad turn if he subjected him to the disadvantages of civilization. After all, remember that wisdom is Eastern; let us accept, as he does, the colonized's wretchedness. The same reasoning is also true for the colonized's notorious ingratitude; the colonizer's acts of charity are wasted, the improvements the colonizer has made are not appreciated. It is impossible to save the colonized from this myth—a portrait of wretchedness has been indelibly engraved.

152   *Appendix 1: Albert Memmi*

It is significant that this portrait requires nothing else. It is difficult, for instance, to reconcile most of these features and then to proceed to synthesize them objectively. One can hardly see how the colonized can be simultaneously inferior and wicked, lazy and backward.

What is more, the traits ascribed to the colonized are incompatible with one another, though this does not bother his prosecutor. He is depicted as frugal, sober, without many desires and, at the same time, he consumes disgusting quantities of meat, fat, alcohol, anything; as a coward who is afraid of suffering and as a brute who is not checked by any inhibitions of civilization, etc. It is additional proof that it is useless to seek this consistency anywhere except in the colonizer himself. At the basis of the entire construction, one finally finds a common motive; the colonizer's economic and basic needs, which he substitutes for logic, and which shape and explain each of the traits he assigns to the colonized. In the last analysis, these traits are all advantageous to the colonizer, even those which at first sight seem damaging to him.

The point is that the colonized means little to the colonizer. Far from wanting to understand him as he really is, the colonizer is preoccupied with making him undergo this urgent change. The mechanism of this remolding of the colonized is revealing in itself. It consists, in the first place, of a series of negations. The colonized is not this, not that. He is never considered in a positive light; or if he is, the quality which is conceded is the result of a psychological or ethical failing. Thus it is with Arab hospitality, which is difficult to consider as a negative characteristic. If one pays attention, one discovers that the praise comes from tourists, visiting Europeans, and not colonizers, i.e., Europeans who have settled down in the colony. As soon as he is settled, the European no longer takes advantage of this hospitality, but cuts off intercourse and contributes to the barriers which plague the colonized. He rapidly changes palette to portray the colonized, who becomes jealous, withdrawn, intolerant and fanatical. What happens to the famous hospitality? Since he cannot deny it, the colonizer then brings into play the shadows and describes the disastrous consequences.

This hospitality is a result of the colonized's irresponsibility and extravagance, since he has no notion of foresight and economy. From the wealthy down to the fellah, the festivities are wonderful and bountiful: but what happens afterward? The colonized ruins himself, borrows, and finally pays with someone else's money! Does one speak, on the other hand, of the modesty of the colonized's life? It is no longer a proof of wisdom but of stupidity—as if, then, every recognized or invented trait had to be an indication of negativity.

Thus, one after another, all the qualities which make a man of the colonized crumble away. The humanity of the colonized, rejected by the colonizer, becomes opaque. It is useless, he asserts, to try to forecast the colonized's actions ("They are unpredictable!" "With them, you never know!"). It seems to him that strange and disturbing impulsiveness controls the colonized. The colonized must indeed be very strange, if he remains so mysterious after years of living with the colonizer.

Another sign of the colonized's depersonalization is what one might call the mark of the plural. The colonized is never characterized in an individual manner; he is entitled only to drown in an anonymous collectivity ("They are this." "They are all the same."). If a colonized servant does not come in one morning, the colonizer will not say that she is ill, or that she is cheating, or that she is tempted not to abide by an oppressive contract. (Seven days a week; colonized domestics rarely enjoy the one day off a week granted to others.) He will say, "You can't count on them." It is not just a grammatical expression. He refuses to consider personal, private occurrences in his maid's life; that life in a specific sense does not interest him, and his maid does not exist as an individual.

Finally, the colonizer denies the colonized the most precious right granted to most men: liberty. Living conditions imposed on the colonized by colonization make no provision for it; indeed, they ignore it. The colonized has no way out of his state of woe—neither a legal outlet (naturalization) nor a religious outlet (conversion). The colonized is not free to choose between being colonized or not being colonized.

What is left of the colonized at the end of this stubborn effort to dehumanize him? He is surely no longer an alter ego of the colonizer. He is hardly a human being. He tends rapidly toward becoming an object. As an end, in the colonizer's supreme ambition, he should exist only as a function of the needs of the colonizer, i.e., be transformed into a pure colonized.

Appendix 2: Alioune Diop

Alioune Diop, "Remarks on African Personality and Négritude," in *Pan-Africanism Reconsidered*, edited by the American Society of African Culture (Berkeley: University of California Press, 1962), 337–345.

We, the inhabitants, the black peoples of these countries of sub-Saharan Africa, have been the victims of slavery; the inhabitants of the Antilles also suffered grievously from it. And we know that movements such as Pan-Africanism, at least on the intellectual level, were born from the struggle carried on by America against racism, and emanated from there, by a sort of gesture of solidarity, to Africa. And we know that the Negro personality, its context and contents, was launched by the Africans in Paris and the Antilles and incarnated by African writers—especially by the people of the Antilles. They are twice-uprooted people, because, unlike the Africans, they have not had the advantage of retaining their roots in African soil and because, unlike the Americans, they have not had the advantage of living in a modern and developed society. Consequently, we had reasons to limit ourselves initially to the history, the art, and the various creation of the Negro, for the Negro has been the most scoffed at by bistory; but for many years now—and you can verify this by leafing through certain issues of *Présence Africaine*—North Africans have been collaborating with us. ...

Pan-Africanism was launched here [in Africa B.N.] and was of an essentially intellectual nature. Many years after its birth, the African peoples and their leaders—some of their leaders—took hold of Pan-Africanism and made an elaborate doctrine of it, adapted to our aspirations and our situation. Each country or each cultural region has its terminology; in France, we invented *Négritude* (negro-ness); in the Anglo-Saxon countries, they invented Pan-Africanism; and together we launched another expression with the same perspective, the African personality.

Well, as to this African personality, we are often asked what does it mean, where does it come from, where does it lead to? I should like simply to recall the moving eyewitness account that our friend from South Africa [Ezekiel Mphahlele] has given us, describing to you the particularly alarming and anxious feelings of those who find themselves in a sort of ghetto. African,

Appendix 2: Alioune Diop   155

especially black Africans, have lived for centuries in a kind of ghetto, a cultural ghetto, and a sort of economic ghetto.

We are reaching a period in history when it would seem that, on a theoretical plane, the problem of independence finds its solution in political independence. But we must not forget that political independence will never be total until the moment when it is assured on both the economic and the cultural levels.

The struggle is far from being over; even on the political level, it is far from over. It is probable that on the economic level we shall encounter still greater difficulties. And, what can be said about cultural independence? For we have finally understood the anxiety of those among our Western friends who mistrust the constant evocation of our originality, and who repeat to us that men are alike. They are perfectly right—men *are* alike—we have always thought so, and we cried it aloud. At that time, we were reminded, however, of differences between us; now we are on the threshold of independence, and we see the emphasis shift to the similarities of humanity in all races.

They are right, but they would be wrong to want to prohibit us from underlining our characteristics, because it is in the name of these very characteristics that we can incorporate ourselves into a general movement ... Africa will ultimately be politically independent. But I believe that the struggle will not be ended thus; for Africa to be politically, formally, independent in a world built along Western lines and Western philosophically and economic options, that world must be remodeled, reconstructed, so that the interests of diverse communities are in equilibrium—and when I say interests, I mean cultural interests; for history, official history, the only one that is widely known, the only one that is heeded and read, is Western and largely influenced and even dominated by the perspectives or problems, if you wish, of the Western hegemony.

History must be remodelled from top to bottom, and I believe that whatever reservations one might harbour toward such a task, toward its hypotheses, we must render homage to the initiative of men such as Cheik Anta Diop who were the first to put their finger on the falsifications of history throughout the centuries, to the advantage of a minority—the white minority—and the disadvantages of the colored peoples.

History must be the histories of all peoples or it is not history. Similarly with other studies. It is certain that in the field of poetry, as in the arts in general, we come face to face with reality—which should be accessible to all temperaments. It has often been said that art knows no homeland; our hearts must be prepared to love all forms of art. We Africans have taken a great stride toward the West as far as integrating ourselves more or less into that culture: we have come to love the great Western musicians, the great sculptors, the great artists, the great writers; ... it is to be desired that the West might display an equal love for the arts that please us, for the arts that enchant our people, and in such a way would communion be possible.

156 *Appendix 2: Alioune Diop*

But if one operates as the leaders of the French Communist Party seem to want to operate, it is probable that this communion will be difficult. You will recall that some years ago the leader of the intellectuals of the French Communist Party, Louis Aragon, a great poet and novelist, began to rule on rights and mete out duties. The French Communist poets were to write only in the sonnet form, which is the product of French emotion. The reaction of some Negro poets—who believed that other forms, another style, other vocables, were better suited to translate fully and authentically the message they had to give—is understandable. This cultural imperialism[,] which men like Aimé Césaire encountered in the Communist Party to such a degree that they left it, is not confined to the Communist Party, but exists in many milieus and many men of the Western cultural world.

You will remember that on many occasions the leaders of the Western cultural world peremptorily affirmed that the experience of the Universal had been attained and exhausted by the West, that the Negro world had nothing to do but docilely insert itself into the Western cultural current, and that it was not only childish but dangerous to speak of other cultures than that of the West. This tendency, which lasted for many years, is today breached; we know that from all parts of the Negro world voices are being raised up to remind us of what the West has forgotten: that the Universal is only a goal and that the Universalist world will only be achieved by all peoples and their geniuses. This will perhaps be more clearly illustrated if we refer to the Christian world. Christianity, as has been remarked, is often considered by militant African nationalists as the quartermaster of colonialism—and simply because Christianity developed in the West and borrowed from Western culture its music, its art, its philosophy, the shape of its dogmatism … Well, Christian Africans and even priests and pastors, have long been raising their voices to point out that if the Christian message is universal, Western forms are simply the means that the churches employ to transmit the Christian message. It is not indispensable to sing Gregorian chants; it is not necessary to refer to Aristotelian philosophy to express what Christ expressed simply: "Love thy neighbour."

It is undeniable that from the resources of our cultural traditions of animism and with the necessary prudence of the true believer, Christianity can legitimately be enriched by legitimate contributions to the music, the liturgy, and the philosophy of the Christian world. What is true of Christianity and history is true in other areas such as economy and sociology. Indeed, I am speaking of a veritable revolution, which Negro poets and all colored men, the cultured men of the non-Western countries, will undertake, not only on the level of their national life (of which I shall speak in a moment), where they will be recruited to affirm their destiny, but also on international levels.

They desire that, on the level of world events, in all studies and all institutions, the initiatives and the responsibilities be mutual. We are not children, we are adults; and it might even be said that we have nothing to learn from the Western culture for which we could not find an equivalent in our own cultures. The only misfortune is that these cultures are based on institutions, on an economy, and on a political freedom which are shaken and frustrated by colonialism. But we are convinced that our cultures are as organic, as deserving of respect and as rich as Western culture—and we have the advantage over Westerners here, for we have for the most part experienced that culture in all its dimensions.

Appendix 3: Frantz Fanon

Frantz Fanon, "The Ordeal of The Black Man" [L'expérience vécue du Noir], chapter five in *Black Skin, White Masks* (New York: Grove Press, 1965), 109–140 (1967 translation by Constance Farrington).

"Dirty nigger!" Or simply, "Look, a Negro!"

I came into the world imbued with the will to find a meaning in things, my spirit filled with the desire to attain to the source of the world, and then I found that I was an object in the midst of other objects.

Sealed into that crushing objecthood, I turned beseechingly to others. Their attention was a liberation, running over my body suddenly abraded into nonbeing, endowing me once more with an agility that I had thought lost, and by taking me out of the world, restoring me to it. But just as I reached the other side, I stumbled, and the movements, the attitudes, the glances of the other fixed me there, in the sense in which a chemical solution is fixed by a dye. I was indignant; I demanded an explanation. Nothing happened. I burst apart. Now the fragments have been put together again by another self.

As long as the black man is among his own, he will have no occasion, except in minor internal conflicts, to experience his being through others . ... [p. 109]

For not only must the black man be black; he must be black in relation to the white man. Some critics will take it on themselves to remind us that this proposition has a converse [double meaning]. I say that this is false. The black man has no ontological resistance in the eyes of the white man. Overnight the Negro has been given two frames of reference within which he has had to place himself. His metaphysics, or, less pretentiously, his customs and the sources on which they were based, were wiped out because they were in conflict with a civilization that he did not know and that imposed itself on him.

The black man among his own in the twentieth century does not know at what moment his inferiority comes into being through the other. Of course, I have talked about the black problem with friends, or, more rarely, with American Negroes. Together we protested, we asserted the equality of all men in the world. In the Antilles there was also that little gulf that exists among the almost-white [la békaille], the mulatto [la mulâtraille] and the nigger [la

Appendix 3: Frantz Fanon 159

négraille]. But I was satisfied with an intellectual understanding of these differences. It was not really dramatic. And then ...

And then the occasion arose when I had to meet the white man's eyes. An unfamiliar weight burdened me. The real world challenged my claims. In the white world the man of color encounters difficulties in the development of his bodily schema. Consciousness of the body is solely a negating activity. It is a third-person consciousness. The body is surrounded by an atmosphere of certain uncertainty ...

For several years certain laboratories have been trying to produce a serum for "denegrification"; with all the earnestness in the world, laboratories have sterilized their test tubes, checked their scales, and embarked on researches that might make it possible for the miserable Negro to whiten himself and thus to throw off the burden of that corporeal malediction ... [pp. 110–111]

In *Anti-Semite and Jew* (p. 95), Sartre says: "They [the Jews] have allowed themselves to be poisoned by the stereotype that others have of them, and they live in fear that their acts will correspond to this stereotype ... We may say that their conduct is perpetually overdetermined from the inside." ...

I move slowly in the world, accustomed now to seek no longer for upheaval. I progress by crawling. And already I am being dissected under white eyes, the only real eyes. I am *fixed*. Having adjusted their microtomes, they objectively cut away slices of my reality. I am laid bare. I feel, I see in those white faces that it is not a new man who has come in, but a new kind of man, a new genus. Why, it's a Negro!

I slip into corners, and my long antennae pick up the catch-phrases strewn over the surface of things—nigger underwear smells of nigger—nigger teeth are white—nigger feet are big—the nigger's barrel chest—I slip into corners, I remain silent, I strive for anonymity, for invisibility. Look, I will accept the lot, as long as no one notices me! ...

Shame. Shame and self-contempt. Nausea. When people like me, they tell me it is in spite of my color. When they dislike me, they point out it is not because of my color. Either way, I am locked into the infernal circle. ... [pp. 115–116]

The evidence was there, unalterable. My blackness was there, dark and unarguable. And it tormented me, pursued me, disturbed me, angered me.

Negroes are savages, brutes, illiterates. But in my own case I knew that these statements were false. There was a myth of the Negro that had to be destroyed at all costs. The time had long since passed when a Negro priest was an occasion for wonder. We had physicians, professors, statesmen. Yes, but something out of the ordinary still clung to such cases. "We have a Senegalese history teacher. He is quite bright ... Our doctor is colored. He is very gentle."

It was always the Negro teacher, the Negro doctor; brittle as I was becoming, I shivered at the slightest pretext. I knew, for instance, that if the physician made a mistake it would be the end of him and of all those who came after him. What could one expect, after all, from a Negro physician?

160   *Appendix 3: Frantz Fanon*

As long as everything went well, he was praised to the skies, but look out, no nonsense, under any conditions! The black physician can never be sure how close he is to disgrace. I tell you, I was walled in: No exception was made for my refined manners, or my knowledge of literature, or my understanding of the quantum theory.

I requested, I demanded explanations. Gently, in the tone that one uses with a child, they introduced me to the existence of a certain view that was held by certain people, but, I was always told, "We must hope that it will soon disappear." What was it? Color prejudice.

> It [colour prejudice] is nothing more than the unreasoning hatred of one race for another, the contempt of the stronger and richer peoples for those whom they consider inferior to themselves and the bitter resentment of those who are kept in subjection and are so frequently insulted. As colour is the most obvious outward manifestation of race it has been made the criterion by which men are judged, irrespective of their social or educational attainments. The light-skinned races have come to despise all those of a darker colour, and the dark-skinned peoples will no longer accept without protest the inferior position to which they have been relegated.[1]

I had it rightly. It was hate; I was hated, despised, detested, not by the neighbor across the street or my cousin on my mother's side, but by an entire race. I was up against something unreasoned. The psychoanalysts say that nothing is more traumatizing for the young child than his encounters with what is rational. I would personally say that for a man whose only weapon is reason there is nothing more neurotic than contact with unreason.

I felt knife blades open within me. I resolved to defend myself. As a good tactician, I intended to rationalize the world and to show the white man that he was mistaken. ... [pp. 117–118]

With enthusiasm I set to cataloguing and probing my surroundings. As time changed, one has seen the Catholic religion at first justify and then condemn slavery and prejudices. But by referring everything to the dignity of man, one had ripped prejudice to shreds. After much reluctance, the scientists have conceded that the Negro was a human being; *in vivo* and *in vitro* the Negro had been proved analogous to the white man: the same morphology, the same histology. Reason was confident of victory on every level. I put all the parts back together. But I had to change my tune.

... In the abstract there was agreement: The Negro is a human being. That is to say, amended the less firmly convinced, that like us he has his heart on the left side. But on certain points the white man remained intractable. Under no conditions did he wish any intimacy between the races, for it is a truism that "crossing between widely different races can lower the physical and mental level... Until we have a more definite knowledge of the effect of race-crossings we shall certainly do best to avoid crossings between widely different races."[2] ...

Appendix 3: Frantz Fanon 161

The Jew and I: Since I was not satisfied to be racialized, by a lucky turn of fate I was humanized. I joined the Jew, my brother in misery.

An outrage!

At first thought it may seem strange that the anti-Semite's outlook should be related to that of the Negro-phobe. It was my philosophy professor, a native of the Antilles, who recalled the fact to me one day: "whenever you hear anyone abuse the Jews, pay attention, because he is talking about you." And I found that he was universally right—by which I meant that I was answerable in my body and in my heart for what was done to my brother. Later I realized that he meant, quite simply, an anti-Semite is inevitably anti-Negro. ... [p. 122]

I made myself the poet of the world. The white man had found a poetry in which there was nothing poetic. The soul of the white man was corrupted, and, as I was told by a friend who was a teacher in the United States, "The presence of the Negroes beside the whites is in a way an insurance policy on humanness. When the whites feel that they have become too mechanized, they turn to the men of color and ask them for a little human sustenance." At last I had been recognized, I was no longer a zero.

I had soon to change my tune. Only momentarily at a loss, the white man explained to me that, genetically, I represented a stage of development: "Your properties have been exhausted by us. We have had earth mystics such as you will never approach. Study our history and you will see how far this fusion has gone." Then I had the feeling that I was repeating a cycle. My originality had been torn out of me. I wept a long time, and then I began to live again. But I was haunted by a galaxy of erosive stereotypes: the Negro's *sui generis* odor ... the Negro's *sui generis* good nature ... the Negro's *sui generis* gullibility ...

I had tried to flee myself through my kind, but the whites had thrown themselves on me and hamstrung me. I tested the limits of my essence; beyond all doubt there was not much of it left. It was here that I made my most remarkable discovery. Properly speaking, this discovery was a rediscovery. ...

I put the white man back into his place; growing bolder, I jostled him and told him point-blank, "Get used to me, I am not getting used to anyone." I shouted my laughter to the stars. The white man, I could see, was resentful. His reaction time lagged interminably ... I had won. I was jubilant.

Notes

1 Sir Alan Burns, *Color Prejudice* (London, Allen and Unwin, 1948), p. 16.

2 Jon Alfred Mjoen, "Harmonic and Disharmonic Race-crossings," The Second International Congress of Eugenics (1921), *Eugenics in Race and State*, vol. II, p. 60, quoted in Sir Alan Burns, *op. cit.*, p. 120.

Appendix 4: Julius Nyerere

Julius Nyerere, "*Ujamaa*—The Basis of African Socialism," in J. Nyerere, *Freedom and Unity: A selection from writings and speeches 1952–65*, Dar es Salaam: Oxford University Press, 1969 (1966), 162–171.

Socialism, like democracy, is an attitude of mind. In a socialist society it is the socialist attitude of mind, and not the rigid adherence to a standard political pattern, which is needed to ensure that the people care for each other's welfare...

In the individual, as in the society, it is an attitude of mind which distinguishes the socialist from the non-socialist. It has nothing to do with the possession or non-possession of wealth. Destitute people can be potential capitalists—exploiters of their fellow human beings. A millionaire can equally well be a socialist; he may value his wealth only because it can be used in the service of his fellow men. But the man who uses his wealth for the purpose of dominating any of his fellows is a capitalist. So is the man who would if he could! ...

In traditional African society everybody was a worker. There was no other way of earning a living for the community. Even the Elder, who appeared to be enjoying himself without doing any work and for whom everybody else appeared to be working, had, in fact, worked hard all his younger days. The wealth he now appeared to possess was not his, personally; it was only 'his' as the elder of the group which had produced it. He was its guardian. The wealth itself gave him neither power nor prestige. The respect paid to him by the young was his because he was older than they, and had served his community longer; and the 'poor' Elder enjoyed as much respect in our society as the 'rich' Elder.

When I saw that in traditional African society everybody was a worker, I do not use the word 'worker' simply as opposed to 'employer' but as opposed to 'loiterer' or 'idler'. One of the most socialistic achievements of our society was the sense of security it gave to its members, and the universal hospitality on which they could rely. But it is too often forgotten, nowadays, that the basis of this great socialistic achievement was this: that it was taken for granted that every member of society—barring only the children and the infirm—contributed his fair share of effort towards the production of its wealth. Not only was the capitalist, or the land exploiter, unknown to traditional African society, but we did not have that other form of modern parasite—the loiterer, or idler, who accepts the hospitality of society as his 'right' but gives nothing in return! Capitalistic exploitation was impossible. Loitering was an unthinkable disgrace.

Those of us who talk about the African way of life, and, quite rightly, take a pride in maintaining the tradition of hospitality which is so great a part of it, might do well to remember the Swahili saying: '*Mgeni siku mbili; siku ya tatu mpe jembe*'—or, in English, 'Treat your guest as a guest for two days; on the third day give him a hoe!' In actual fact, the guest was likely to ask for the hoe even before his host had to give him one—for he knew what was expected of him, and he would have been ashamed to remain idle any longer. Thus, working was part and parcel, was indeed the very basis and justification of thus socialist achievement of which we are so justly proud.

There is no such thing as socialism without work. A society which fails to give its individuals the means to work, or, having given them the means to work, prevents them from getting a fair share of the products of their own sweat and toil, needs putting right. Similarly, an individual who can work—and is provided by society with the means to work—but does not do so, is equally wrong. He has no right to expect anything from society because he contributes nothing to society.

The other use of the word 'worker', in its specialised sense of 'employee' as opposed to 'employer', reflects a capitalist attitude of mind which was introduced into Africa with the coming of colonialism and is totally foreign to our own way of thinking. In the old days the African had never aspired to the possession of personal wealth for the purpose of dominating any of his fellows. He had never had labourers or 'factory hands' to do his work for him. But then came the foreign capitalists. They were wealthy. They were powerful. And the African naturally started wanting to be wealthy too. There is nothing wrong in our wanting to be wealthy; nor is it a bad thing for us to want to acquire the power which wealth brings with it. But it is certainly wrong if we want the wealth and the power so that we can dominate somebody else. Unfortunately there are some of us who have already learnt to covet wealth for that purpose, and who would like to use the methods which the capitalists use in acquiring it. That is to say, some of us would like to use, or exploit, our brothers for the purpose of building up our personal power and prestige. This is completely foreign to us, and it is incompatible with the socialist society we want to build here.

Our first step, therefore must be to re-educate ourselves; to regain our former attitude of mind. In our traditional African society we were individuals within a community. We took care of the community, and the community took care of us. We neither needed nor wished to exploit our fellow men.

And in rejecting the capitalist attitude of mind which colonialism brought into Africa, we must reject also the capitalist methods which go with it. One

164 *Appendix 4: Julius Nyerere*

of these is the individual ownership of land. To us in Africa land was always recognized as belonging to community. Each individual within our society had a right to the use of land, because otherwise he could not earn his living and one cannot have the right to life without also having the right to some means of maintaining life. But the African's right to land was simply the right to use it: he had no other right to it, nor did it occur to him to try and claim one. ...

We must not allow the growth of parasites here in Tanganyika. The TANU Government [Tanganyika African National Union] must go back to the traditional African custom of land holding. That is to say, a member of society will be entitled to a piece of land on condition that he uses it. Unconditional, or 'freehold', ownership of land (which leads to speculation and parasitism) must be abolished. We must, as I have said, regain our former attitude of mind—our traditional African socialism—and apply it to the new societies we are building today. TANU has pledged itself to make socialism the basis of its policy in every field. The people of Tanganyika have given us their mandate to carry out that policy, by electing a TANU government to lead them. So the Government can be relied upon to introduce only legislation which is in harmony with socialist principles.

But, as I said at the beginning, true socialism is an attitude of mind. It is therefore up to the people of Tanganyika—the peasants, the wage-earners, the students, the leaders, all of us—to make sure that this socialist attitude of mind is not lost through the temptations to personal gain (or to the abuse of positions of authority) which may come our way as individuals, or through the temptation to look on the good of the whole community as of secondary importance to the interests of our own particular group.

Just as the Elder, in our former society, was respected for his age and his service to the community, so, in our modern society, this respect for age and service will be preserved. And in the same way as the 'rich' Elder's apparent wealth was really only held by him in trust for his people, so, today, the apparent extra wealth which certain positions of leadership may bring to the individuals who fill them, can be theirs only in so far as it is a necessary aid to the carrying out of their duties. It is a 'tool' entrusted to them for the benefit of the people they serve. It is not 'theirs' personally; and they may not use any part of it as a means of accumulating more for their own benefit' nor as an 'insurance' against the day when they no longer hold the same positions. That would be to betray the people who entrusted it to them. If they serve the community while they can, the community must look after them when they are no longer able to do so.

In tribal society, the individuals or the families within an ethnic group were 'rich' or 'poor' according to whether the whole ethnic group was rich or poor. If the ethnic group prospered, all the members of the ethnic group shared in its prosperity. Tanganyika, today, is a poor country. The standard of living of the masses of our people is shamefully low. But if every man or woman in the country takes up the challenge and works to the limit of his or her ability for

Appendix 4: Julius Nyerere   165

the good of the whole society, Tanganyika will prosper; and that prosperity will be shared by all her people.

But it must be shared. The true socialist may not exploit his fellows. So that the members of any group within our society are going to argue that, because they happen to be contributing more to the national income than some other groups, they must therefore take for themselves a greater share of the profits of their own industry than they actually need; and if they insist on this in spite of the fact that it would mean reducing their group's contribution to the general income and thus slowing down the rate at which the whole community can benefit, then that group is exploiting (or trying to exploit) its fellow human beings. It is displaying a capitalist attitude of mind.

There are bound to be certain groups which, by virtue of the 'market value' of their particular industry's products, will contribute more to the nation's income than others. But the others may actually be producing goods or services which are of equal, or greater, intrinsic value although they do not happen to command such a high artificial value. For example, the food produced by the peasant farmer is of greater social value than the diamonds mined at Mwadui. But the mine-workers of Mwaduiu could claim, quite correctly, that their labour was yielding greater financial profits to the community than that of the farmers. If, however, they went on to demand that they should therefore be given most of that extra profit for themselves, and that no share of it should be spent on helping the farmers, they would be potential capitalists.

This is exactly where the attitude of mind comes in. It is one of the purposes of Trade Unions to ensure for the workers a fair share of the profits of their labour. But a 'fair' share must be fair in relation to the whole society. If it is greater than the country can afford without having to penalize some other section of society, then it is not a fair share. Trade Union leaders and their followers, as long as they are true socialists, will not need to be coerced by the government into keeping their demands within the limits imposed by the needs of society as a whole. Only if there are potential capitalists amongst them will the socialist government have to step in and prevent them from putting their capitalist ideas into practice!

As with groups, so with individuals. There are certain skills, certain qualifications, which, for good reasons, command a higher rate of salary for their possessors than others. But, here again, the true socialist will demand only that return for his skilled work which he knows to be a fair one in proportion to the wealth and poverty of the whole society to which he belongs. He will not, unless he is a would-be capitalist attempt to blackmail the community by demanding a salary equal to that paid to his counterpart in some far wealthier society.

European socialism was born of the Agrarian Revolution and the Industrial Revolution which followed it. The former created the 'landed' and the 'landless' classes in society; the latter produced the modern capitalist and the industrial proletariat.

166 *Appendix 4: Julius Nyerere*

These two revolutions planted the seeds of conflict within society, and not only was European socialism born of that conflict, but its apostles sanctified the conflict itself into a philosophy. Civil war was no longer looked upon as something evil, or something unfortunate, but as something good and necessary. As prayer is to Christianity and to Islam, so civil war (which they call 'class war') is to the European version of socialism—a means inseparable from the end. Each becomes the basis of a whole way of life. The European socialist cannot think of his socialism without its father—capitalism!

Brought up in tribal socialism, I must say I find this contradiction quite intolerable. It gives capitalism a philosophical status which capitalism neither claims nor deserves. For it virtually says 'Without capitalism, and the conflict which capitalism creates within society, there can be no socialism!' This glorification of capitalism by the doctrinaire European socialists, I repeat, I find intolerable.

African socialism, on the other hand, did not have the 'benefit' of the Agrarian Revolution or the Industrial Revolution. It did not start from the existence of conflicting 'classes' in society. Indeed I doubt if the equivalent for the word 'class' exists in any indigenous African language; for language describes the ideas of those who speak it, and the idea of 'class' or 'caste' was non-existent in African society.

The foundation, and the objective, of African socialism is the extended family. The true African socialist does not look on one class of men as his brethren and another as his natural enemies. He does not form an alliance with the 'brethren' for the extermination of the 'non-brethren'. He rather regards all men as his brethren — as members of his ever extending family. That is why the first article of TANU's creed is: '*Binadamu wote ni ndugu zangu, na Afrika ni moja.*' If this had been originally put in English, it could have been: 'I believe in Human Brotherhood and the Unity of Africa.'

'*Ujamaa*', then, or 'familyhood', describes our socialism. It is opposed to capitalism, which seeks to build a happy society on the basis of the exploitation of man by man; and it is equally opposed to doctrinaire socialism which seeks to build its happy society on a philosophy of inevitable conflict between man and man.

We, in Africa, have no more need of being 'converted' to socialism than we have of being 'taught' democracy. Both are rooted in our own past — in the traditional society which produced us. Modern African socialism can draw from its traditional heritage the recognition of 'society' as an extension of the basic family unit. But it can no longer confine the idea of the social family within the limits of the ethnic group, nor, indeed, of the nation. For no true African socialist can look at a line drawn on a map and say 'The people on this side of that line are my brothers, but those who happen to live on the other side of it can have no claim on me'; every individual on this continent is his brother.

It was in the struggle to break the grip of colonialism that we learnt the need for unity. We came to recognize that the same socialist attitude of mind

Appendix 4: Julius Nyerere   167

which, in the tribal days, gave to every individual the security that come of belonging to a widely extended family, must be preserved within the still wider society of the nation. But we should not stop there. Our recognition of the family to which we all belong must be extended yet further—beyond the ethnic group, the community, the nation, or even the continent—to embrace the whole society of mankind. This is the only logical conclusion for true socialism.

Index

Note: Locators in *italics* represent figures and **bold** indicate tables in the text. Endnotes are indicated by the page number followed by "n" and the note number e.g., 24n16 refers to note 16 on page 24.

Abaluhya tribe 113
Abbas, Ferhat 111
Abidjan 71
Académie française 39n3
Accra conferences 12, 42–43
Addis Ababa (Ethiopia) 44, 119
African anticolonial movements 41, 86–110 passim; continent map 5; democracy 58; fang mask *34*; historical and cultural heritage 52; ideologies passim; languages 20, 30, 38, 47–50, 63, 71–76, 103, 14–151, 166; modernization 56, 70–75, 85–87; nationalism passim; national movement 54, 58, 64–76, 85–88, 112; personality (African/Negro) 8, 24n16, 134–139, 154; political identity 6; political-territorial nationalism in 23, 29, 51; resistance to White rule/occupiers 58–60; scripts *75*; socialism 58, 67, 79–80, 86–89, 95–99, 105–106, 162; society in era of independence 94, 105; soldiers in colonial armies 116
African-Americans 4–25 passim, 137–138, 146n2
African and Malagasy Union 47, 51n5, 119
African churches and chapels 16, 65, 72–73, 79
African-European cultural fusion 37–38
African and Pan-African identity 5–6, 31, 98, 149
African kingdoms 55
African League 48
African Mission in Sudan (AMIS) 129

African National Congress (ANC) 67n12, 76, 104
African Union (AU) 119–130 passim; establishment 122–123; Constitutive Act 123–128; and Darfur 128–130; institutions of *124*; Peace and Security Council 123–124, 129
Afro-Asian solidarity conference in Bandung 41
Afro-Zionism 131; *see also* Black Zionism
Ahidjo, Ahmadou 113
Akan and Yoruba states 55
Algeria 42, 65, 91, 99–104, 107n22, 111, 119, 121
Al-Bashir, Omar 129, 130n8
Ali, Duse Muhammed 140
All-African People's Conference (AAPC) 43
American Colonization Society 137
AMIS *see* African Mission in Sudan (AMIS)
ANC *see* African National Congress (ANC)
Anderson, Benedict 2–3
Anglophone states 47, 119
Angola 73, **78**, 85, 91, 94–95, 99
anticapitalism 83–87
anticolonialism 2, 83–86
anticolonial movements 41, 86, 98, 102, 104, 106n, 108n34, 109
anticolonial nationalism 29, 83, 85, 105, 109, 112, 142
anticolonial resistance 3
antiracist racism (Sartre) 38
anti-Westernism 83–86

Index 169

Ashanti federation 55; War 61; region and people 113
Association of Independent African States 43
AU *see* African Union (AU)
Avineri, Shlomo 75
Awolowo, Obafemi 22
Azikiwe, Nnamdi 22, 68, 79n2

Back-to-Africa movement and concept 12–18, 24n16, 24n19
Balkanization of Africa 56, 66n4
Banda, Hastings Kamuzu 22, 62, 68, 80, 81n9
Barue revolt 61
basic concepts and the struggle for independence **85–86**
Basuto Gun War 61
Battle of Adwa 13, 25n24
Bello, Ahmadu 113
Benin, art exhibits *55–57*
Black-African civilization 10
Black Literary Renaissance (or Harlem Renaissance) 134
Black missionaries 20
Black national awakening 2, 3, 7, 10, 20–22, 52, 117n6, 148
Black nationalist movements 13
Blacks passim; use of the term 4, 23n1; *see also specific entries*
Black Skin, White Masks (Fanon) 158–161
Black Zionism 13–18; the idea of 131–137; praxis of return 137–142; and Zionism 142–146
Blyden, Edward Wilmot 8, 12, 14, *15*, 16, 24n13, 24n16, 132–139, 143
Bolshevik revolution 82, 84
Brazzaville Conference (1944) 110
Britain 18, 23n4, 26, 29, 51, 76, 80–83, 88n9, 90
British Labour party 68
British South Cameroon 47
Buganda 55, 89n10

Cabral, Amilcar 94, 98, 106n7, 107n9, 107n32, 107n17–19
Cameroon 29–142 passim; French 43, 47, 88n6, 116n2; British 43; German 43
Cameroonian Union (UC) 113
Cape Verde islands 85, 91, 94, 106n7, 106n8, 123
capitalism 82–87, 88n1, 166
Capitula 84, 88n5

Caribbean Islands 7–8, 18, 20, 24n16, 31, 39n4, 132, 137, 142
Césaire, Aimé 8, 31, *33*, 39n4, 40n5, 84, 139, 156n2
child labor *59*
Chilembwe, John 22
Chissano, Joaquim 107n20, 116
Christianity 16, 20, 65, 66, 71, 115, 115, 140, 143, 156, 166
churches 16, 20, 65, 71–72, 137, 156
civil equality 23; struggle for, in America 9
class-national unity (Cabral) 98
colonial administration 43
colonialism passim; especially 82–89, 90–109
Colonial Nations 38
colonial officialdom as an enemy 93
Colonizer and the Colonized, The (Memmi) 150–153
color prejudice 160, 161n1
communalism 87
Congo 12, 55, 68, 72, **78**, 80n7, 81n13, 116n2
conquest of Africa 58–62
consciousness (national, political, racial, self-awareness) 2, 3, 9, 23, 27, 36, 71, 85, 103, 144, 149n1, 159
Conservative Francophones 119
Constitutive Act of the African Union 123–130
continental Pan-Africanism 6, 28, 41–51, 148; emergence of 41–42; first Pan-African unification efforts 42–47; forces of cohesion and division in Africa 47–50
continental territorial nationalism 28
Convention People's Party 51n1, 76
Crowther, Samuel 20
Crummell, Alexander 138
Cuba 20, 43, 84, 85, 89n8, 99, 108n33, 122, 132, 137
Cuffee, Paul 137
Cullen, Countee 133–134
culture(al): assimilation 31; colonialism 33; diversity 28; inferiority 9; intellectual movement 31; neocolonialism 39; racial identity 6; racial nationalism 27; rehabilitation 38; Zionism 134

Dahomey 48, 51n7, 55, 116n2, 137
Dar es Salaam 71
Darfur 122; case study: and the African Union 128–130

170 Index

Declaration of Human Rights 45–46, 69, 76, 127
Declaration of the Rights of the Negro Peoples of the World 17–18
decolonization 1–2, 3, 3n1, 26, 42, 52, 79n1, 85, 87, 90–92, 100–103, 110, 112, 116, 117n5, 118n17, 118n18, 142, 148;
de Gaulle, Charles 38, 89
Dei-Annang, Michael Francis 87, 89n12
de Klerk, Frederik 67n12
Delaney, Martin R. 10, 12
Democratic Party of Guinea (PDG) 89n8, 113–114
Democratic Republic of Congo (DRC) 29, 80, 123, 124
Diop, Alioune 154–157
discrimination 8–10, 69, 72, **77**, 91, 117n7, 131, 139, 145
discriminatory legislation 7
disenfranchisement 131
diversity, ethnic and cultural 28
Djibouti 29, 116n2, 122, 124; *see also* French Somaliland
Du Bois, W.E.B. 8, 12, 19, 84, 132, 142–146 passim

East Africa passim; *see also* map *49*
East African Community 47, *49*, 51n6
East African Federation 43
Economic Community of West African States (ECOWAS) 47, 51n7
(socio-)economic development 52, 63, 85, 90, 126, 128
economic liberty **78**
education: 8, 9, 14, 19, 22, 24n16, 25n25, 27, 38, **46**, *49*, 51n6, 58, 66n2, 68, 71, **77**, 80n3, 80n4, 80n5, 91, 94–95, *97*, 104, **124**, 138–140, 160; radical nationalism 94–95; traditional 95
Egypt/Egyptian 9, 16, 24n10, 41, 43, 119, 124, 132, 135, 140, 145
enslavement of Africans 9, 12, 16, 92; political 26
equality 5, 7–9, 18, 22–23, 24n19, 45, 46, 52, 58, 63, 68, 71, 87, 105, 110–11, 127, 128, 131, 135–136, 144, 158; under the law **77**; racial **78**
Equality of the Human Races, The (Firmin) 9
Eritrea 29, 121–124 passim
Essay on the Inequality of the Human Races, An (Gobineau) 9
Ethiopia 13, 19, 25n24, 29, 41, 43, 44, 61, **78**, 119–124 passim, 130n5, 144,

145, 146n5; Ethiopian Anthem 17–18, 25n21, 25n24; UNIA anthem 140–141, 145, 146n5; Ethiopian churches 20
ethnic groups: *see also* (partial list); Ashanti 113; Bamileke 43; Basotho 61; Fanti Ghana 113; Giriama 113; Hausa-Fulani 113; Hehe 61; Herero 61; Hutu 112; Ibo 113; Kalenjin 113; Kikuyu 116; Maasai 113; Ndebele 61; Ngoni, 59–60; Oyo 55; Shona 61; Tutsi 112; Yoruba 113
ethnic nationalism 28, 148
European industrialization 31, 85, 87
Eurocentric worldview 24n10, 53
exploitation 9, 18, 26, 38, 58, 82, 84–85, 92, 94, 95, 99, 139, 163, 166

Fanon, Frantz 8, 100–103, 107n22, 107n23, 142, 158–161
Firmin, Anténor 9
FNLA (Frente Nacional de Libertação de Angola) 104, 108
Fourah Bay College 20, 25n23, 146
Fouta Djallon region, Guinea 113
Francophone states 47, 51n5, 119; bloc 39n3; African supporters 110
francophonie 38
Freedom and Unity: A selection from writings and speeches (Nyerere) 162–167
free elections **78**, 80n9
Freetown, Sierra Leone 13–14, *14*
FRELIMO (Liberation Front of Mozambique) 93–99, 104–105, 106n3, 106n5, 106n6; economic system 99; hospital *96*; Makonde woodcarvers *96*; school *97*
French-African community, union, federation 88n7, 109–11
French colonialism 31
French Revolution 68
French Socialist party 68
French Sudan [or Mali] 43, 55, 88n6, 89n9, 110, 116n2
Fugitive Slave Act (1850) 13
Fulani empire 55

Garden of Eden, Black 9, 133
Garvey, Amy 19, 145
Garvey, Marcus 8, 9, 16–19, 21, 24n19, 134–146
Geiss, Immanuel 4, 23n2, 24n11, 24n20, 132, 137–138, 146
Gellner, Ernest 3
genocide 67n10, 121, 123, 128, **128**

Index 171

Germany/German 37, 43, 59–62, 64–65, 66n9, 67n10, 67n14, 67n17, 82, 108n35

Ghana 12, 21, 22, 23n5, 41–44, *48*, 51n1, 51n7, 55, 66n3, 68, 71, 74, 79n1, 80n9, 89n12, 113, *114*, 119, 125, 138, 142, 145; Gold Coast (now Ghana) 20–21, 43, 51n1, 51n7, 55, 61, 71, 74, 76, 89, 113, 138, 142

Ghana-Guinea Union 43

Gobineau, Arthur de 9, 131

Gold Coast *see* Ghana

government by consensus **78**

Great Mosque of Jenné in Mali *58*

Great Zimbabwe *54*

guerrilla warfare 92

Guinea-Bissau 85, 91, 94, 100, 104–105, 106n7, 106n8, 107n11, 120, 125

Gun War, Basuto 61

Haiti 8, 19, 23n3

Harlem Renaissance (1920s) 134

Hausa-Fulani 29, 113; Fulani empire 55

Herero Revolt 61, 67n10

Horton, Africanus 20

Houphouët-Boigny, Félix 84, 88n7, 109–112

Hughes, Langston 133–134

human dignity 12, 14, **78**, 126, 131

Hut Tax War 61

Hutu 112

imperialism 55, 75–76, 82–84, 88n1, 88n5, 94, 140, 156

Imperialism: The Highest Stage of Capitalism (Lenin) 82–83

individualism 71, 87, 95

intellectualism 33

Ita, Eyo 22, 25n25

Italy 13, 25n24, 29

Jewish Zionism 131–146 passim

Johnson, James W., editor *New York Age* 12

Justice and Equality Movement (JEM) 128

Kampala 71

Kano 56

Kasavubu, Joseph 68, 80n8

Kaunda, Kenneth 68–69, *70*, 81n11; letter to British Secretary of State for the Colonies 69–70

Keïta, Modibo 84, 89n9

Kennedy, John F. 80n4

Kenya 22, 23n5, 29, 43; languages 47–49; 62, 66, 68, 71, **77–78**, 80n4 passim; especially 91–129

Kenya National African Union (KANU) 80n4

Kenyatta, Jomo 19, *22*, 62, 68, 80n5, 84

Kilwa 56

King, Martin Luther 80n4

King's African Rifles **78**, *115*

Knox, Robert 131

Ku Klux Klan 131

Lagos 71

Languages: African languages 49, 71, *75*; colonial languages 47, *50* (distribution), 149; Kinyarwanda 49; Kirundi 49; Malagasy 49; Somali 49; Swahili 49; Swati (Eswatini) 49

Lenin, Vladimir Ilyich 82–84, 86, 88n1, 88n3, 98; *see also* Marxism-Leninism

liberal European nationalism 52

liberal concepts (racial equality, national self-determination, gov. by consensus, majority rule, free elections, basic liberties, human dignity, economic liberty) **78**

liberation passim

liberation movements passim; *see also* FNLA, MPLA and UNITA (Angola); FRELIMO (Mozambique); PAIGC (Guinea Bissau); PAC and ANC (South Africa); SWAPO (South Africa); UNITA, ZANU and ZAPU (Rhodesia, today's Zimbabwe)

Liberia passim; especially 5–51, 119–142

Liberia Herald (Blyden) 14–15

Libya 41, 43, 119, 121, 125, 126

Lincoln's Emancipation Proclamation 131

L'Ouverture, Toussaint 8

Low, D. Donald Anthony 60

Lumumba, Patrice 68, *69*, 80n7, 81n13

lynchings 7, 13, 131

Macaulay, Herbert 20

Macleod, Iain 69

Maji-Maji rebellion 59–60, 62, *64*, 65, 66n9

majority rule **78**

Makonnen, Ras 8, 19, 23n5, 142, 145

Madagascar/Malagasy 45, 47, 49, 51, 51n5, 116, 119, 125, 127

172   Index

Malawi (Nyasaland) 55, 62, 68, 80n9, 81, 125
Mali 43, 48, 51n7, 55, 58, 65, 66n3, 84, 89n9, 110, 116n2, 119, 125, 145; Mali Federation 43
Manchester Congress (1945) 19, 27
Mandela, Nelson *63*, 64, 67n12, 67n13, 76, 81n20
Martinican Progressive Party 39n4
Marxism-Leninism 86, 97–99, 105–106, 107n19, 108n33; influence on radical African ideologies 98; *see also* Lenin
Masinde, Elijah 66
massacres: Mueda (1960) 104; Pijiguiti (1959) 104; Sharpeville (1960) 104; Sétif 104; Xinavane (1961) 104; *see also* genocide
Matisse 32
Mau-Mau uprising 80n5, 113, 115
Mboya, Tom 68, 80n4
Memmi, Albert 150–153
missionaries 20, 25n23, 71, *81*; missions 52, 71, 104 (civic), 123
modernization 56, 70–75, 85, 87
modern nationalism 7, 9, 27–28, 52
modern racism 7, 9, *10*, *59*
Modibo Keïta 84, 89n9, 110
Mombasa 56
Mondlane, Eduardo 68, 81n12, 97
Monomotapa (King) 55
monopolies **77**, 82–84
Monroe, James 13, 137
Moody, Harold 8, 23n4
Morocco 41, 43, 119, 121
Mozambique 61, 68, **78**, 85, 90–105 passim, 106n2, 106n5, 113, 116, 118n16, 118n20, 120–122, 125
MPLA (People's Movement for the Liberation of Angola) 104, 105, 106n4, 107n12, 107n33, 108, 108n36
Mueda massacres (1960) 104
Muslims/Muslim 29, 30n4, 65, 111, 113, 117, 128, 143; Islam/Islamic 124–25, 166

Nairobi (Southwest Africa) 71
Namibia 61, 91
National Emigration Convention 137
nationalism as protest against White racism 8–10
National Liberation Council 79n1
National Liberation Movement 3, 113
national self-determination **78**

national-territorial consciousness 71
Ndebele and Shona wars 61; *see also* ethnic groups
Négritude 6, 31–40 passim, 111, 139, 154
Negro passim; regarding the use of the term Negro 146n2
Negroism and Pan-Negroism 5–6, 7–25, 41, 52, 132
"Negro-African Civilization" 35
"Negro African society" 86
"Negro Empire" in Africa 16
Negro Hatikvah 140
neo-colonialism 93, 106n6
NESAM (Mozambican Secondary-School African Students) 90
new nationalism 52–67 passim
New Negro Movement 134
Nigeria 17, 20, 22, 24n16, 25n25, 29, 43, 48, 51n7, 55, 76, 79, 82, 87n2, 113, 117n14, 119, 125, 137, 142
Niger Valley Exploration Party 137
Nkomo, Joshua 65, 108n34
Nkrumah, Kwame 12, 19–23, 23n5, 41, 42, 44, 51n1, 51n3, 62, 68, 79n1, 82–84, 88n1, 88n4, 107n9, 111, 113, *114*, 119, 139, 142
NPC (Northern People's Congress) 113
Nova Scotia (Canada) 137
Nyasaland 22, 80; British 55, *114*
Nyerere, Julius 62, *62*, 67n11, 67n16, 68, 79n3, 86, 87, 162–167

Obote, Milton 68, 81n10
October Revolution in Russia (1917) 83–84
Ogot, Bethwell 109, 116n1
Omar, El-Haj 65
opponents of national independence 109–118 passim
oppression in America 8
Organization of African Unity (OAU) 44–45, 119–122; Charter 50; establishment 45; mandate 44–47; membership 46; principles 46; purpose 46; rights and duties of member states 47
Oyo empire 55

PAC (Pan-African Congress, South Africa) 104
Padmore, George 8, 19, 23n6, 30n1, 84, 139, 142, 145

Index 173

PAIGC (African Party for Independence of Guinea and Cape Verde) 104, 105, 106n7, 106n8
Pan-African Conferences and Congresses 8, 18–19, 23n7, 144
Pan-African Congress 21, 23n5, 25n22, 28, 30n1, 51n1, 145; 1919 resolutions 19; 1945 resolutions 26–27
Pan-African Federation 23n5
Pan-Africanism passim
Pan-Africanism Reconsidered (Diop) 154–157
Pan-African movement 12, 19, 22, 23n2, 32, 146
Pan-African nationalism 4–5
Pan-African unification 119
Pan-African unity 41, 47
Pan-Negroism 5–6, 12, 41; on Africa 20–23; emergence of 7–8; identification with African homeland 10–13
Pan-Negro movement 27
Pan-Negro nationalism 4–25 passim
Pan-Negro solidarity 19; *see also* Negroism and Pan-Negroism
peace 26, 35, 45, 46, 60, 70, 71, 86, 100, 120, 123, **124**, 126–129, 130n10
Picasso 32; cubism *34*
Pijiguiti massacres (1959) 104
political-territorial nationalism in Africa 23, 29, 51n1
political unification in Africa 6, 41, 47
Portuguese colonialism and colonies **77**, 85, 93–94, 100, 106n7, 109, 113
positive action 51n1
PPMP (Parti progressiste martiniquais) 39n4
precolonial African civilization 55; culture 32; socialism 87; society 38
Príncipe 85, 91, 125
private entrepreneurship 74
Protestant Christianity 71
PSC (Peace and Security Council) 123
PSS (Senegalese Socialist Party) 111

Queen Elizabeth II and Commonwealth leaders *114*

Races: hierarchy 9–11
racial-cultural nationalism 111, 148
racial discrimination passim; especially 8, 72–73, 91
racial empowerment 11
racial equality **78**

racial identity of Blacks 8–9; cultural-racial 6
racial rioting (1829) 13
racism 7–10, 18–27, 38, 59, 92, 107, 131–135, 139, 148, 151, 154
racist theories 9
radical nationalism: 85, 88n6; aims 91–95; armed struggle 99–106; ideological sources of influence 95–99; origins 90–91; political struggle 99–106
RDA (Rassemblement démocratique africain) 84, 88n6
rebellion 10, 60, 61–67, 113, 118n16; amongst others: Maji-Maji 59, 60–62, 64–65, 66n9 ; Mau-Mau 80n5, 113, 115; Nat Turner's slave rebellion 137; *see also* revolt, uprisings
rehabilitation of Africa 38, 92
resistance to independence 109–118; Also Supporters of the French African Union 110–112; Ethnic Opposition 112–113; Opposition by the Traditional Leadership 113–115; Opportunists 116
Resolution on West Africa 26–27
Responsibility to Protect (R2P) 123
revolt 42, 53, 60–61, 62, 65, 67n10, 73, 98, 116n1, 137, 148; *see also* rebellion and uprisings
Rhodes, Cecil 55, 82
Rhodesia 13, 55, 60, 61, 65–66, 67n20, 73, **78**, 81n11, 88n3, 100, 104–105, 108n34, *114*, 120
romantic nationalism 35, 40n6
Roumain, Haitian Jacques 133
rule of law 68, 71, **77**, 126, 128(m)
Rwanda 49, 112, 117n11, 121–122, 123, 125, 142

salvation 131–132
São Tomé 85, 91, 125
Sartre, Jean-Paul 36, 37, 38, 40n20, 135, 159
secular democratic political systems 68
Sékou Touré 65, 79n1, 84, 89n8, 110, 111, 114, 117n9, 142
self-consciousness 3
self-determination 145
self-governance 54, 113
Senegal 35, 38, 39, 39n3, 39n4, 43, *48*, 51n7, 68, 71, 109, 111, 116n2, 119, 122, 125, 159

174   *Index*

Senghor, Léopold Sedar 31–38 passim, 39n3, 39n4, 40n7, 40n12, 40n15, 40n17, 40n18, 40n19, 68, 80n6, 86, 109–111; passim, 117n4, 117n8, 139
Sharpeville massacres (1960) 76, *77*, 81n19, 104
Sierra Leone 13, 17, 20, 24n16, 25n23, *48*, 51n7, 61, 119, 125, 134, 137, 139, 146
Sissoko, Fily Dabo 110
slave ship *Marie Séraphique* of Nantes *59*
slavery/enslavement/slave 4, *6*, 7–20 passim, 26, 38, 58, *59*, 92, 111–112, 131, 132, 135, 137, 139, 154, 160
slave trade 4, *6*, 7, 8, *10*, 13, *59*
Smith, Anthony 3n4, 28, 30n3
social justice 24, 68–69, 71, 99, 128
social modernization process 56
social system and exploitation 92
solidarity 4, 8, 11, 19, 41, 45, 46, 71, 87, **125–127**, 135, 139, 154
Somalia/Somali Republic/Somali (Italian) 29, 30n2, 43, 49, 121, 122, 123, 125, 128, 142; Somali Northern Frontier District (NFD) 29
Somaliland (British) 29, 43, 51
Somaliland (French) 29; *see also* Djibouti
South Africa 91–100, 104–105, 108, 108n35, 117n7, 120, 125, 154
Soviet communism 97–99
spectator segregation in sports stadium *79*
sub-Saharan Africa 6, 39n3, 41, 47, 154
Sudan 29, 41, 43, 51, 55, 65, 88n6, 89n9, 110, 112, 116n2, 117n13, 121–129 passim, 130n8, 130n9, 130n10; *Union soudanaise* 89n9; South Sudan 29, 37, 112, 121–122; Sudan Liberation Movement/Army (SLM/A) 128
Swahili: uprising 60; language 49, 66; expressions 66n9 (maji-maji), 79 and 87 (Ujamaa), 163 (saying) *see* languages
SWAPO (South West Africa People's Organisation) 104, 108n35
Swati (Eswatini) language 49; *see also* languages

Tanganyika 43, 47, 59, 60–62, 67n11, 67n15, 78, 79n3, 114, 118n19, 164–165; *see also* Tanzanyia
TANU (Tanganyika African National Union) 65, 67n11, 114

Tanzania 43, 49, *49*, 51n6, 64, 65, 67n11, 67n17, 68, 71, 79n3, 80, 88n3, 88n4, *96*, 120, 122, 125; *see also* Tanganyika
Taxes 61, 67n14; hut taxes 53
Territory/Territorial: passim; especially 26–30
Timbuktu 56
Togo: British Togo 43; French Togo (today's Togo) 29, *48*, 51, 116, 125, 137
To New York (poem by Senghor) 37–38
Touré, Samori 65
Touré, Sékou 65, 79n2, 84, 89n8, 110, 114, 117n9, 142
Towards Colonial Freedom (Nkrumah) 82–83
trans-Atlantic slave trade 4, 8, 9, *10*
transportation 50, 70, 71, 74
Tunisia 41, 43, 119, 125
Turner, Henry McNeal, Bishop 131, 134, 138
Turner, Nat 137; *see also* rebellion
Tutsi 112; *see also* genocide

UDIHV (Union for the Defense of the Interests of Upper Volta) 114
Uganda (Buganda) 29, 43, 47, 49, 51n6, 55, 67n11, 68, 71, 80n3, 80n4, 81n10, 121, 123, 125, 128
Ujamaa 79n3, 87, 162, 166
UNAMID (United Nations African Mission in Darfur) 129
UNIA (Universal Negro Improvement Association) 16, 140; UNIA anthem *see* Ethiopia
Union of African States 43
UNITA (National Union for the total independence of Angola) 104, 108
United States of Africa 44, 51n1, 119, 120
Universal Declaration of Human Rights 45, 46, 76, 127
Universal Ethiopian Anthem 17–18, 25n21, 146n5
uprisings 8, 13, 60–61, 62–63, 65, 68, 80, 92, 107n22, 116n1; *see also* rebellion and revolt
urbanization 56, 70
US Civil War 7
UTP (United Tanganyika Party) 114

Wassoulou Empire 65
West Africa passim *see also* map *48*
Western democratic ideas on African nationalism 68–70; nationalist concepts and modernization processes 70–76; Western liberal concepts 76–79

Westernized Africans, struggle for independence **77–78**
White culture 7, 36
White racism 9–10, 38, 133–135, 148; nationalism as protest against 8–10
White settler colonies 91
Whither O Africa? (poem by Dei-Anang) 87
Williams, Henry Sylvester 8, 23n7
World War I and II passim
Wretched of the Earth, The (Fanon) 100, 107n22, 107n23
Wright, Richard 133

Xinavane massacres (1961) 104

Zaire (Congo) 29, 51n5, 68, 71, 108n33, 122
Zambia 29, 68, 69, 73, 81n11, 81n14, 125
ZANU (Zimbabwe African National Union) 104, 105, 108n34
Zanzibar 12, 43, 47, 112, 117n12
ZAPU (Zimbabwe African Peoples Union) 104, 108n34
Zimbabwe (Rhodesia) 55–56, 73, 81, 88n3, 91, 100, 104–105, 108n34, 121–122, 125, 129–130, 130n3, 130n4, 145
Zionism passim; *see also* chapter 11 on Black Zionism
Zionist Garveyite mass-movement 138
Zulu wars 64

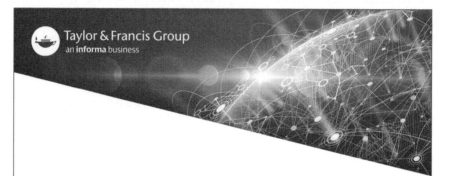